D0759524

THE SECOND COMING OF THE INVISIBLE EMPIRE

MERCER UNIVERSITY PRESS

Endowed by

TOM WATSON BROWN
and
THE WATSON-BROWN FOUNDATION, INC.

THE SECOND COMING OF THE INVISIBLE EMPIRE

The Ku Klux Klan of the 1920s

William Rawlings

MERCER UNIVERSITY PRESS | *Macon, Georgia*
2016

MUP/ H917

© 2016 by Mercer University Press
Published by Mercer University Press
1501 Mercer University Drive
Macon, Georgia 31207

9 8 7 6 5 4 3 2 1

Books published by Mercer University Press are printed on acid-free paper
that meets the requirements of the American National Standard for
Information Sciences—Permanence of Paper for Printed Library Materials.

ISBN   978-0-88146-561-7
Cataloging-in-Publication Data is available from the Library of Congress

*For Uncle Charlie, who, unfortunately,
got to know the Klan better than most.*

Contents

Author's Preface

I suspect my grandmother might have been a supporter of the Ku Klux Klan, at least at the outset. As a young widow struggling to raise a child in the trying days of the early 1920s, she would have found some resonance in their avowed philosophy and willingness to take positive action to right the wrongs that seemingly plagued then-modern America. When I knew her decades later, she had mellowed somewhat, but remained a staunch member of the Women's Christian Temperance Union, a faithful occupant of the family pew at the Sandersville Methodist Church, and a firm believer in the separation of the races. A Southerner to the core, she would scold me if I made the mistake of mentioning the Civil War, correcting me with its proper name, the War Between the States. She feared to the very end that America was on the path to perdition, afflicted by creeping immorality, a weakening of religious resolve, and beset from afar by the threat of international communism. Thus it would be only natural that my grandmother, born in the 1880s, would approve of the Klan, an organization that stood for One Hundred Percent Americanism, Prohibition, supported Law and Order, and endorsed the tenets of Protestant Christianity.

My interest in the Ku Klux Klan came to me via my grandmother, albeit indirectly. It stemmed from her brother-in-law, her late husband's younger sibling, my Great Uncle Charlie. She always described him in carefully chosen words, but it was clear that he was someone she despised. Nearly three decades older than my grandmother, he was a wealthy man at his peak, the owner of tens of thousands of acres of land, a bank, a hotel, a railroad, and multiple other businesses. By the time I was born he had been dead nearly a decade, but not before losing everything and spending much of the latter part of his life in prison, convicted of the murder of his first cousin. His story of spectacular success followed by dismal failure piqued my interest as a writer, and eventually became the central theme of a non-fiction book, *A Killing on Ring Jaw Bluff*.

Over the years I had heard hints and suggestions of the specifics of Uncle Charlie's life. I recall my grandmother referring to his "manifold sins and wickedness," euphemistically quoting the Book of Common Prayer. He was wealthy, true, but in her eyes immoral. I learned the details, such as they were, from my father in a long conversation that took place over several days on New Zealand's South Island, part of a father-son trip we'd taken to celebrate his retirement and seventieth birthday. Perhaps the one thing I recall most vividly was Charlie's encounter with the Ku Klux Klan. The exact date was uncertain, but we decided it was most likely in 1921. Besides being a successful businessman, Charlie was also a noted philanderer whose tastes often crossed racial lines. His actions drew the eye of the newly formed local Klan. He was warned to change his ways. When he did not, they waylaid him on a lonely country road and castrated him.

It would have been difficult to write about Uncle Charlie's life without mentioning the Klan incident. In truth, it would be difficult to write anything about America in the 1920s without mentioning the Klan. A key element of being an author of non-fiction is the mastery of one's subject. As part of my background preparation for writing *A Killing on Ring Jaw Bluff*, I read extensively on the Ku Klux Klan. Like many—perhaps most—Americans, I had vaguely assumed that the Klan was some sort of secret organization formed around the time of the Civil War (apologies, grandmother!) and persistent to the present day. I assumed the organization was primarily Southern, and that its guiding philosophy was one of racial animus directed toward African-Americans. I was essentially wrong on all counts.

Over the past century and a half, there have been three separate and distinct "Ku Klux Klans." The first was the Ku Klux Klan of the Reconstruction Era, dating from the late 1860s to the early 1870s. That Klan was one of dozens of loosely organized groups that sprang up spontaneously in the states of the former Confederacy during the post-war period of martial law and occupation by Federal troops. It was, fundamentally, an organization that pursued its social and political ends via terrorism, a part of what has been termed "the Ku Klux Movement." Generally, the goal of these groups was two-fold: the restoration of local order in the unsettled years after 1865, and the return of power to the former ruling class, the latter frequently accomplished by suppression of the voting and other rights of the newly freed slaves. For multiple reasons, the various "Klans" faded and died by the mid-1870s.

The second Klan and the subject of this book is that formed by William Simmons in 1915. Other than the name, it had little in common with the Klan of the Reconstruction Era. Simmons's Klan was created as a beneficial, fraternal order, not unlike hundreds of others in the day. The name was inspired by the depiction of the 1860s Klan in a then-popular movie, *The Birth of a Nation*. Within a decade and for a few brief years, Simmons's Klan became one of the more powerful social and political voices in American life before fading into obscurity by the late 1920s. That body, whose formal name was The Knights of the Ku Klux Klan, Inc., was disbanded in 1944. The third group of various "Klans" that sprang up after World War II do, in fact, fulfill the stereotype of what I and many associate with the name. Their central theme is commonly one of white supremacy; they exist far from the American mainstream.

Almost everything I thought I knew about the Ku Klux Klan of the 1920s was wrong. Though Southern in origin, at its peak the greatest numbers of its members were in the cities of the upper Midwest. It was not formed primarily to promote a given agenda, but rather as a money-making scheme for its founders and officers. While it espoused racism through its endorsement of white supremacy, its position on the subject was not far from the mainstream of American thought in the era. It was also anti-Catholic, anti-Semitic, anti-immigrant, and in favor of Prohibition (despite the drinking habits of its leaders). The rapid growth of the Klan during the early 1920s was due not so much to the intrinsic attractiveness of its philosophy, but instead accomplished through skillful marketing.

There is little doubt that the Ku Klux Klan of the 1920s was a corrupt organization whose message of religious and racial hatred profoundly affected the conversation of American life for nearly a decade. Despite this, the order spread to every state in the Union, attracting millions of members in the process. It is an interesting episode in American history, to say the very least.

Several talented authors have written general histories of the Ku Klux Klans, including the Klan of the 1920s. The subject is a massive one, encompassing nearly a hundred and fifty years and forty-eight disparate states. More recently, the extensive internet availability of historical newspapers has provided the opportunity for a much broader and more detailed view of the events of the era. In this account, I have attempted to provide the reader with sufficient background to understand both the "original" Klan of the 1860s, and the details of the formation and evolution of Simmons's successor "Klan" of 1915. The course of the revived order was driven by its leaders, thus to a great extent I focus on their actions. During the nearly three decades of the legal existence of The Knights of the Ku Klux Klan, Inc., its headquarters and base of operations were (for the most part) in Atlanta, Georgia. While the narrative is a national one, I have, when appropriate, chosen events and/or examples from the Klan's home state. I have devoted particular attention to Julian LaRose Harris, the son of the celebrated Southern writer and creator of Uncle Remus, Joel Chandler Harris. Julian Harris, via his newspaper, the *Columbus (GA) Enquirer-Sun*, was one of the outstanding voices in opposition to the Klan during the early 1920s, leading to his award of the Pulitzer Prize in 1926.

I believe that many readers who have some familiarity with the 1920s Klan will find much in this account that is new. To give a few examples, understanding the Lost Cause movement and the rise of fraternalism in the late nineteenth and early twentieth centuries helps provide some insight as to why Simmons would name his new "Klan" for what was basically a terrorist organization. The activities of the American Protective League during World War I provided the model for the Klan's conversion to a secret order. The competing Klans—themselves inspired by *The Birth of a Nation*—that vied for members during the initial years of Simmons's Klan have been little discussed in previous works. The details of the infighting among insiders of the Klan in the years 1922-1924 is key to the understanding of subsequent events. The W. J. Coburn and Madge Oberholtzer murder cases provide a window into the minds of Klan leaders. Finally, I devote a long chapter to the details of the post-Klan lives of several of the major figures in this saga.

The Ku Klux Klan of the 1920s is a fascinating, controversial, and often ugly subject, but it is an inescapable part of our American history. I trust that readers will find this account both interesting and informative.

William Rawlings
Sandersville, Georgia
January 1, 2015

Introduction

To the average American of the early twenty-first century, mention of the Ku Klux Klan evokes images of burning crosses and hooded men espousing a foul agenda of white supremacy, far from the mainstream of the nation's core values. Indeed, such an image would be correct. Those fringe elements that today make up the loose-knit groups that represent themselves as the Ku Klux Klan are nearly universally reviled, existing on the margins of society, protected in their rights of free speech under the First Amendment.

But in the 1920s, the Ku Klux Klan was a potent force in American life and politics, active in every state in the Union, promoting its nativist agenda of "One Hundred Percent Americanism" while democratically electing officials on all levels from local councilmen to congressmen, senators and state governors. Though never firmly representing the consensus of American thought, the Klan at its peak boasted of millions of members drawn from across the social and economic spectrum of the nation's population. The order's phenomenal growth from mere hundreds of members in 1920 to several million in mid-decade is the story of one of the most successful marketing efforts in American history.

In popular thought, the Klan of today is often believed to be part of the unbroken lineage of an unholy cabal formed in the post-Civil War South as a white supremacist organization, its prime reason for existence being the suppression of the civil rights of African-Americans. Such a perception is erroneous. It is important to understand that the group known as the Ku Klux Klan has had three separate and distinct incarnations since its birth in the Reconstruction Era. While bearing the same name, each "Klan" was different in organization, agenda, and impact on society at large. Though each iteration is of social and historical interest, it was the second Klan of the 1920s that rose to a position of national prominence and is the subject of this book. While each "Klan" lays claim to the heritage of those that preceded it, it is a mistake to assume that their history represents an unbroken timeline. Likewise, while there are some—perhaps many—similarities in thought and deed, the prime driving force for the formation of each of the three Klans was quite different.

The Ku Klux Klan of the 1860s was one of many local resistance and regulatory organizations that spontaneously arose in the South as a result of the social, political, and economic turmoil that existed following the defeat of the Confederacy. In current parlance it would be considered a terrorist organization. As conditions improved in the years following the war, and faced with vigorous Federal prosecution, the loosely affiliated organizations that made up the so-called "Ku Klux Movement" quietly faded away in the early 1870s.

A half-century after the end of the Civil War, a man named William Joseph Simmons, a failed Methodist minister and fraternal society organizer, formed a "beneficial, fraternal order" known as the Knights of Ku Klux Klan. His prime goal in doing so was not to promote a specific agenda, but rather to create a business enterprise. His choice of naming his order after the Ku Klux Klan of the Reconstruction Era was based largely on the then-current popularity and public awareness of the Klan's rehabilitated reputation. Atlanta, Georgia, Simmons's home at the time, had become one of the major cities of the New South. Rebuilding from the ashes left by Sherman's March to the Sea, the city's recovery accompanied that of the revision of Southern history and the glorification of the Lost Cause. Yes, the Confederacy had suffered defeat, but not through lack of valor, military prowess, or the righteousness of the Confederate cause. This veneration extended not only to the soldiers and officers who fought the South's battles, but also to those who served in local resistance movements during Reconstruction, specifically the Ku Klux Klan. The innovative 1915 movie, *The Birth of a Nation*, became America's first blockbuster while glorifying the image of the Klan. Simmons, capitalizing on the publicity generated by the movie and usurping the film's props of costume and burning cross for his order's regalia and prime icon, launched his new Knights of the Ku Klux Klan shortly after the film's debut.

For the first four-and-a-half years of its existence, Simmons's Klan struggled, attracting perhaps two thousand or so members in Georgia and Alabama. Although organized as a social order, the First World War offered the new Klan an opportunity to demonstrate its own form of public service by the intimidation of draft dodgers, slackers, and those who failed to support the war effort. This militancy, apparently not part of Simmons's original organizational plan, gave the Klan a sense of purpose. With the end of hostilities, the Klan faltered, and by the mid-1920 was essentially bankrupt.

Hoping to save his organization, Simmons approached Edward Young Clarke, an Atlanta promoter doing business as the Southern Publicity Association. The original idea was to have Clarke organize a recruitment campaign for the Klan. Clarke, however, sensing a lucrative commercial opportunity, agreed to merge his firm into the Klan. The Southern Publicity Association became the in-house Propagation Department of the Knights of the Ku Klux Klan, and Clarke became one of the order's officers. Klan recruiting agents, known as Kleagles, were dispatched across the nation. Based on their aggressive efforts, within a year-and-a-half the Klan's membership had risen to nearly 100,000. At its peak around mid-decade, the order would count an estimated five million-plus members.

Simmons was often described as a dreamer and a talented orator, but clearly lacking organizational skills. Under the guidance of Clarke, the Klan grew rapidly. Accompanying this growth, a phenomenal amount of income poured into the order's headquarters in Atlanta. This money, plus the untapped political potential of the Klan, attracted men more conniving than either Simmons or Clarke. In late 1922 and early 1923, both were deposed and eventually banished from the Klan. Hiram W. Evans, a former dentist, took over the helm of the order, serving as Imperial Wizard until 1939. Evans attempted to restructure the Klan to stem the violence attributed to it while emphasizing its potential political strength. He failed. The political and social power of the Klan, as well as its membership, peaked around 1925, and thereafter went into a precipitous decline. Although local branches retained some strength in certain areas of the country, by 1930 the Ku Klux Klan was essentially defunct as a national order. It remained a functioning organization until 1944 when it officially disbanded under the demand of the Internal Revenue Service for the payment of back taxes.

In the years following World War II, there were efforts to revive the Klan as a national order similar to that of the 1920s. They were unsuccessful, to be replaced by the current group of white supremacist organizations that carry the name of Ku Klux Klan. At present, it is estimated that there are more than forty different "Klans" in existence in the United States with a total of around 5,000 members.[1] There is little or no affiliation between individual groups. While adopting the regalia and iconography of the 1920s Klan, the actions and agendas of present day Klans vary widely.

The history of the Ku Klux Klan of the 1920s is one of the most fascinating in the myriad of tales that make up the American story. It is an account of an organization that seemingly recognized no paradox in its embrace of national patriotism and Protestant Christian values while espousing racial and religious hatred directed toward many of America's citizens. Its avowed support of the Constitution and the Rule of Law did not prevent its members from acting on their own as judge and jury in their enforcement of perceived moral and legal infractions. Its support of Prohibition, while an excellent marketing tool, did nothing to curtail the drinking habits of its leaders. It is a saga that includes all the elements of a work of popular fiction: violence, greed, murder, treachery, blackmail, lust, and off-camera sex thinly veiled under an aura of Christian values and moral chastity. Most importantly, a careful examination of the history of the Ku Klux Klan of the 1920s contradicts the proposition that the order was driven primarily by a single principled agenda or creed. The avowed tenets of Christianity, patriotism, white supremacy, the rule of law, and the rejection of things foreign were fundamentally secondary to the accumulation of wealth and power by its leaders. It was this simple fact that in the end would lead to the order's demise.

---

[1] Estimate from the Anti-Defamation League (http://archive.adl.org/learn/ext_us/kkk/default.html, accessed 6 December 2014)

Part I

The Roots of the Invisible Empire:

The Ku Klux Klan of the 1860s

We may, I think, forbear argument and take it for granted that the Ku Klux movement was an outcome of the conditions that prevailed in the Southern states after the war. It was too widespread, too spontaneous, too clearly a popular movement, to be attributed to any one man or to any conspiracy of a few men. Had it existed only in one corner of the South, or drawn its membership from a small and sharply defined class, some such explanation might serve. But we know enough of its extent, its composition, and the various forms it took, to feel sure that it was neither an accident nor a mere scheme. It was no man's contrivance, but an historical development. As such, it must be studied against its proper background of a disordered society and a bewildered people.

William Garrott Brown
The Lower South in American History
Published 1903

Chapter 1

The Roots of the Klan

There is no stranger chapter in American history than the one which bears for a title, "Ku Klux Klan." The organization which bore this name went out of life as it came into it, shrouded in deepest mystery. Its members would not disclose its secrets; others could not.... The veil of secrecy still hangs over its grave.[1] These words, penned in 1884 in one of the first histories of the Klan, refer to it in past tense, for it had ceased to exist. The Ku Klux Klan and similar groups formed in the South of the 1860s were products of the historical period known as Reconstruction. They were its spawn, their presence and purpose a response to the social, political, and economic conditions that existed in the former states of the Confederacy in the years following the Civil War.

By the early 1870s the Klan and dozens of other local and regional organizations of similar purpose had for the most part faded from existence. Their demise can be attributed not only to vigorous prosecution by state and federal authorities, but also to changing political conditions and public revulsion at the many "outrages" committed in their name. By the decade of the 1880s, the deeds of the Ku Klux Klan were rapidly morphing into legend, often reviled in the North as atrocities, while seen in the South as the actions of bold men willing to stand up to the oppression of an occupying army and imposed government in a time of wrenching social upheaval. To some extent both views were correct.

Were it not for a man named William J. Simmons, the Ku Klux Klan would have remained a historical curiosity, a footnote among the many strange events of the Reconstruction Era. Simmons, a failed Methodist minister, insurance salesman and self-described "fraternalist,"

---

[1]Lester and Wilson, *Ku Klux Klan: Its Origin, Growth and Disbandment,* 47.

had a vision of starting his own fraternal order. In 1915—capitalizing on the by-then-legendary reputation of the 1860s Klan—he did just that, resurrecting the organization in both name and spirit. Within a decade, it had become one of the more powerful voices in American life and politics. Like its predecessor, however, this new incarnation of the Invisible Empire was doomed to fail, but not before indelibly staining a transitional period in the nation's history with its existence and actions.

To understand the Ku Klux Klan of the early twentieth century it is necessary to understand its beginnings, how an organization originally rooted in principles of terrorism could—some six decades later—muster public parades of tens of thousands of supporters and elect governmental officials on local, state and national levels as it inflicted its message of exclusion and *über*-nationalism on American society.

The Ku Klux Klan was formed in the spring of 1866 in rural Pulaski, Tennessee, some sixty miles south of Nashville. Once a prosperous agricultural community, Pulaski had suffered from the collapse of the slave-based economic system that had driven the prosperity of the South since the invention of the cotton gin in the 1790s. According to accepted lore, the idea of forming a social club was hatched on December 24, 1865, during an informal gathering of six young Confederate veterans. The initial purpose was apparently one of benign recreational diversion intended only for amusement, not unlike the college fraternities of the day. In casting about for a name, someone suggested the Greek word *kyklos* (κύκλος), meaning circle, with "klan" added for alliteration. [2]

The first formal meetings of the Klan were held in the spring of 1866, and by all accounts constituted of little more than mystery, silly rituals, and social interaction. The organizers had chosen imposing names for the Klan's officers—the Grand Cyclops as president, the Grand Magi as Vice President, and so forth. Outrageous disguises were

---

[2] Sources differ as to whether the initial meeting of the organizers of the Klan took place in December 1865, or later in May or June of 1866. The version presented here is that of an initial meeting during which the idea was formulated, and a later series of organizational meetings. *See Chapter Notes for additional information on the alleged first site of the meeting of the Klan, as well as an alternative explanation for the name.*

worn, not so much to prevent identification of members but rather to impress and intimidate new inductees who—once members themselves—carried on the tradition. There were no standard costumes, uniforms, or regalia. At the outset, this secret, mysterious society was nothing more than a local social club, a pleasant diversion from a community and culture that had been ripped apart by the ravages of war.

The historical record sheds little light on when this recreational society transitioned into something more, a vigilante group whose purpose was to enforce its goals through extralegal means. Tennessee, among all the states of the Confederacy, had retained a strong Unionist element and fell under federal control early in the war. Andrew Johnson, a pro-Union Tennessean, had been chosen as Lincoln's running mate for the 1864 election, hoping to send a message of national unity with the foreseen end of the war. He had previously served as the state's governor in the 1850s, then as military governor under federal occupation from 1862 to 1864, generally aligning himself with the more radical elements of the Republican party. With his transition to Washington in 1865, the role of provisional governor was assumed by William G. ("Parson") Brownlow.

Brownlow, a former Methodist minister, newspaper editor and rabid Unionist, had been imprisoned by the Confederacy early in the war on a charge of treason for his vocal and often virulent anti-secession rhetoric. Pardoned and exiled to the North, he became a celebrity of sorts, closely allied with the Radical Republicans. As Tennessee's governor, he was quick to disenfranchise ex-Confederates. Within days of taking office he had overseen the ratification of the Thirteenth Amendment, the formal acknowledgment of the end of slavery. Freed slaves were soon granted full suffrage and were encouraged to organize under the auspices of the Union League, an extension of the Radical wing of the Republican Party. Rapidly consolidating political power, Brownlow forced through the ratification of the Fourteenth Amendment in 1866, after which Tennessee became the first former Confederate state to be readmitted to the Union.

Meanwhile in the towns and villages about the state, the months and years following the end of the war witnessed an unraveling of the previously stable social and political order.[3] Pulaski, the birthplace of the Ku Klux Klan, was situated in Giles County bordering the Alabama state line. The county's population of roughly thirty thousand included some twelve thousand-odd freed slaves, giving a black-white ratio that reflected the average for the lands of the former Confederacy. For the most part uneducated and unaccustomed to self-direction, the freedmen now constituted the majority of voters, easily swayed by Union League organizers and others. A breakdown of civil institutions, crime, and general lawlessness were on the increase, not to mention the general social disorder that resulted from the practical exclusion from power of the former ruling classes. It was this environment that gave rise to the local Klan's self-appointed role as regulator, enforcer, and resistor to change. To understand the spread of this shadowy organization, it is necessary to understand more fully one of the darkest eras in American history, that of Reconstruction.

---

[3] Trelease, *White Terror: The Ku Klux Klan Conspiracy and Southern Reconstruction*, 9-13.

Chapter 2

A Brief History of Reconstruction

One of the seeming paradoxes of history is the reverence often expressed by Southerners toward Abraham Lincoln in the years following the Civil War. Lincoln, above all, was the Union commander-in-chief, the ultimate leader of the military forces that crushed the Confederacy. Political feelings aside, much of this adoration can be traced to his stated hopes for a relatively benign post-war reunion between North and South. With Lincoln's assassination in April 1865 and the assumption of the office by the staunch Unionist Andrew Johnson, it was assumed that the reintegration of the states of the former Confederacy would be far more arduous. Initially, to the surprise of many, this turned out not to be the case.

The Reconstruction Era is generally divided by historians into three phases: Presidential Reconstruction from war's end in 1865 to 1867, Radical Reconstruction beginning in March 1867 and ending when the last of the rebel states was formally readmitted to the Union in 1870, and a final period characterized by increasing local political power by southern Democratic parties, terminated by the withdrawal of federal troops in 1877.[1]

In the spring and summer of 1865, the body politic in Washington was sharply divided as to the fate of the conquered South. One prominent faction, the Radical Republicans, declared the former rebel states should be punished severely, suggesting the long-term disenfranchisement of ex-Confederates, the confiscation of their property with redistribution to the freed slaves, as well as onerous reparation payments. The other major faction, moderate Democrats, took a more

---

[1] Some historians date the beginning of the Reconstruction Era from 1863 with the Emancipation Proclamation and the admission to the Union of the breakaway state of West Virginia.

nuanced approach. They were willing to allow a more rapid path to rehabilitation, but agreed that the rebel states should not be quietly forgiven and allowed to rejoin the Union as if the more than half a million deaths brought by war represented mere a spat between family members.

In the summer heat of 1865, the South lay in ruins. Not only was there physical damage—the destruction of hundreds of miles of rail lines, manufacturing facilities, and the like—but also economic and social devastation. A way of life built around the production of cotton, America's major export and the fountainhead of much of the young nation's positive balance of trade, lay in shambles. The 1860 census had recorded the population of the eleven Confederate states as approximately 8.73 million, of whom 40 percent (3.5 million) were slaves employed primarily in agriculture. At war's end these new freedmen found themselves in a physical and political limbo, unchained but without a clear direction as to their future.

Although each area of the former Confederacy had its unique concerns, the problems faced by the conquering North fell broadly into three categories. First was a general breakdown of societal and governmental function. With the old system dead, its former leaders now defeated and disenfranchised, a new democratic and more egalitarian society had to be created. Order had to be maintained. Crime, ranging from petty theft to murder and mayhem, was common. Second, and integrally related to the first, was the question of the role of the freed black slaves in a society dominated by their former white masters. The animus between the two groups—now separate but unequal—was sharply divided by racial lines. Third was economic chaos rooted in the death of the plantation system and its dependence on slave labor that characterized much of the antebellum South. What was to be the new economic relationship between those who worked the land and those who owned it?

While Congress and the President dithered over which direction to take with the Confederate states, enforcement fell to the military.[2] At the

---

[2] Coakley, *The Role of Military Forces in Domestic Disturbances 1789-1878*, 269.

end of hostilities, there were approximately 202,000 Federal troops occupying the conquered states. By January 1866, this number had fallen to 88,000 and continued to decline as soldiers were mustered out. After October 1866, only about 20,000 widely dispersed troops were charged with maintaining law and order for a population of more than eight million spread over the vast range of eleven states. Two years later this number was further reduced to approximately 11,000, with additional draw downs in the subsequent years of occupation. The relatively small number of troops meant law enforcement fell to local resources. Additionally, many of the military forces were composed of black regiments, whose presence in an enforcement role aroused resentment among the white population.[3]

Assisting the Federal troops were representatives of the Freedmen's Bureau,[4] created in 1865 as a division of the War Department to deal with the challenges of millions of freed slaves. In addition to providing aid and assistance to both ex-slaves and many destitute whites, the Bureau focused on establishing some degree of local order by arranging labor contracts and adjudicating minor disputes and legal infractions while promoting education for all. At times working with Northern aid and missionary societies, the Bureau's presence and efforts to impose an inclusive society were often deeply resented by local communities, seen as a further attempt to destroy a way of life that had existed for generations.

In the months following the end of hostilities in the spring of 1865, President Andrew Johnson's attitude toward the former Confederacy seemed to soften. He promoted a path of accelerated reconciliation, the goal being the readmission of the rebel states within a year. The main requirement was the ratification of the Thirteenth Amendment, renouncing slavery but granting no further rights to those freed from its bonds. The provisional state governments rapidly complied, leading to its formal adoption in mid-December 1865. Presidential pardons to ex-Confederates were dispensed freely, planting the seeds of a nascent political resurgence of the South's old leadership.

---

[3] See Singletary, *Negro Militia and Reconstruction.*
[4] More properly, the Bureau of Refugees, Freedmen, and Abandoned Lands.

While the ex-slaves were now free men and women, they continued to occupy the place of second-class citizens in the new order. In both the North and the South, citizenship was not equated with the right to vote; only six of the Northern states "allowed blacks to vote on any terms."[5] Southern legislatures quickly enacted so-called Black Codes, limiting and regulating the civil rights of freedmen, much to the annoyance of the Radical Republicans. Even more worrisome to the congressional Republicans was their own political future. The passage of the Thirteenth Amendment effectively nullified Article 1, Paragraph 2, Section 3 of the United States Constitution, the so-called Three-Fifths Compromise. Under this clause, "other Persons" (a euphemism for those enslaved), would be counted as three-fifths persons for the purpose of determining Congressional representation. Forty percent of the population of the former Confederate states was now composed of freed slaves, raising the specter of increasing the number of Southern representatives by nearly twenty percent at the time of the next reapportionment. Majority-black states such as Mississippi and South Carolina would see the greatest gains, with Florida, Georgia, and Louisiana close behind. Although the provisional legislatures were pro-Union, the power of the Democratic Party was increasing. The ex-slaves counted now as full persons, but under the provisional governments had little chance of participating in the electoral process.

As 1865 became 1866, the ideological differences between the President and Congress widened. Johnson increasingly aligned himself with the Democrats, while in the occupied states of the South, former Confederates were growing gradually more powerful. In April 1866, Congress passed the Civil Rights Act, designed to protect the rights of the freed slaves. President Johnson vetoed it, only to have his veto overridden. In Norfolk, a crowd of some 800 blacks marching in celebration of its passage were fired upon by a white man, who was in turn attacked and killed by the mob. Two days of rioting were quickly suppressed by a show of military force. In May, an unruly group of black soldiers recently mustered out of service clashed with the police in Memphis, resulting in a white mob that slaughtered some forty-seven

---

[5] McPherson, *Ordeal By Fire: The Civil War and Reconstruction*, 500.

blacks, while suffering the deaths of only two whites. In July in New Orleans, several days of political rallies by the newly emboldened freedmen resulted in clashes that left nearly forty dead, again the vast majority of them black. Delegates to the events were said to have been "hunted down" by whites.[6] These and other "outrages" increasingly turned public and political opinion in the North against Johnson's policies of benign reconciliation.

Emboldened by gains in the 1866 elections, the positions of the Radical Republicans garnered more legislative converts. Over a period of months, Congress debated and finally passed on March 2, 1867, the first of the so-called Reconstruction Acts, euphemistically titled "An Act to Provide for the More Efficient Government of the Rebel States." The act removed the provisional governments of the ten remaining ex-Confederate States, divided the South into five military districts, and imposed martial law.[7] Under military rule, the states were required to grant suffrage to freedmen, draft new constitutions, and—as a condition of readmission to the Union—approve the Fourteenth Amendment granting equal protection under the law to all. President Johnson promptly vetoed the measure. Congress immediately overrode his veto, turning the act into the law of the land.

To those in the conquered South, still suffering nearly two years after the end of the war, the imposition of military rule added insult to injury. Just at a time when there appeared a glimmer of hope for the right of regaining self-rule and the restoration of civil society, it was all snatched away. State and local governments were arbitrarily dismissed by the actions of a Congress in which they had little representation. De facto political and legislative power was handed to the former slaves, who at best were politically naïve, and at worst easily swayed by those who sought to punish their former masters. More so than any other single factor, it was the period of Radical Reconstruction ushered in by this Act that gave rise to the first incarnation of the Ku Klux Klan.

---

[6] Coakley, 284.
[7] Tennessee had been readmitted to the Union in 1866.

Chapter 3

The Arc of Terrorism

In August 1868, General Nathan Bedford Forrest revealed to a correspondent for the *Cincinnati Commercial* that the Ku Klux Klan boasted "over 40,000" members in Tennessee, and "about 550,000" in the Southern States.[1] Reason might suggest the numbers were exaggerated, but less than a year into Radical Reconstruction there was no doubt the Klan had become the subject of national interest. Its true membership will never be known, but the fact that it had grown from a handful of members to perhaps tens of thousands in slightly more than two years suggests its philosophy and actions had wide appeal.

Military rule, especially after March 1867, had been accompanied by the rise of local chapters of the Union (or Loyal) League.[2] They were, for practical purposes, disciples of the Radical Republicans whose primary purpose was to organize the freed slaves into politically active supporters of the party. The various names and organizational structures often differed, but commonly local units were framed as secret or semi-secret societies into which new members were inducted with elaborate ritual.[3] A pervading fear among whites was the possibility of black-led rebellion stemming from these clandestine groups. The 1790s slave uprising in Haiti in which some 4,000 whites were murdered was still recent enough to evoke comparison and dread of the possibility of a similar event. Nat Turner's 1831 rebellion in southern Virginia with its brutal slaughter of men, women, and children was even more recent. In response, "throughout the South, there began spontaneously to spring up local

---

[1] Reported in *New Albany (IN) Daily Commercial,* 10 September 1868.
[2] The terms Union League and Loyal League are often used interchangeably.
[3] Avary, *Dixie After the War,* 263.

[white] defensive groups, generally in the form of secret societies, designed primarily to offset the aggressiveness of the Loyal Leagues."[4]

The Ku Klux Klan of Giles County, Tennessee, had gradually assumed the role of an extra-legal regulatory organization, a covert group serving in a self-appointed police function. Its primary purpose initially was to maintain social order, much of which involved the intimidation of politically active Negroes or those perceived to have crossed some ill-defined boundary of acceptable social behavior. Other loosely affiliated dens (chapters) had been formed in adjacent territories. With the passage of the first Reconstruction Act and the prospect of years of military occupation of the South, many felt the Klan needed to assume a larger role. In April 1867, delegates from the existing dens met at the Maxwell House hotel in Nashville, Tennessee for the purpose of creating a formal organizational structure for the Klan.[5] A Prescript (constitution) was drawn up, declaring the territory in which the Klan operated to be an "Empire" and laying out its goals in high-toned phrases: "To protect the weak, the innocent, the defenseless, from the indignities, wrongs and outrages of the lawless, the violent and the brutal...," "To protect and defend the Constitution of the United States, and all laws passed in conformity thereto...," "To aid and assist in the execution of all constitutional laws, and to protect the people from unlawful seizure...."[6]

Officials and titles were designated, their powers and duties defined. A list of questions posed to potential members served to exclude those who were or had been "a member of the Radical Republican Party, or either of the organizations known as the 'Loyal League' and the 'Grand Army of the Republic.'" The opposition to "negro equality" and the belief in "a white man's government" were necessary requirements.[7]

Former Confederate General Nathan Bedford Forrest was named the first Grand Wizard, the "supreme officer of the Empire." Politically, he was an excellent choice. Both pragmatic and driven, he was held in

---

[4] Horn, *Invisible Empire: The Story of the Ku Klux Klan 1866-1871*, 29.

[5] Interestingly, Maxwell House Coffee traces its name to this hotel, as does the expression, "Good to the last drop," allegedly uttered by President Theodore Roosevelt while a guest there in 1907.

[6] Horn, 397.

[7] Ibid., 406.

high esteem in the South for his brilliant leadership during the war. A millionaire planter and speculator prior to the outbreak of hostilities, Forrest joined the Confederate Army as a private, rising rapidly through the ranks to lieutenant general. Though untrained in military command and cavalry tactics, his innovative strategies led to a string of victories from 1862 through the end of the conflict.

The existence of the Ku Klux Klan, this strange, secret Southern society, first caught the interest of the national press in early 1868. In the spring of the year, the *Rochester (NY) Standard* playfully explained this "new-coined compound word which is at the present time on everyone's lips" was more than "a mere cabalistic expression." [8] With tongue-in-cheek prose the paper speculated as to the origin of the name, offering possible word roots in old English, Greek, and Latin. A Texas newspaper referred to it as "an abominable hoax," while quoting a Tennessee paper alleging the Klan to be "a purely political organization."[9] By mid-year, however, national papers were filled with frequent accounts of "outrages" committed by masked men said to be members of the "shadowy organization." The light-hearted reporting gave way to reliable reports of whippings, beatings, and even murder of Negroes and Unionists whose activities had drawn the attention of the group.

The Northern press developed a certain perverse fascination with the Klan as reporting often gave way to exaggeration and outright falsehood. In May 1868, the *Illustrated News* printed a lurid tale supposedly recounting the details of a Klan initiation.[10] According to the unidentified informant, the ceremony took place in a cavern lit by flaming pine knots and "lined with rows of grinning skeletons," conducted by "the Grand Cyclops, a gigantic man, naked to the waist, with a dagger in his right hand and the whole upper portion of his body smeared with warm, smoking blood." A "lusty negro," bound and gagged, was thrust upon an altar, whereupon the novice was required to stab the victim in the heart, "staining his hands in the gushing life

---

[8] *Rochester (NY) Standard*, 21 May 1868.
[9] *Flake's Daily Bulletin (Galveston, TX)*, 14 February, 1868.
[10] Recounted in Horn, 43.

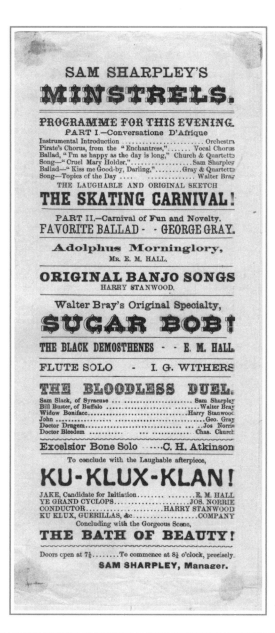

In the early Reconstruction Era of the late 1860s, the Ku Klux Klan was considered by some in the North an object of ridicule, as evidenced by this comedic program from a traveling minstrel troupe. (From the collections of the Center for Popular Music, Middle Tennessee State University.)

blood." Fearful for his own life, he complied, but horrified by what he had been forced to do, allegedly reported it to the *News* to warn others of the depravity of this wretched group. The public's fascination with the Klan lapped over into popular entertainment. Sam Sharpley's Minstrels, a variety troupe operating in New York in the late 1860s, concluded their show with a "laughable afterpiece" titled "Ku-Klux-Klan," apparently a comedic take on a Klan initiation.[11]

To some degree, the news coverage of the Klan took on a political bias. Commentary varied widely depending on the location and politics of the given newspaper or its editor. The *Galveston (TX) Daily News* opined, "We presume the Klan to be one of those secret societies which are often formed in troublous times; and though the course it pursues may be condemned, we think it very doubtful whether any innocent persons will suffer at its hands, but believe, rather, than many such will be protected or avenged by it."[12] In contrast, an Ohio daily reported, "The horrors practiced by these wretches grow more intensely black every day. They roam through the country and perpetrate their crimes with apparent impunity, and a Satanic determination and disregard of consequences perfectly appalling."[13]

By 1868, the Klan's actions had drawn international interest. In late September of that year the *London Morning Post* featured a long article on the situation in Tennessee, focusing on Governor Brownlow's struggle against the insurgency, the near-state of "civil war," the anti-Klan laws, and the state's appeal to Washington for assistance. The correspondent, more balanced in his reporting than most American accounts, was unwilling to speculate on the eventual political outcome of the struggle.

---

[11] The fascination and literary fabrication extended to popular literature as well. *The Terrible Mysteries of the Ku-Klux-Klan*, a contemporary (1868) novel by Edward H. Dixon, depicts the group as possessing supernatural origins and semi-magical powers. The fictional *The Masked Lady of the White House: Or The Ku-Klux Klan* depicts a female Klan spy who is actually working for the Radical Republicans in an effort to defeat the Klan.

[12] *Galveston (TX) Daily News*, 30 March 1868.

[13] *Benton Tribune (Oxford, OH)*, 21 July 1868.

The Klan was not the only such organization that sprang up across the enormous territory of the former Confederacy. Other local movements, more or less structured, assumed comparable roles in other locations both during and after Reconstruction. The Knights of the White Camellia were active in a number of states, using violence and intimidation to resist Republican rule.[14] In addition to the Klan, Tennessee had the Pale Faces and the Red Jackets. Mississippi citizens joined the Native Sons of the South, the Society of the White Rose, the Knights of the Black Cross, or the Seventy-Six Association. There were numerous others, numbering perhaps in the dozens. Their goals varied but shared the common purpose of restoring and maintaining self-rule, most often through both overt and covert—sometimes violent— support of the Democratic Party. In both current and subsequent thought, these organizations were often considered "Klans" or Klan-like. Their number and uniformity of purpose have led historians to often refer to "The Ku Klux Movement" as a generic name inclusive of the various resistance organizations that sprang up in the South in the 1860s and 1870s.

According to a number of accounts, Grand Wizard Nathan Bedford Forrest ordered the Klan disbanded in early 1869, and its paraphernalia and records destroyed. His reasoning, it seems, held that the organization had accomplished its mission of restoring some degree of civil rule. In truth, this order—if it was in fact given by Forrest—had little effect on the actions of the loosely affiliated member-dens of the Invisible Empire. "In most sections of the South the dissolution of the Ku Klux was governed solely by local conditions; and generally speaking, the Klan's end was more in the form of a spotty, slow, and gradual disintegration than a formal and decisive disbandment."[15] Among prime reasons cited for the organization's end was the increasingly pervasive use of violence and the resulting loss of the quiet public support it had once enjoyed. It appears well established that as time went forward others used the name or reputation of the Klan as a cover for criminal activity or acts of personal vengeance. The role of suppressive activity on the part of

---

[14] Also (mis)spelled as "Camelia." The use here is the correct English spelling of the flower, but note that in Spanish, it is spelled with a single "l".

[15] Horn, 360.

state and federal authorities is not to be understated, but like any insurgency, the Klan's basic existence was fundamentally dependent on the tacit support of the populace at large.

In Georgia, from whose red clay hills the seeds of a revived Klan would spring some half century hence, the group was active from at least 1868 until 1871 or later. As early as the spring of 1868, General George G. Meade, Commander of the Department of the South which included Mississippi, Alabama, Georgia, and the Carolinas, issued suppressive orders aimed at Klan activity, threatening offenders with trial before a military commission.[16] While the Klan's presence appears to have been statewide, the two regions seeing the most action were the northwest foothills region, and counties of the upper cotton belt south and west of Augusta. The demographics of these areas were fundamentally different. In the more mountainous region, farms were small and former slaves few in number. Whites composed a comfortable majority of the population. In the cotton-producing counties, however, blacks made up sixty percent or more of the population, theoretically holding the key to political power. A study of Reconstruction in Georgia published by Columbia University in 1915 makes a number of interesting observations on how the actions of the Klan differed in these two areas.[17] In the northwest of the state, the Klan took on a more regulatory role, enforcing social order. Clashes between whites and blacks were framed more as a struggle between classes, as freedom had removed the last formal wall between the status of the former slaves and poor white farmers. In the counties with majority-black populations, Union and Loyal League organizers were aggressively active, often working in conjunction with agents of the Freedmen's Bureau. Here, the actions of the former slaves often took on a political nature. In turn, Klan action was more violent and directed toward the suppression of black voting rights.

As Congressional hearings in 1871 would later document, presumed Klan-related violence and intimidation was common in Georgia in the years between 1868 and 1870. At the same time, there were a number of "insurrections," caused at least in part by the attempt of the freedmen to

---

[16] *New York Herald*, 7 April 1868.
[17] Thompson, "Reconstruction in Georgia," 361-388.

exercise their new-found civil and political freedoms. In September 1868, some dozen or more blacks marching in a political rally were killed in the so-called Camilla Massacre in Mitchell County. [18] In the North this incident became a *cause célèbre*, seen as yet another sign of Southern intransigence and a clear justification for the rigors of Radical Reconstruction. In the South, the specter of a crowd of marching blacks, some of whom were armed, raised fears of race-fueled rebellion. In December of the same year, a dispute over land ownership by armed blacks in an area of former rice plantations near Savannah became known as the "Ogeechee Insurrection."[19]

In August 1870, a Union League organizer named Cudjo Fye led an armed mob of blacks in an attempt to free a prisoner from the Jefferson County jail in Louisville, Georgia. He alleged to his followers that he was operating under direct orders of Republican Governor Rufus Bullock. Initially dissuaded in their efforts by local officials, Fye returned the next day with a band of "fifty or sixty armed followers," "damning the white man promiscuously," as well as threatening to burn the town "and kill every man, woman and child in it." They broke into the jail and freed the prisoner. In response, as many as a thousand armed whites from surrounding counties descended on Louisville, later assisted by Federal troops. The affair ended fairly peacefully, with a number of the leaders of the mob later sentenced to prison.[20]

While none of these "insurrections" directly involved the Klan, they were used by locals to justify its existence in Georgia. The years of military rule saw countless episodes of threats, beatings, and other forms of intimidation of politically active blacks, Union League organizers, carpetbaggers, and scalawags who were deemed threats to the resumption of local political rule.[21] Murders were not uncommon: G. W. Ashburn, a

---

[18] Formwalt, "The Camilla Massacre of 1868: Racial Violence as Political Propaganda," 399-426.

[19] Bell, "The Ogeechee Troubles": Federal Land Restoration and the 'Lived Realities' of Temporary Properties, 1865-1868," 375-97.

[20] Coulter "Cudjo Fye's Insurrection," 213-25.

[21] The term "carpetbagger" was used to refer to outsiders, most commonly from the North, who moved to the South following the Civil War, often to participate in Reconstruction activities or take advantage of the economic, social,

politically active scalawag judge, was assassinated in Columbus in March 1868. A year later, a group of Klansmen in Warren County took from jail and executed the man—a physician—accused of the murder of one of their leaders. The matter was clearly a private one, but speaks to the self-assurance of the Klan's sense of justice. There were numerous other examples.[22]

The Klan's violence and utter opposition to imposed Republican rule was of increasing concern in Washington. In response, Congress passed a series of Enforcement Acts under the provisions of the Fourteenth Amendment, the first in 1870 and two more in 1871. Aimed at the activities of the Klan, they were designed to stop intimidation of blacks, especially with regard to their voting rights. The third act, known informally as the Ku Klux Act, specifically addressed issues of conspiracy and disguises, suspending the right of *habeas corpus* and meting out harsh punishment to those who violated its provisions. The law was vigorously enforced under President Grant's direction, resulting in a number of high-profile trials and convictions of alleged members of the Klan.

Meanwhile, Congress had launched its own investigation into the matter. Between May and December 1871, Congressmen held a series of hearings both in Washington and in the South for the purpose of documenting the anti-government activities of the Klan. Testimony was heard from a wide range of individuals, ranging from those thought to be

---

and political opportunities afforded by the turmoil of the era. The name derives from the soft-sided luggage in which they packed their belongings. "Scalawags" (also spelled "scallawag" or "scallywag") were native Southerners who cooperated with the imposed order during the era, often holding political office. The origin of this word is less clear. It is possibly derived from Scalloway, a small city on the largest of Scotland's Shetland Islands. At one time it was used as a derisive descriptor of low-grade farm animals. Both terms were used in a pejorative manner for many years after the end of the Reconstruction era. For example, in the 1895 romantic novel, *Ku-Klux Klan, No. 40* by Thomas J. Jerome, the amorous rival of a young Klansman for the love of his lady is described as a "miserable, South-hating, carpet-bagger."

[22] By the 1870s, the name of the Ku Klux Klan was so inextricably associated with violence that it was verbalized and used as such. An example from *The Sandersville (GA) Herald*, 7 October 1875: "Two negro men attempted to ku-klux a negro woman near Augusta. They first tried to cut her throat and then drown her but failed in both."

at the highest levels of the Klan to those who had suffered at its hands. While the methods of the Klan were generally condemned by all, it should be remembered that their desired outcome of the intimidation and violence was often a political one: the suppression of Republican support in the South. Hence, the hearings had a definite political undertone. According to one historian:

> The Republican members diligently sought to establish from the witnesses that the Ku Klux Klan was a political organization, composed exclusively of Democrats, and designed primarily for the persecution of Republicans, black and white, and especially for the intimidation of negro voters. The Democrats on the other hand, worked just as hard to sustain the theory that the Ku Klux had no political purposes whatsoever, that they did not concern themselves with the politics of their victims, but were organized and operated entirely as a widespread vigilance committee for the preservation of law and order.[23]

At the outset, the Committee agreed by default to allow a broad range of testimony, thus the inclusion of many rumors and hearsay. Perhaps the star witness was General Nathan Bedford Forrest, the reputed former Grand Wizard. Forrest's testimony was coy and evasive, marked by frequent and seemingly selective memory lapses. He stated that he had been told of the existence of an organization known as the Ku Klux Klan, but knew scarcely more than that. The investigators gained little from his testimony.[24]

Based on the testimony of hundreds of witnesses there was no doubt that the Klan (or those representing themselves as the Klan) had visited a reign of terror upon the South. The oft-repeated tales of intimidation, beatings, and murder were explicit and for the most part consistent with the order's designation as a terrorist organization. The verbatim testimony before the committee was published in 1872 under the lofty title of "Testimony Taken by the Joint Select Committee to Inquire into the Conditions of Affairs in the Late Insurrectionary States," with the succinct subtitle, "The Ku-Klux Conspiracy." The report is spread over

---

[23] Horn, 298-299.
[24] *See Chapter Notes for additional information on Gen. Forrest and the Ku Klux Klan.*

thirteen volumes of small-print type, one of which contains the Majority
and Minority summary reports of the hearings. While there was no
attempt to justify the crimes and atrocities of the Klan, the final written
opinions of the Majority and Minority members of the Committee
diverged sharply based on political orientation.[25]

By 1870, the Republican-dominated legislatures of all the former
rebel states had ratified the Fourteenth and Fifteenth Amendments,
allowing their readmission to the Union. The last was Georgia, admitted
in July of that year. While Federal troops still occupied the South, local
white-oriented political parties were rapidly gaining strength. Tennessee
and Virginia came under Democratic control in 1869, followed by North
Carolina in 1870 and Texas in 1871. By 1877, the eleven former
Confederate states were solidly back in Democratic hands. Klan and
other politically motivated violence ebbed as the nation, weary of war and
its aftermath, turned its eyes to other issues of the day. While the last
two of the Reconstruction Amendments had guaranteed both civil and
voting rights for freedmen, newly empowered Southern governments set
about to systematically dismantle their mandates.

The disputed presidential election of 1876 brought an end to the
Reconstruction Era. After years of Republican rule it was clear that the
Democratic candidate, Samuel J. Tilden, had won the popular ballot,
exceeding Rutherford B. Hayes's total by nearly a quarter million votes.
The problem arose with the electoral vote. While both parties had advo-
cated an end to Reconstruction, the campaign had been vicious, with the
Democrats attacking the corruption of the Grant presidency and the
Republicans reminding voters that the former rebel states were heavily
Democratic. In the South, there were active attempts to suppress the
black vote, the overwhelming majority of which would have gone to the
Republicans. Reports of voter fraud were widespread. The nineteen
electoral votes of Louisiana, Florida, and South Carolina were especially
suspect, as was the eligibility of one of the three electors from Oregon.

---

[25] See the Report of the Joint Select Committee (1872). The interested
reader is directed to the complete report, which is readily available from several
sources in electronic format. The Georgia-related testimony alone consists of
more than 1200 pages in two volumes.

Together, the twenty disputed votes could swing the election in either direction.

As the Constitution gave no specific guidance as to how the impasse should be resolved, Congress created an Electoral Commission whose decision would be final unless overturned by both houses of Congress. After a series of hearings, the Republican-majority commission voted to give the disputed votes to Hayes, thus awarding their candidate victory by the slim electoral margin of a single vote out of the 369 cast. While the Republican-controlled Senate was content with the vote, the Democrat-controlled House of Representatives sought to obstruct the decision, going so far as to pass a resolution stating that Tilden had been "duly elected President of the United States." It was all for naught, as on March 5, 1877, Rutherford B. Hayes took the presidential oath without event.

It was rumored that Hayes's ascension to the presidency was made possible by an unwritten back-room agreement between the parties, the so-called Compromise of 1877 that, among other things, brought a formal end to Reconstruction. In the month following his inauguration, Hayes ordered the remaining Federal troops withdrawn from the South, paving the way for complete political control by the Democratic Party, thus forming a regional voting block that would last for the next century.

While the intentions and legacy of Reconstruction have been debated since its end, there seems little doubt that its policies did more harm than good. Beyond the horror of war and the shame of defeat, the years of military occupation and imposed political will left a legacy of enmity between the South and the North that lingers nearly a century and a half later. If the purpose of Reconstruction was to rebuild the economy and the society of the South into something more nearly resembling that of the North, it also failed in this regard. For the remaining years of the nineteenth century, much of the South—especially the rural areas—became an economic backwater, an agrarian region characterized by poverty, disease, and hopelessness. The well-meaning intentions of the Fourteenth and Fifteenth Amendments to the Constitution were soon diluted by legislative action and court decision. In the years that followed, the freed slaves—now nominally full citizens with constitutionally-protected rights and privileges—were once again relegated to the status of second-class persons. Their freedoms abridged by Jim Crow laws and their place in society limited by segregation, they entered an era of physical and intellectual poverty that would last for decades.

The one legacy of Reconstruction that was to persist and burst upon the national scene some half-century later was that of the Ku Klux Klan. Its exploits transformed and magnified into myth, its terrorist image softened by time, robed figures of the Klan would ride once again, no less dangerous but all the more powerful.

Part II

The Lost Cause Years 1865-1915:

From Terrorists to Knights in White Sheets

The history of the vanquished has too often fallen to the pen of the victor, and to insure justice to the Southern cause, the pen must be taken by some Southern man who is willing to devote his time and talents to the vindication of his countrymen, in a history which shall challenge the criticism of the intelligent, and invite the attention of all honest inquirers.

From a solicitation for *The Lost Cause: A New Southern History of the War of the Confederates*
Published 1866

The victim of the Lost Cause legend has been history, for which the legend has been substituted in the national memory.

Alan T. Nolan, in "The Anatomy of the Myth"
The Myth of the Lost Cause and Civil War History
Published 2000

Chapter 4

The Apotheosis of the Fallen

Approximately fifteen miles northeast of downtown Atlanta, a massive rocky outcropping known as Stone Mountain rises more than 800 feet above the surrounding countryside, a remnant of the formation of the Blue Ridge Mountains. Visible from as far as forty miles away, it is reputedly the world's largest piece of exposed granite. It is now the center of a state-owned recreational park originally designed as a memorial to the men and women of the Confederacy. Access is via Jefferson Davis Drive. The mountain itself is ringed by Robert E. Lee Boulevard while the park's golf links lie to the east of Stonewall Jackson Drive. On the monolith's sheer north face, a colossal carving measuring some 90 feet tall by 190 feet wide depicts these three, Davis, Lee, and Jackson, the men who form the pinnacle of the Confederate pantheon.[1]

Stone Mountain's Confederate monument came into being through the efforts of Helen Plane, a Confederate widow and one of the original organizers of the Atlanta Chapter of the United Daughters of the Confederacy (UDC).[2] In 1914, at age eighty-five, she was instrumental in forming the UDC's Stone Mountain Confederate Memorial Association, serving as its first president. The original idea was to honor General Robert E. Lee with a seventy-foot tall bust carved on the mountain's north side. After consideration of a number of candidates to complete the project, the Association chose John Gutzon de la Mothe Borglum, at the time one of the nation's most distinguished sculptors.

Arriving in Atlanta in August 1915, Borglum spent three days examining the mountain. He reported to the Association that the proposed bust of Lee would be dwarfed by the tremendous size of the

---

[1] And their horses, Blackjack, Traveler, and Little Sorrel, respectively.
[2] Freeman, *Carved in Stone: The History of Stone Mountain*, 55-63.

rock face, that something much grander was needed. Borglum proposed a veritable army of marching figures—between 700 and 1,000 of them ranging in height from 35 to 50 feet—facing east toward the new dawn. There would be groups of cavalry, infantry and artillery plus others surrounding a central group with the images of Davis, Lee, and Jackson. Overall, the carving would be some 1,200 feet in length. And there was more. At the base of the rock face, Borglum proposed a carved colonnade behind which a massive room would be cut into the mountain, a Memorial Hall to be dedicated to the women of the Confederacy.

Borglum's vision of a Confederate Memorial never came to fruition. War, financial considerations and politics intervened. Borglum abandoned the project, moving on to carve the colossal presidential heads of Mr. Rushmore. After various fits and starts the carving was abandoned in 1928, only to be completed under the auspices of the State of Georgia in the early 1970s. The carving that today graces the mountain's scarp is a mere wisp of Borglum's original glorious vision. Despite this, it remains the largest and most impressive of hundreds of such monuments across the Southland, a testament also to the power of the way of thinking known as The Lost Cause.

The wounds marking the shattered forests and fields that hosted the far-flung battles of the Civil War had scarcely begun to heal when Edward A. Pollard, a former editor of the *Richmond Examiner*, published a 752-page opus titled *The Lost Cause: A New Southern History of the War of the Confederates*. Virulently pro-Southern while condemning the politicians and military leaders of the North, it was released in 1866 to wide commercial success. Pollard's work is best remembered, however, for lending its title to the informal crusade that came to represent mainstream Southern thought in the latter years of the nineteenth century. The so-called Lost Cause, promoted by Confederate veterans, their former leaders and descendants, sought to bestow the moral high ground to the men and women of Confederacy while depicting the South's defeat as the inevitable result of the North's numeric superiority in men and matériel.

In the decades that followed the war, the political leaders of both sides published prolifically, often in the form of memoirs subtly slanted to provide the proper narrative for their place in history. Alexander H.

Stephens, the vice president of the Confederacy, was among the first, releasing his two-volume *A Constitutional View of the War Between the States* in 1868. President Jefferson Davis's *The Rise and Fall of the Confederate Government* in 1881 was followed four years later by the *Personal Memoirs of Ulysses S. Grant.*

The first major work by a military leader, however, was that of Confederate Lieutenant General Jubal Early in his *Memoir of the Last Year of the War for Independence in the Confederate States of America,* published in 1867. Despite having been relieved of command by General Lee for his failures in the Shenandoah Valley in 1864-65, Early was to emerge at the forefront of the post-war movement that glorified the Southern cause and the men who fought for it. He took an active role in the Southern Historical Society and its journal, the *Southern Historical Society Papers,* which served as a platform for Southern thought and revisionism in the latter quarter of the nineteenth century. First published in 1876, the lead article of its first issue, titled "Origin of the Late War," was a justification of the Confederacy's formation and resulting conflict as the South's defense of "her constitutional rights and liberties." Through personal correspondence, lectures, and authorship of articles, Early did much to elevate Generals Robert E. Lee and Stonewall Jackson to heroic status, stalwart icons of a righteous cause.

Recollections of the war were kept alive by memorial services, veterans' organizations, publications, and monuments. Within a few years of the end of the war, every state of the former Confederacy had established a formal Memorial Day to honor those who had served in the conflict. Veterans' groups sprang up spontaneously across the South, first on a local basis, then nationally. The United Confederate Veterans (UCV) was formed in 1889, followed by the United Daughters of the Confederacy (UDC) in 1894, and the Sons of Confederate Veterans (SCV) in 1896. The monthly *Confederate Veteran* magazine began publication in 1893. Produced in popular format in contrast to the more academic tone of the *Southern Historical Society Papers,* its content sought to glorify the men who had fought for the South and the memory of those who had died. Permanent mementos took the form of more than

500 Confederate memorial monuments erected in towns and cities from Virginia to Texas between 1865 and 1912.[3]

Among the many projects promoted by the UCV, UDC, and others, was the campaign to ensure that school textbooks were free of the "false history" of the war often produced by Northern publishers.[4] If the texts were to be acceptable for use in the former Confederacy, the interpretation of historical events necessarily needed to follow the Southern view of the conflict, its causes and its outcomes. Their efforts were successful; by the first decade of the twentieth century, state-level textbook committees were the norm, ensuring that a "proper" historical narrative was presented to young minds.

By the latter years of the nineteenth century, the Legend of the Lost Cause had been firmly established, so widely accepted and so pervasive in Southern thought that some historians have likened it to the equivalent of a popular religion.[5] Its truths were simple and direct: The primary reason for the Civil War was the defense of States' Rights, not slavery. The South was just in seeking to establish a new independent republic. It was the failure of the Northern states to acknowledge this reality that lead to war. Despite wise leaders, able soldiers, and heroic generals, Confederate armies were defeated by the North's overwhelming superiority in troops and resources. The Southern way of life, including the institution of slavery, was unique and superior to that of the North. The post-war years of so-called Reconstruction represented punishment inflicted upon the South by a vengeful North. In the end, Southern spirit and culture rebounded, leading to the hackneyed phrase, "The South Shall Rise Again." Henry Grady, de facto spokesman for the New South, summarized the viewpoint well in his address to the New England Society in December 1886: "The South has nothing for which to apologize. She believes that the late struggle between the States was war

---

[3] Foster, *Ghosts of the Confederacy*, 273.
[4] Fahs and Waugh, *The Memory of the Civil War in American Culture*, 64-76.
[5] Wilson, *Baptized in the Blood: the Religion of the Lost Cause 1865-1920*, 1-17.

and not rebellion, revolution and not conspiracy, and that her convictions were as honest as yours."[6]

To a greater or lesser degree, this view of history persisted and grew well into the twentieth century to the point of gaining wide acceptance across the American landscape, often displacing other, less flattering narratives. So national in scope was the rehabilitation of the South and many of its leaders that over the ensuing years the United States government would honor General Robert E. Lee by issuing no fewer than five postage stamps and one coin bearing his image, a strange honor for a once bitter foe.

As the legacy of the war years persisted in American memory, the era served as the setting for numerous popular literary works, ranging from the forgettable to such classics as Stephen Crane's *The Red Badge of Courage*.[7] Even Jules Verne, the noted French author, published in 1887 *North Against South*, a novel set in Confederate Florida.[8] The Reconstruction Era exploits of the mysterious Klan attracted writers as well. Among the first was an anonymously published 1872 work, *The Nation's Peril*, subtitled "The Ku Klux Klan" and purporting to be "A Complete Exposition of the Order." In lurid prose based primarily on the Congressional hearings of the prior year, the author warned, "The standard bearers of the devil himself, coming from the lowest depths of the infernal regions, with seething vials of wrath and an earnest intention to do the bidding of their master, could scarcely have set on foot a conspiracy more damnable than this."[9]

---

[6] Harris, *The Life of Henry W. Grady*, 91.

[7] Undoubtedly, the best remembered work that encompassed The Lost Cause theme was the 1936 book by Margaret Mitchell, *Gone With The Wind*. Made into a movie in 1939, it incorporates all the elements of the Southern view of the war, ranging from contented slaves to brutish Yankees to the valor and pluck of Southern men and women.

[8] Originally titled *Nord Contre Sud* in the French edition.

[9] Anonymous, *The Nation's Peril*, 12. As a further example, in describing the punishment inflicted by alleged Klan members on "an exceedingly intelligent colored man" living in Lowndes County, Georgia, and "thoroughly imbued with Republican principles," the anonymous author writes, "His wife was subjected to the most revolting indecencies. The last garment that covered her nakedness was wrenched from her person and torn into shreds, leaving her utterly exposed to the malicious and lecherous eyes of the intruders." Tangentially, Arthur Conan

Perhaps the first novel on the Ku Klux Klan to achieve major success was *A Fool's Errand*, originally published anonymously in 1879 by Albion Tourgée, a carpetbagger attorney who moved to North Carolina in 1866 and served as a superior court judge under the Republican government. Firmly committed to universal suffrage and the ideals of the Radical Republicans, his book detailed Klan violence based on his experiences during the height of Reconstruction.[10] Only six months after its release, Tourgée shed his anonymity and published an expanded version of the book containing a non-fiction addendum, now retitled *The Invisible Empire*. Similar to *The Nation's Peril* and drawn primarily from the Congressional hearings, Tourgée documented in precise prose page after page of Klan "outrages," while condemning Southern society and thought in general.

By the 1890s, the violent legacy of the Klan had become a fading memory, blending with the greater violence of the war. The tone of popular literature had changed, no doubt influenced by the legends of The Lost Cause. "The standard bearers of the devil himself," were now seen in some quarters as resistance fighters, brave men willing to risk all for the good of a society oppressed by an imposed government whose power was enforced by "foreign"—i.e., Federal—troops. For example, in the preface to the 1895 novel, *Ku-Klux Klan No. 40*, the author states, "...While the hand of Ku-Kluxism is stained with blood, yet, considering the sufferings of the South endured during the brief existence of that organization, it is the purest and whitest hand ever raised by an outraged people to repel the assaults of their oppressors."[11] Though fictional, the scenes of the book were said to be "founded on well-authenticated historical facts."[12] The Klan's legacy was moving to join that of other

---

Doyle's Sherlock Holmes is pitted against ex-members of the Klan in the 1891 short story "Five Orange Pips." In a rare exception to Holmes's prowess, the presumed murderers escape, only to meet their fate at the Hand of God when they are lost at sea in a violent storm.

[10] *See Chapter Notes for more information on the interesting subsequent career of Albion Tourgée.*

[11] Jerome, *Ku Klux Klan No. 40*, 3.

[12] Ibid., 4.

resistance movements past and hence, from the Sicarii of Roman-occupied Judea to the Maquis of Nazi-occupied France.

Undoubtedly the most influential fiction works featuring the Ku Klux Klan were those of Thomas F. Dixon, Jr. Born in rural North Carolina in 1864, as a youth Dixon observed first-hand the rigors of Radical Reconstruction. He was aware of his father's membership in the Klan and watched from the doorway of his home as a Negro accused of raping a white woman was lynched by a group of alleged Klansmen.[13] In 1883, Dixon graduated with highest honors from Wake Forest University,[14] his record earning him a scholarship to attend Johns Hopkins University to study political science. At Hopkins he became close friends with another graduate student, Woodrow Wilson, a Virginian and fellow Southerner. Thanks to Wilson's connections, Dixon was offered a job as drama critic for the *Baltimore Mirror*.

Aside from his interest in the political system, Dixon had also developed a keen interest in the theater. Apparently deciding graduate study was not for him, and over his friend Wilson's objections, he dropped out of Hopkins after only a semester to pursue a brief stage career in New York. When this path failed, he returned to North Carolina and earned a degree in law, after which he served briefly in the North Carolina General Assembly. Turning next to religion, Dixon became a successful and well-respected Baptist minister in the Northeast. While a pastor in Boston, he was invited to give a commencement address at his alma mater, Wake Forest. A talented lecturer, he impressed a member of the school's Board of Trustees so much that it was suggested that he be nominated to receive an honorary Doctor of Divinity degree. Modestly declining the offer, Dixon in turn suggested that his friend Woodrow Wilson would be an excellent choice for such an honor.[15] Because of this recommendation, Wilson was awarded the degree, something that he would remember years later when called upon by Dixon. By the mid-1890s, Dixon had become disenchanted with

---

[13] Cook, *Thomas Dixon*, 23.
[14] Dixon was a founding member of Wake Forest chapter of the Kappa Alpha Order.
[15] Cook, 41.

Baptist doctrine, and opened a new, non-denominational church in New York. He became more and more politically active, eventually giving up the ministry entirely in 1899 to spend the next few years as a traveling lecturer in wide demand for his oratory skill.

Dixon finally discovered his niche in life as a writer. While on the lecture circuit, he attended a theatrical production of Harriet Beecher Stowe's *Uncle Tom's Cabin.*[16] Incensed by what he saw as a misrepresentation of the South and her people, he was determined write a novel exposing the "truth" of the Reconstruction Era. His vow resulted in a three-book "Trilogy of Reconstruction": *The Leopard's Spots* in 1902, *The Clansman* in 1905, and *The Traitor* in 1907. The books' villains were carpetbaggers, freed slaves, and the occupying Federal troops, many of whom were black.[17] Their heroes were the members of the Ku Klux Klan, presented most poignantly as champions of Southern rights and defenders of Southern womanhood. The third and final book in the series was dedicated to "The Men of the South Who Suffered Exile, Imprisonment and Death for the Daring Service They Rendered Our County as Citizens of the Invisible Empire."

Considered patently racist even by the standards of the day, the works became instant bestsellers in both the North and the South. Doubleday, Page & Company, Dixon's publisher, advertised the first book in the series as "giving the Southern point of view of [the Negro's sufferings], and as a picture, it is as graphic and striking as Mrs. Stowe's book. No matter what may be the opinion about the race problem, it is certainly right that an adequate presentation of the Southern view in the form of fiction, which is easy to read and which carries conviction by its very sincerity, should be studied by people who have not known the facts."

---

[16] Ibid., 51.

[17] Even Simon Legree, the villain of Stowe's book, reappears in *The Leopard's Spots* after having avoided service in the Confederate military by cross-dressing to pose as a German immigrant woman during the war. Now a supporter of the Radical Republicans but no less vicious and unprincipled, he has become a Union League organizer, eventually rising to Speaker of the House in the General Assembly under the corrupt Republican regime.

Emboldened by his success as a novelist, Dixon went on to pen more than twenty novels, as well as several works of non-fiction. Not having lost his love of the stage, he wrote a screenplay adaption of the second work in his trilogy, *The Clansman*.[18] A decade later this work, renamed for the silver screen *The Birth of a Nation*, would become the inspiration for a revival of the Ku Klux Klan.

---

[18] In addition to his printed works, through 1937 Dixon is given credit for writing eighteen screenplays, as an actor in four movies and as a director of two. ("Thomas Dixon, Jr.," IMDb, accessed 1 November 2014, http://www.imdb.com/name/nm0228746/?ref_=fn_al_nm_1)

Chapter 5

The Golden Age of Fraternalism

The Ku Klux Klan of the 1860s was by any measure a product of the era, an amorphous and spontaneous crusade that for a brief period coalesced into a formal structure, then quietly faded away as the world around it changed. The organization that was to adopt the same name some half-century later was also a product of its time. Unlike the original version, which represented the culmination of a grassroots movement, the second incarnation of the Klan was primarily the creation of one man, William J. Simmons. Despite anything else that it was or might become during the three decades of its existence, the Ku Klux Klan of the 1920s was first and foremost a fraternal order. In many ways, this was the key to its initial success.

From the perspective of the early twenty-first century, it may seem somewhat bizarre that grown men would voluntarily don costumes resembling bed sheets, wear headgear not unlike dunce caps with masks, and rally around burning crosses singing hymns of Christian praise while condemning those of different birth and color. The alliterative names awarded to all things Klanish—Klavern, Klectoken, Kloran, Kligrapp, Klonvocation and the like—sound simply silly. The use of secret phrases to identify other members, "Ayak?" with the response, "Akia," as well as occult signs and symbols suggest a childhood fantasy world.[1] Yet at the height of its power, the Klan attracted millions of members and was thus able to wield immense political and economic power. Why?

The answer lies in part in the rise of fraternalism in America in the late nineteenth and early twentieth centuries. Secret fraternal societies have existed from the dawn of recorded history. Perhaps the oldest and best known in North America are the Freemasons, whose lodges date

---

[1] Ayak? (Are you a Klansman?) Akia. (A Klansman I am.)

from the early colonial era. De Tocqueville, traveling in the young United States in the 1830s, observed:

> Americans of all ages, all conditions, and all dispositions, constantly form associations. They have not only commercial and manufacturing companies, in which all take part, but associations of a thousand other kinds—religious, moral, serious, futile, extensive, or restricted, enormous or diminutive. The Americans make associations to give entertainments, to found establishments for education, to build inns, to construct churches, to diffuse books, to send missionaries to the antipodes; and in this manner they found hospitals, prisons, and schools. If it be proposed to advance some truth, or to foster some feeling by the encouragement of a great example, they form a society.[2]

The years between the end of the Civil War and the start of the Great Depression saw an explosion in the number of fraternal organizations in the United States. Most had at their core some public or private beneficial purpose while providing social interaction, insurance, or other rewards for their members. Many, perhaps most, were structured as secret societies whose inductions often involved elaborate ritual. It was, as one writer described it, "The Golden Age of Fraternity."[3] By 1896, it was reported that some 6,400,000 men in the country belonged to secret fraternal orders. Considering the possibility that some men belonged to more than one such group, it was estimated that "every fifth, or possibly every eighth, man you meet is identified with some fraternal organization, for the preservation of whose secrets he has given a solemn oath, a pledge more binding in its nature than perhaps any other known among men."[4] By 1911, as many as 9,000,000 men, or one out of every five in the country, were members of the orders, the majority of which had been formed within their generation.[5] By 1926, there were said to be some 800 secret orders inhabiting the American landscape, accounting for a total membership of 30,000,000

---

[2] De Tocqueville, *Democracy in America*, 114.
[3] Moore and Tabbert, *Secret Societies in America*, 7.
[4] Ibid., 1.
[5] Ibid., 35.

individuals.[6] It was estimated that half of all the county's adults were members of one or another society.[7]

The names of orders themselves belied their perceived worthiness. There were "Ancient and Illustrious" orders, "Improved" orders, and "Benevolent and Protective" orders. Their members were Knights, Mystics, Hibernians, Odd Fellows, Shepherds, Blue Friars, and Transylvanian Saxons. The animal kingdom was well represented through orders named for the Moose, Elks, Yellow Dogs, Camels, Eagles, Owls, Beavers, and Lions. The titles of their officers were equally arcane. To quote one contemporary commentator on the subject, perhaps writing a bit tongue-in-cheek: "On the dais sits a Monarch or a Master, a supreme Seignior, an Illustrious Potentate, a Grand Illuminator, or a Maharajah. No secretary is a secretary in this world of dreams come true; he is a Thrice Illustrious Scribe. No treasurer is a treasurer; he is an August Keeper of the Strong-Box. No citizen is a citizen; he is a knight, a monk, a priest, a dervish, or an ogre."[8] Membership in orders spanned and blurred the social spectrum. Once adorned in the lodge's finery, hod-carrier and banker stood side by side as equals. Even Warren Harding, elected President in 1920, was an Elk, a Moose, a Mason, a Shriner, and a Tall Cedar of Lebanon.[9]

So it was in 1915 that William J. Simmons, a thirty-five year-old insurance salesman and failed Methodist minister, made the decision to form his own fraternal order. A member at one time or another of "about twelve or fifteen" orders including the Masons, Royal Arch Masons, and the Great Order of Knight Templars, he was well aware of the potential financial and social rewards of such an endeavor. After usurping the then-legendary name and Prescript (constitution) of the 1860s Ku Klux Klan, borrowing for regalia movie-prop costumes from the silver screen,

---

[6]This time frame represented the peak of the Ku Klux Klan's membership. It is reasonable to assume a significant proportion of this number was accounted for by members of the Klan and associated organizations. *See Chapter Notes for comments on the decline of Fraternalism in the United States in the 1920s and beyond.*

[7] Moore and Tabbert, 50.

[8] Ibid., 56.

[9] Ibid., 54.

and injecting his own personal biases and iconography, he set out to do so. The result was what would become for a moment in time one of the most powerful political and social organizations in American history.

Chapter 6

The Man Who Would Be Emperor

The philosophy that was to take the second incarnation of the Ku Klux Klan to great heights was that of its founder, William Joseph Simmons. It was this same philosophy, put into action, which bore responsibility for its downfall. Thus, in many ways, it is impossible to fully understand the Klan without understanding the creed of its first Imperial Wizard, the man anointed as Emperor of the Invisible Empire.

Some years later, Simmons would recall that in reviving the Klan in 1915, his purpose was: "to establish a fraternal, patriotic, secret order for the purpose of memorializing the great heroes of our national history, inculcating and teaching practical fraternity among men, to teach and encourage a fervent practical patriotism toward our country, and to destroy from the hearts of men the Mason and Dixon line and build thereupon a great American solidarity and a distinctive national conscience which our country sorely stands in need of."[1] Despite the eloquence of this high-minded statement, the truth belied a far darker agenda.

Simmons, known to his friends as "Joe" or "Colonel" was a tall, bespectacled redhead of Irish ancestry, born in north Alabama. Prior to the founding of the Klan, he had led a singularly undistinguished life. A fawning Klan-sponsored biography of the early 1920s described Simmons as "a remarkable man in many ways. He is 6 feet 2 inches tall, weighs about 220 pounds, is perfectly proportioned, has a most engaging personality, and the whole impression of the man is pleasing," going on to say that he had been a "conspicuous success" in life prior to organizing the Klan's revival.[2]

---

[1] Committee on Rules, *The Ku Klux Klan: Hearings Before the Committee on Rules*, 68.

[2] Jones, *The Story of the Ku Klux Klan*, 57.

In September 1921, an exposé of the Klan in the *New York World* sought to damage the order by exposing its secrets and corrupt nature. This brought calls for a Congressional investigation, resulting in hearings before the House Committee on Rules the following month. Imperial Wizard Simmons, shown here in the hearing room, skillfully portrayed the Klan as a patriotic, Christian organization with a positive social agenda. Paradoxically, what had begun as an effort to destroy the Klan resulted in a massive influx of new members. (Library of Congress.)

The facts were less flattering. The son of a country physician, Simmons's biographers recount that after leaving home he pursued a pre-medical education at Johns Hopkins University in Baltimore, an uncertain bit of history that is not supported by the records of the institution.[3] Supposedly forced to drop out for financial reasons, he enlisted in the military for a brief stint during the Spanish-American War. Returning home after his discharge, he experienced a religious conversion at a Methodist camp meeting, and decided on a career in the ministry. For more than a decade he was a circuit-riding preacher, never achieving any degree of success but honing his speaking skills with such rousing sermon topics as "Women, Weddings, and Wives," "Red Heads, Dead Heads, and No Heads," and "Kinship of Kourtship and Kissing."[4] In 1912, he was charged by the church conference with "incompetence" and suspended.[5] A church spokesman recalled that Simmons "had a much higher estimate of his ability than was entertained by the conference."[6]

Simmons next took jobs selling garters and as a history instructor before taking a position as a promoter with the Woodmen of the World. It was here that he found his niche. The Woodmen of the World was a fraternal beneficial order founded in Nebraska in 1890. Like others of the day, it had secrecy and ritual at its heart, with membership limited to white males between sixteen and fifty-two years of age. Although there was a strong social component to the "camps" (as lodges were known), from the start a primary purpose of the society was to provide insurance to its members. With his experience as a preacher and salesman, Simmons was immediately successful, rising rapidly to an income of some $15,000 a year, more than sixty times his salary as a minister, and earning the honorary title of "Colonel" in the process.[7] Importantly, he

---

[3] Jackson, C.O. "William J. Simmons: A Career in Ku Kluxism," 351.

[4] Shepherd, "How I Put Over the Klan," 14 July 1928, 7. Simmons related this to a writer in 1928, making a bit of a joke of the fact that he was fascinated with "three K's" a decade before he formed the revived Ku Klux Klan.

[5] Ibid.

[6] Ibid., 32.

[7] This figure is based on Simmons's comments regarding his income, and should be viewed with a great deal of suspicion. If true, he would have been

recognized the financial rewards to be reaped by those who held office and power in the order.

In 1923, Simmons would find himself locked in a struggle over control of the Klan. Hoping to win support from Klansmen and those sympathetic to his position, Simmons decided to "make a public statement descriptive of our organization."[8] This took the form of a book titled, *The Klan Unmasked*, in which he laid out in detail the reasoning behind the masked order's philosophy. The Emperor's photograph formed the book's frontispiece, the image of a confident man dressed in a starched high-necked collar, costumed in a suit with vest and watch chain, and staring intently at the reader through his signature pince-nez glasses. In gentle pedantic prose, not unlike that of a father calmly explaining the ways of the world to a son on the cusp of manhood, Simmons explained his—and the order's—beliefs. The purpose of the Klan, he explained, was to confront the many imminent threats facing America. Its creed was based on One Hundred Percent Americanism as found in the United States Constitution and the tenets of Protestant Christianity. The Klan's organization as an exclusive secret order was not unusual; there were many such others that limited their memberships to those in certain religious or ethnic groups. It was not founded "on racial or sectarian animosities and hatreds. The Klan is neither anti-racial nor anti-sectarian. It is pro-American," he explained.[9]

America's threats were both internal and external. America's genius, her democracy, was founded on Anglo-Saxon principles not shared by those recent waves of immigrants who were swelling the nation's cities. The American West was in danger of being overrun by Japanese immigrants, just as the porous Mexican border attracted newcomers from Latin America. The cities of the East were teaming with ghettos full of Germans, Italian, French, and others. Such "immigrant people are not

---

doing quite well. Although estimates could vary widely, a simple calculation based on the Consumer Price Index (CPI) would suggest that $15,000 in yearly income in 1915 would be roughly equivalent to a salary of greater than $300,000 per year a century later. *See Chapter Notes for more on William J. Simmons and the Woodmen of the World.*

[8] Simmons, *The Klan Unmasked*, 8.
[9] Ibid., 38.

Americans. They are Europeans."[10] Granted, America was originally populated by immigrants, but in Simmons's view, "[t]he new immigration is totally different. This later swarm has come mostly to get jobs and money," originating from "the lowest grade of the working class and includ[ing] a large percentage of beggers (*sic*) and peddlers, of thieves and criminals."[11]

The ethnic threat was intimately connected to a religious one. Many of the newcomers were Catholic. Their loyalty lay not in their adopted homeland and its ideals, but rather to the Pope in Rome, ignoring America's Jeffersonian concept of separation of Church and State. As for the Jews, they were perhaps acceptable if they chose to convert to Christianity, in which case they might even be considered for membership in the Klan.

Simmons reserved his harshest rhetoric for blacks. Stating simply that the "African Negro can not realize democracy" because of his "state of biological evolution."[12] Simmons went on to aver that despite attempts at education, the black race is incapable of progressing "beyond the age of twelve years."[13] Granting them the right to vote in significant numbers "would endanger democracy."[14] As to the general issue of suffrage, it should be limited to those individuals who could both pass an examination in American history and achieve an acceptable score on an intelligence test.[15]

America was, in Simmons's thought, a "peculiar Nordic civilization, the creation, par excellence, of the whitest of the white European races."[16] Failure to squarely face and take action against the threats of alien immigration, foreign religions, and less worthy ethnic minorities would result in the collapse of the "American civilization." It was for this

---

[10] Ibid., 74.

[11] Ibid., 127.

[12] Ibid., 141.

[13] Ibid., 148. In addition to Negroes, Simmons also states Australian Bushmen and gypsies are incapable of democracy.

[14] Ibid., 159.

[15] Ibid., 252-59.

[16] Ibid., 170.

reason that the Klan was formed, and for this reason the nation's fate rested on such men willing to take action.

By any measure, Simmons's description of the Ku Klux Klan's philosophy might be described as a virulent strain of jingoist racism, a promotion of the concept that those having a perceived difference in color, ethnicity, or religion represented by their very presence a threat to all that America stood for and all that true Americans held dear. Yet by 1925, some ten years after the formation of the Klan, this message had attracted millions of members to the order.

Chapter 7

White Knights to the Rescue

By the second decade of the twentieth century, the reputation of the Ku Klux Klan of the 1860s had taken on a new light. The South was now reasonably prosperous; the horror of war and the privations of Reconstruction had been relegated to the hoary tales of old men. With a new generation in charge and groups like the United Daughters of the Confederacy determined to keep the memory alive, there was renewed interest in the war and its legacy. Not unlike the adoration given members of "The Greatest Generation" some half century after the end of World War II, the dwindling numbers of Civil War veterans were venerated for their service and sacrifice.

In journals, magazines, and books, writers and historians seemed willing to take a fresh look at the events of the Reconstruction Era. The author of a 1912 history of the Klan in Alabama reflected the thinking of the day, particularly that of the South. Apparently referring to Albion Tourgée's *The Invisible Empire*, she wrote:

> Only one writer has ventured far into this field of research, which until then seemed forbidden, and in his contribution to history, fact and fiction are so interwoven as to be almost indistinguishable. But the widespread and intense interest manifested in his revelations of the origin and purposes of the Klan indicates that the present generation eagerly imbibes knowledge of the sacrifices and achievements of the men who in the awful crisis of reconstruction, and against almost insuperable obstacles, rescued the commonwealth from the control of corrupt adventurers and ignorant freedmen, and established orderly government, without which the subsequent marvelous development of natural resources and advancement in education which have placed the state in the forefront of progress would have been impossible.[1]

---

[1] Damer, *When the Klan Rode*, 5-6.

For practical purposes, the rehabilitation of the Klan was nearly complete.

If a single inspiration could be given credit for the revival of an organization named the Ku Klux Klan, surprisingly, it would be a movie. In the early years of the new century, Thomas Dixon, the lecturer, former minister, and author of the trilogy of books that included *The Clansman*, was sailing on a sea of artistic and financial success. Having adapted the book's plot for the theater, the stage version of *The Clansman* opened to initial rave reviews in September 1905, the first of many performances in a nationwide tour. Like the book, the play was highly controversial, most prominently for its overt racism. Praised by many and condemned by others, it drew sell-out audiences despite threats of mob violence in some cities, in the process reaping "a fortune" for its author.[2]

The success of *The Clansman* as a stage play naturally drew Dixon to the then-new medium of silent motion pictures. As early as 1911, he had attempted to form a corporation to produce a movie version but could not secure adequate funding. In 1913, he found someone willing to undertake the project, but only if Dixon would agree to accept a twenty-five percent interest in the picture as his payment. Dixon reluctantly agreed, a fortuitous decision that would later make him a millionaire. Working with an unknown director named David Wark Griffith, Dixon tweaked the plot for the silver screen. Filming took place in Hollywood over a total of nine weeks between July and October 1914 using actors who were for the most part unknowns willing to work for minimal salaries.[3] Production was plagued by cost overruns, with the final movie being the longest commercial film yet made. Its prospects were uncertain at best.

Dixon was deeply worried about the film's success. He should not have been. He first saw the finished version of *The Clansman* at a private viewing in New York in February 1915. The small, select audience was ecstatic. His biographer recounts, "Dixon, himself deeply moved, immediately caught the infectious enthusiasm of the group; he shouted

---

[2] Cook, 104.
[3] Among them was Lillian Gish who played the lead female role, later going on to become one of America's best known film idols.

to Griffith across the building that *The Clansman* was too tame a title for such a powerful story; it should be called *The Birth of a Nation*, the title which the motion picture subsequently bore."[4]

From a cinematographic standpoint, the movie was indeed marvelous. Griffith's genius as a director, together with the skill of his cameraman, Billy Bitzer, produced a film that became the nation's first blockbuster. It set the standard for those who followed, and for decades held all-time records for attendance and profit. Its content and storyline, however, were troubling to many. For all its technical accomplishments, there was a darker side that reflected the themes of Dixon's *Clansman*. Though based on historical events, its "dramatic incidents [gave] the audience a definite feeling of Negro depravity and white virtue."[5] Negro characters—often played by whites in blackface—were portrayed as ignorant simian brutes lusting after white women. It was the Ku Klux Klan to the rescue, the knights in white sheets whose decisive action avenged evil and saved the honor of the fragile heroine.

Even before its public release, the film had ignited a storm of protest. The National Association for the Advancement of Colored People (NAACP), organized only six years earlier, launched a concerted effort to have the movie banned. Anticipating the potential problems, Dixon contacted fellow Johns Hopkins alumnus and now-President Woodrow Wilson. Wilson no doubt recalled Dixon was responsible for his receiving an honorary doctorate at a time when the recognition helped advance his political career. The President, thinking that Dixon was seeking a governmental appointment, was relieved to find that his old friend was merely requesting that he enjoy a private viewing of Dixon's new movie, *The Birth of a Nation*. Wilson readily agreed. On February 18, 1915, the movie was shown in the East Room of the White House to the President and his daughters, as well as members of his cabinet and their families. Wilson, who as a youth had lived in Georgia and the Carolinas during the Reconstruction years, was clearly moved by the film. "When the two hours and forty minutes of camera reporting were over, he rose from his chair and wiped his eyes. 'It is,' he said, 'like

[4] Cook, 112.
[5] MacKaye, "The Birth of a Nation," 46.

writing history with lightning. And my only regret is that it is all so terribly true."[6]

With the President's tacit endorsement, Dixon sought further support the next day, this time from the Chief Justice of the Supreme Court, fellow Southerner Edward D. White of Louisiana. White, himself a former Klansman in post-Civil War New Orleans, readily agreed to attend a screening of the movie once he heard of the Klan's role in the drama. That evening, the film was shown under the auspices of the National Press Club in the ballroom of Washington's Raleigh Hotel to a large audience that included the Chief Justice and his wife, "together with many members of Congress and members of the diplomatic corps."[7] The response was overwhelmingly positive.

Political support in hand, Dixon and Griffith headed for New York for a formal review by the National Board of Censors. Despite the NAACP's efforts, the Board cleared the movie to open as scheduled on March 3, 1915. With the billboards of Times Square emblazoned with gigantic figures of robed Klansmen bearing burning crosses, *The Birth of a Nation* had its grand premiere at the Liberty Theatre on West 42nd Street, half a block away. Ushers dressed in Union and Confederate uniforms showed patrons to their seats. Movie reviewers showered accolades on the production as show after show played to sell-out crowds willing to pay the then-astounding sum of two dollars for admission. At the Liberty Theatre alone, the film ran continuously for some forty-seven weeks. Following its initial success in New York, the picture toured nationally throughout the United States and internationally in Europe, South Africa, and Australia.

Reaction to the film was polarized to positive and negative extremes. Reviewers gushed praise: "Stupendous masterpiece,"[8] "realistic beyond the power of words," with "scenes whose historical correctness are unquestionable,"[9] "The greatest presentation of one of the greatest dramas in the South."[10] The *Charlotte Observer* reported: "But for real

---

[6] Ibid., 69.

[7] *Evening Star* (Washington, DC), 20 February 1915.

[8] *San Jose (CA) Mercury News*, 12 April 1915.

[9] *State (Columbia, SC)*, 23 November 1915.

[10] *Augusta (GA) Chronicle*, 18 November 1915.

excitement when the nerves tingle and the applause grows uproarious at times, let one choose the presentations of Reconstruction scenes and the reign of terror that threatened the whole South till the 'Invisible Empire' of the Ku Klux Klan appeared on the scene, beginning with the conception of the idea to its fullest realization, when the mysterious riders saved women, children, and a whole town from the dangers of a mob of negroes incited by carpet-baggers."[11] Dorothy Blount Lamar, Georgia author and later National President of the United Daughters of the Confederacy, referred to *The Birth of A Nation* as "the greatest production of the day," observing, "Our people know too little of what gave birth to the Ku Klux Klan."[12]

On the other side, the attempts of the NAACP to halt distribution of the film bore little fruit. A brief note in the *New York Times* observed, "So far the association has found no way to interfere with the film, which has been viewed by crowded houses at every projection."[13] Letters to the editor and the rare editorial decried the movie, e.g., "not only is the conduct of the negro largely and darkly exaggerated, but the virtues of the Ku Klux Klan are extolled in an altogether untrue light."[14] Theaters were occasionally the scene of protests or demonstrations, but nothing seemed to deter the eager crowds.[15] "*The Birth of a Nation* is wonderful! The Ku Klux Klan! What they suffered, lost, and braved! This was a band of knights sent to make things work out as it was desired and none but these men could have accomplished it."[16] If there had ever been any doubt as to the contribution of the Ku Klux Klan to the salvation of the South and the restoration of order after the Civil War, *The Birth of a Nation* had effectively erased it.

---

[11] Quoted in the *Augusta (GA)Chronicle*, 18 November 1915.

[12] *Macon (GA)Telegraph*, 24 November 1915.

[13] *New York Times*, 7 March 1915.

[14] *Rockford (IL) Republic*, 13 December 1915.

[15] By late 1922, five years after the movie's release, it was estimated that some five million people, or one out of every eighteen Americans, had seen the movie. (From response by Albert H. T. Banzhaf, General Counsel to D. W. Griffith, to objection to the showing of *The Birth of a Nation* filed by the NAACP with the Motion Picture Commission of the State of New York, 2 December 1922.)

[16] *Charlotte Observer*, 13 November 1915.

As moviegoers thronged to theaters during the long hot summer of 1915, there was another incident which may have contributed to the reemergence of the Ku Klux Klan: the lynching of Leo Frank. The case of *The State of Georgia v. Leo M. Frank* was, and continues to be, one of the most contentious legal proceedings of the twentieth century. At approximately 3:00 AM on the morning of April 27, 1913, a night watchman discovered the body of thirteen-year old Mary Phagan in the basement of the National Pencil Company Building on South Forsyth Street in Atlanta. She had been raped and murdered, apparently the preceding day. Her body showed evidence of a blow to the head, with death from strangulation inflicted by a length of white cord. Initial suspicion fell on two factory employees, but further investigation by detectives resulted in the arrest and subsequent indictment of Leo Max Frank, the factory's superintendent.

Leo Frank was from a prosperous New York family. He was well educated with an engineering degree from Cornell, and some two and a half years earlier had married a lovely young wife from a prominent Atlanta family. He was also Jewish, and had been elected president of the local chapter of B'nai B'rith in 1912. Relatively speaking, he was wealthy, earning a salary of $180 per month plus a portion of the company's profits, a stark contrast to many of his production employees who were paid pennies per hour. Many were teenagers like Mary Phagan, who earned 7 and 4/11 cents per hour—roughly four dollars for a standard fifty-five hour week.

Frank's trial began on July 28, 1913, and lasted twenty-nine days. The sensational nature of the case alone was enough to warrant intense public interest and press coverage, but the fact that the defendant was an outsider and a Jew, described in some local media as a Northerner-come-South to take advantage of ignorant lowly paid workers, elevated it to an issue of nationwide interest. The testimony against Frank was damning despite allegations that he was being persecuted because of his religion and ethnicity. It took a jury of twelve men just four hours of deliberation to find him guilty. He was sentenced to death by hanging. The case was appealed multiple times, eventually reaching the United States Supreme Court. Each appeal resulted in an affirmation of the jury's verdict. With no hope of a new trial, Frank's defenders next turned to the state Pardon and Parole Commission, seeking to have his death sentence commuted to one of life imprisonment. By a two-to-one margin, this appeal was also rejected. Frank was sentenced to die on June 22, 1915.

Meanwhile, the state had become the focus of national disparagement for Frank's conviction, especially in the North. Many, perhaps acting more on emotion than reason, were convinced of his innocence. Governor John M. Slaton, whose mercy represented the last potential chance to save Frank from the noose, received an estimated hundred thousand letters from around the nation urging him to halt the execution of an innocent man. In response to mounting pressure, Slaton undertook a reexamination of the case on his own, visiting the site of the crime and reviewing the voluminous documents. In the mind of the local public, the fact that the governor was even considering his options in the case led to cries of bias, as Slaton had been the law partner of one of Frank's attorneys.

On the day prior to the scheduled execution, and five days before the end of his term as governor, Slaton commuted Frank's sentence to life in prison. The reaction was immediate. A mob estimated to number as many as 2,000 marched on the governor's country home where he had taken refuge. He was saved by a battalion of National Guard troops who dispelled the crowd with fixed bayonets.[17] Several days later an angry mob attempted to seize the governor at the state capitol, again only to be dispersed by several regiments of National Guard troops.[18]

On the day of the pardon, Frank had been quietly moved to the State Penitentiary in Milledgeville, situated in the midst of 4,000 acres of state-owned farm land. He issued a brief statement to reporters proclaiming his innocence and saying that he was "deeply moved and gratified" by the governor's action. Meanwhile, there were reports of "an oath-bound organization" formed at Mary Phagan's grave in Marietta which had sworn to "get" both Slaton and Frank, "no matter how long it takes."[19]

---

[17] *New York Times*, 22 June 1915.
[18] *New York Times*, 27 June 1915.
[19] Ibid.

Security at the prison farm was relatively minimal; it was assumed that Frank would be safe among the prison population there. He was not. Rather than being kept isolated in a cell, he was housed in an open bunkroom with about a hundred other prisoners. On the night of July 17, less than four weeks after his arrival, he was attacked by a butcher-knife wielding convict serving a life sentence for two murders. The assailant managed to slash Frank's neck, severing one of his jugulars and resulting in severe blood loss before he was restrained by guards and other prisoners. It was only the quick action of another prisoner, a physician serving a life sentence for murder, that saved Frank's life.[20]

While the mobs protesting Frank's commutation faded after a few days, the battle in the press continued. A number of national newspapers applauded Slaton's action. In Georgia, the reaction was mixed, but for the most part negative. One of the most outspoken advocates for Frank's guilt during the entire trial had been Thomas E. Watson, the fiery attorney, ex-congressman, man-of-the-people, and former 1896 Populist Party vice-presidential candidate with William Jennings Bryan. Now in his late fifties, Watson devoted his time to writing, most notably his monthly *Watson's Magazine* and his weekly *Jeffersonian* tabloid. Although still widely respected, he had become a rabid anti-Semite, railing against the money and influence of Jews, in addition to his opposition to the Catholic Church, the Liquor Dealers' Association, the L&N Railroad, and the Atlanta Chamber of Commerce, to name a few of the many he considered enemies of the South and nation. For him, the Frank case had been the epitome of much that was wrong with America. From early in the course of the case he had dedicated page after page in his publications to analyses supporting Frank's guilt. Essentially the entire March 1915 issue of the magazine was devoted to the subject, definitively confirming the jury's verdict—in Watson's mind, at least— and referring to the accused as "a canker and a pest."[21] Time after time, he called for vengeance.[22] With Slaton's commutation of Frank's sentence, Watson was livid, viciously attacking the governor's decision.

---

[20] *New York Times*, 7 July 1915.
[21] Watson, "A Full Review of the Leo Frank Case," 278.
[22] Woodward, *Tom Watson: Agrarian Rebel*, 439.

In Marietta, the group that had allegedly formed over the dead girl's grave now took action. Calling themselves "The Knights of Mary Phagan," they openly discussed freeing Frank from prison in order to lynch him. And they did so in a meticulously planned raid, carefully including among the twenty-eight men who participated those with the skills needed for the job at hand. On the night of August 16, 1915, the highly organized mob traveled in a convoy of cars to Milledgeville, cut the prison's telephone lines, and handcuffed the warden before departing with Frank. They drove all night to arrive in Marietta early on the 17th. There, at approximately seven in the morning, they lynched the prisoner in front of a house that was once Phagan's home.

For the most part the national press, which only two months earlier had expressed some degree of relief at Slaton's commutation, rose up once again in a single voice to denounce the lynching. The reaction in Georgia was more tempered. *The Macon Telegraph* was less firm in its denouncement of the lynching, opining that the perpetrators of the hanging "were firmly convinced Frank was guilty, honestly convinced, of that there can be no doubt," continuing, "They really believed they were avenging angels." The writer observed, "Doubtless they can be apprehended, doubtful they will."[23] The mayor of Atlanta, in San Francisco for the Dixie Day celebration on August 17, likewise failed to condemn the mob's action, "startling his hearers by rushing to the defense of the lynching of Leo M. Frank."[24]

The men who participated in the lynching of Leo Frank were never brought to justice despite the fact that their identities were widely known. Tom Watson, for his loud and persistent calls for "justice" over the course of the case, became the lightning rod for blame. Louis Marshall, who argued the Frank case before the United States Supreme Court, said unequivocally, "Tom Watson is the murderer of Leo Frank," continuing, "He was the scoundrel who stirred up the agitation of which Frank was the victim for nearly three years before his death. *The Jeffersonian* bristles with vulgar lies and the basest kind of

---

[23] *New York Times*, 18 August 1915.
[24] Ibid.

misrepresentation, designed to incite an ignorant populace into committing murder."[25]

Watson responded with his usual venom, attributing the personal attacks against him to Northern Jews and others who would interfere with the rights of the South, "a new form of alien dictation and carpet-bag rule." If the interference with Southern life did not cease, he prophesied, *"another Ku Klux Klan may be organized to restore HOME RULE."* [26] Though the words may have stung at the moment, the castigation seemed to do Watson little harm. His views—however removed from mainstream American thought they may have seemed at the moment—resonated with the state's voters. Five years later they elected him to represent Georgia in the United States Senate. As to the Klan, Watson could not have been more correct. His prediction was to come true by the end of the year.

---

[25]Ibid.

[26] *The Jeffersonian (Thomson, GA),* 2 September 1915. The italics and capitalization were Watson's.

Chapter 8

Lighting The Fiery Cross

A believer of the conventional story of the founding of the second Invisible Empire might only think this to be a noble enterprise conceived in the mind of a unique individual bent on making the world a better place. Most of the widely-accepted accounts of the 1915 revival of the Ku Klux Klan, however, were written at a later date by its publicists, a fact that suggests the reader should view them with a healthy sense of skepticism. As William J. Simmons recounted the story, the concept came to him in a vision shortly after the turn of the century:

> He was then a poor minister in Alabama, and one summer night was sitting at his window watching the clouds as they drifted in front of the moon. Suddenly he thought he caught sight of something mysterious and strange in the sky, and as he looked at the clouds a row of horses seemed to be galloping across the horizon. White-robed figures were on the steeds. The clouds seemed to disperse, and a rough outline of the United States appeared as a background. The horses remained, and then one big problem after another of American life moved across the map. He fell to his knees and offered a prayer to God to help solve the mystery of the apparitions he had seen in the sky. He then registered a vow that a great patriotic fraternal order should be built as a memorial to the heroes of our nation. That was the real beginning of the Knights of the Ku Klux Klan....[1]

Other accounts differ. According to a 1925 article in *The American Mercury*, the Knights of the Ku Klux Klan was originally conceived by Simmons as an Atlanta "locker club," the local name for a nominally private club formed to circumvent the state's prohibition of alcohol. The account was written by Ward Greene, who at the time worked as a reporter for the *Atlanta Journal*. According to Greene, Simmons

---

[1] Jones, 59.

approached Atlanta City Clerk Walter Taylor with a proposed constitution for a locker club to be known as the Knights of the Ku Klux Klan. The city had many of them; most were organized as fraternal orders with names such as Moose, Elks, Owls, Beavers, Badgers, and the like. Simmons demanded, "What do you think of it, Walter? The name, I mean. For a locker club? Will they join?" Taylor replied, "Naw—They all want to be animals!" [2]

Greene's story is perhaps apocryphal, but there is some suggestion that the idea of forming a fraternal organization named the Ku Klux Klan was not Simmons's alone. A 1924 exposé written under a pseudonym by an ex-Klan insider attributes the original idea to Jonathan B. Frost, at the time an Atlanta magazine editor and former fraternal organizer who had been inspired by the representation of the Klan in *The Birth of a Nation*.[3] According to this source, Frost presented the idea at a convention of the Woodmen of the World, for whom Simmons was working at the time. Simmons allegedly aligned himself in a partnership with Frost to start the revived Klan. In fact, the name "J. B. Frost" appears on the original petition for incorporation of the Knights of the Ku Klux Klan. In later testimony before Congress, Simmons referred to "a traitor in our ranks who held under me a position of trust, who embezzled all of our accumulated funds in the summer of 1916 and went off and attempted to organize a counterfeit order." [4] The issue of the missing money was taken to court, the result of which was Simmons winning an $800 judgment against Frost, all of which was eaten up by legal fees.[5] This was not the end of the matter, however. Frost moved to

---

[2] Greene, "Notes for a History of the Klan," 240-241. Greene later went on to greater things, achieving success as a playwright, novelist, and author. He is perhaps best remembered for a 1940s piece titled "Happy Dan, the Whistling Dog," published in *Cosmopolitan* magazine. Walt Disney purchased the rights to the story, which morphed into the 1955 animated film, *Lady and the Tramp*. Greene is credited as the author of the book version of *Lady and the Tramp*.

[3] Moneval, *The Klan Inside and Out*, 11.

[4] Committee on Rules, 101. The petition was filed on April 26, 1916, Confederate Memorial Day.

[5] According to an account given by Simmons to a journalist in 1928, Frost came along "when the Klan was a few weeks old." He was sent to Birmingham to organize a new Klavern there, but absconded with the fees that he'd collected

Nashville and formed his "counterfeit" Soveren Klan, which would compete with Simmons's Knights of the Ku Klux Klan for the next several years.

Whatever the exact details of its origins, the new order's formation came to practical fruition in October 1915. The reputation of the Reconstruction Era Klan was at an all-time high courtesy of *The Birth of a Nation*. In villages, towns, and cities across the South there was an increasing sense that traditional America was changing—perhaps in the process losing her sense of direction. Cities were growing rapidly, many of them populated by foreign immigrants. Automobiles offered new freedom, especially to the young. The new medium of the motion picture graphically displayed a world very different from that of the traditional agrarian heartland. Meanwhile, with turmoil in Europe, a wave of patriotism was sweeping the country, even though the United States was still a year and a half away from her entry into World War I. The concept of a fraternal order with the goal of promoting true American values was an appealing one.

By Simmons's account, he made the final decision to form a revived Klan while he was laid up in bed for three months following an automobile accident. Having little else to do, he worked out the details of the proposed order, including the regalia, the "KL" alliterative names and titles, and a constitution based on the Prescript of the 1860s Klan. [6] It was Simmons's lawyer, a man named E. R. Clarkson, who gave him the final push to start on his new venture. Clarkson had been hired to sue the driver of the car that struck Simmons. When presented with his client's idea, Clarkson immediately encouraged it, volunteering by saying, "I'll join."[7] Simmons marketed the idea: "I went around Atlanta talking to men who belonged to other lodges, about the new Ku Klux Klan. The Negroes were getting pretty uppity in the South along about that time.

---

in the process. Simmons sued him in the local court and won a judgment of $800. (Shepherd, "How I Put over the Klan," 35.)

[6] To quote Simmons exactly, "It was while I was in bed that I struck upon what I call the 'KL' idea—putting those two letters in front of every title. It was rather difficult sometimes to make the two letters fit in, but I did it, somehow." (Shepherd, "How I Put over the Klan," 32.)

[7] Ibid.

The North was sending down for them to take good jobs. Lots of Southerners were feeling worried about conditions."[8]

On October 26, 1915, Simmons gathered thirty-four like-minded men in Clarkson's office to present the idea of a revived Klan. Among them were two members of the 1860s Klan as well as several members of the Knights of Mary Phagan, the group that lynched Leo Frank.[9] The meeting was led by John W. Bale, a representative in the Georgia legislature and himself a member of the Odd Fellows, the Elks, the Shriners, the Knights of Pythias, the Woodmen of the World, the Sons of Confederate Veterans, and the Knights Templar Masons.[10] Simmons spoke for an hour, laying out his vision for the new Ku Klux Klan with all the skill of an ex-minister and fraternal organizer. The group, evidently convinced, voted to apply for a state charter. They agreed to meet the next month for a formal swearing-in ceremony.

The thirty-four charter members reassembled at Atlanta's Piedmont Hotel on Thanksgiving night, November 25. The venue was the city's premiere hotel, located at Peachtree and Luckie Streets. But the ceremony was not to take place there; Simmons had "a surprise" in mind. The oath was to be administered at midnight, atop Stone Mountain, some eighteen miles distant. A tourist bus hired for the occasion waited outside to transport the group. Simmons's choice of Stone Mountain for the ceremony may have been due to the well-publicized plans of the United Daughters of the Confederacy to create a massive stone monument to the Confederacy in the form of a carving on the mountain's sheer face. Gaining permission was no problem. Samuel H. Venable, the mountain's owner, was among the Klan's initial inductees. The weather was said to be "terrible," and only fifteen men elected to follow. Earlier in the day Simmons and A. C. Dallas, a realtor, had hiked up the mountain carrying boards for a sixteen-foot high cross which they hammered together and left at the top.

The fifteen would-be Knights of the Ku Klux Klan trudged up the barren mountain's rocky trail, guided only by flashlights and whipped by

---

[8] Ibid.
[9] Ibid.; Golden, *A Little Girl is Dead*, 300.
[10] Knight, *A Standard History of Georgia and Georgians, Vol. 5*, 2689.

cold autumn winds.[11] On the summit, Simmons instructed each man to gather a boulder. Together they propped up the cross, forming a makeshift altar on which Simmons laid an American flag, a Civil War sword, and a Bible open to the twelfth chapter of Romans.[12] He then put a match to the cross, which had been wrapped in excelsior soaked in a mixture of gasoline and kerosene. In the light of the flaming cross he administered the initiation oath to the assembled, thus marking the rebirth of the Klan.[13]

---

[11] Simmons's exact quote on the initial ceremony from a contemporary pamphlet on the Klan read, "And thus on the mountain top that night at the midnight hour, while men braved the surging blasts of wild wintery mountain winds and endured a temperature far below freezing, bathed in the sacred glow of the Fiery Cross, the Invisible Empire was called from its slumber of half a century to take up a new task and fulfil a new mission for humanity's good, and to call back to mortal habitation the good angel of practical fraternity among men." (*New York World*, 13 September 1921).

[12] Romans 12 (NIV) refers to action in Christ's name, beginning, "Therefore, I urge you, brothers and sisters, in view of God's mercy, to offer your bodies as a living sacrifice, holy and pleasing to God—this is your true and proper worship."

[13] The cross burned that Thanksgiving night may not have been the first cross set aflame on Stone Mountain in the fall of 1915. *See Chapter Notes for further information on this detail, and the use of the flaming cross as the symbol of the Klan.*

Part III

The Klan Reborn

The Ku Klux Klan of the Twentieth Century

It can not be too strongly stressed that this pseudo-Klan, as well as other subsequent organizations with similar name, had not the slightest, remotest connection with the original Klan which was formed in Pulaski, Tennessee, in 1866, and which was formally and officially disbanded in 1871, thus ending its existence.

The primary difference has always been in motivation. The original Klan sprang into being in 1866 to meet the chaotic, abnormal and intolerable conditions of that era for which no normal and lawful remedy seemed immediately available. None of the modern organizations using the name of Klan would pretend, however, that there is now or ever was any such impelling reason for their existence. Another conspicuous difference has been that whereas there was never any suspicion or accusation of commercial motive in the original Klan, pecuniary gain seems to have been obviously a strong and prominent factor in the formation and promotion of many of the modern users of the name.

Stanley F. Horn
Invisible Empire: The Story of the
Ku Klux Klan 1866-1871
From the Epilogue of the Second Edition,
Published 1969

Chapter 9

The Battle of the Klans

Following days of an intensive publicity campaign characterized by huge newspaper ads and anticipatory reviews, *The Birth of a Nation*, "The Greatest of All Spectacular Productions," opened at the Atlanta Theatre on December 6, 1915. Viewers were assured of the most moving visual experience of their lives, a "sublime epic" of some 5,000 scenes, a production requiring 18,000 people and 3,000 horses, and costing $500,000, all of which were gross exaggerations.[1] But such details didn't matter. It *was* the greatest "movie" of the day, its plot a champion of the Southern cause, its heroes "white-clad horsemen" "determined upon a last desperate chance to rescue women and homes and civilization from an unspeakable curse" manifest in the form of scheming carpetbaggers and Negro militia. The *Constitution's* reviewer gushed in a long write-up the following day, "It makes you laugh and moves you to hot tears unashamed. It makes you love and hate. It makes you forget decorum and forces a cry into your throat. It thrills you with horror and moves you to marvel at vast spectacles. It makes you actually live through the greatest period of suffering and trial that this country has ever known."[2] And in the process, vividly glorified the heroic exploits of the Ku Klux Klan.

Two days later, a crudely hand-drawn two-column, seven-inch high advertisement appeared on the *Constitution's* pages, sandwiched between grocery ads and routine news of the war in Europe. Dominating the ad was the image of a rampant horse on whose back was a robed figure holding high a flaming cross. It had been copied directly from an advertising poster for the movie. The ad promoted "The World's

---

[1] According to a later account, the actual cost of the movie was between $90,000 and $100,000. The maximum number of people on the payroll during its production was estimated to be 600. (MacKaye, 42.)

[2] *Atlanta Constitution*, 7 December 1915.

Greatest, <u>Secret</u>, Social, <u>Patriotic</u>, <u>Fraternal</u>, Beneficiary Order," the Knights of the Ku Klux Klan, noting that it had been chartered by the State of Georgia on December 6, 1915, the same day as *The Birth of a Nation's* local premiere.[3] The advertisement had been drawn by "Col. W. J. Simmons, Founder & Imperial Wizard." It specified that this was "A High Class Order for Men of Intelligence and Character" and gave an address on West Peachtree Street, presumably for those interested in joining.

By Sunday, December 12, 1915, movie ads boasted that 19,759 people had seen the production in Atlanta during the first six days of its local run, a questionable figure if for no other reason than the physical capacity of the theater. Simmons's Klan was off to a somewhat slower start. Originally, he had intended it to be a "Beneficiary Order" as his ad in the *Constitution* had indicated, a fraternity with secret ritual perhaps, but one whose membership was something to be acknowledged publically with pride. Its goals, according to the charter filed the following year, were "purely benevolent and eleemosynary."[4] It promised "no profit or gain to the members thereof."

Within a few months the Atlanta Klan No. 1 had ninety members, all of whom had paid the $10 "donation" and spent $6.50 on the robe and regalia, the latter allegedly designed by Simmons himself but bearing a striking resemblance to the costumes of the actors in *The Birth of a Nation*. It should be emphasized that the Ku Klux Klan of the 1860s had no "uniform" per se, simply disguises designed to mask the identity of the wearer while intimidating its perceived enemies. Simmons's Klan, in contrast, had a formal series of robes, caps, and masks, similar but displaying minor variations indicating the rank and/or office of the Klansman. The basic design of these robes was lifted directly from the costumes of the actors in *The Birth of a Nation*. This meshed neatly with the public's then-current perception of the Klan, much of which had been shaped by the popular movie. As with his former employer, the Woodmen of the World, Simmons's new fraternity offered life insurance, a potentially lucrative sideline for Simmons as the sole owner

---

[3] The underlined words were the work of the ad's creator.
[4] "Eleemosynary": Defined as of, or relating to, charity.

of the franchise. Some forty-two of the initial members purchased $53,000 worth, no doubt yielding a handsome commission.[5]

After the initial burst of activity, the Klan grew slowly. It was, at the outset, essentially a one-man operation, poorly funded and dependent almost entirely on the efforts of its founder and Imperial Wizard. A formal charter for the Knights of the Ku Klux Klan was not granted until mid-1916, about the same time Simmons registered a copyright for the Kloran, the formal embodiment of the Klan's ritual. By multiple accounts Simmons may have been an excellent orator skilled at presenting his vision of the new order, but was poorly organized and ill-equipped to advance its spread. One of his first efforts ended in failure.

In the spring of 1916, Confederate veterans were scheduled to hold their annual convention in Birmingham, Alabama. Simmons wanted to have a local Klavern of the Klan "in full running order" by the time of the meeting. To this end, he dispatched Jonathan B. Frost, one of the co-founders of the Klan who at the time held the office of "state organizer of Alabama."[6] Frost, like Simmons, had long been associated with fraternal orders and was quite familiar with the recruitment process. On the other hand, Simmons's choice of Frost for this important mission appears indicative of his naivety or his inability to judge the character of those around him, a deficit that would later lead to his being deposed as Imperial Wizard.

Jonathan Frost had been one of the founders and head of the Columbian Woodmen, a fraternal beneficial order similar to the Woodmen of the World. By 1910, the order had some 15,000 members in Georgia and surrounding states, yielding a steady source of income.[7] One newspaper report noted the organization possessed "a large cash

---

[5] Shepherd, "How I Put over the Klan," 35.

[6] *Atlanta Constitution*, 30 September 1916.

[7] On the occasion of Columbian Woodmen being banned from doing business in South Carolina, the *Life Insurance Independent* (21, No. 7, July 1909) described the order as one of "those money-seeking autocratically-controlled organizations which get their business not through the spontaneous promptings of fraternal spirit, but through a medium of a corps of well-paid organizers." The same could later have been said about the Knights of the Ku Klux Klan.

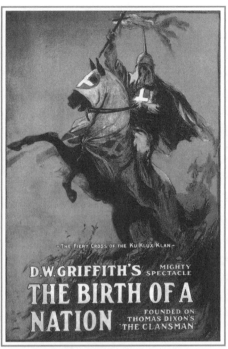

D. W. Griffith's silent movie, *The Birth of a Nation*, (above) was the first national blockbuster, holding all-time attendance records until the release of *Gone With the Wind* more than two decades later. It extolled the role of the Ku Klux Klan in the Reconstruction South, and served to inspire W. J. Simmons to take the Klan name for his fraternal order. Klan regalia, including the burning cross, were taken directly from the movie. The cover of the official Klan news publication (below) is a near-copy of the movie poster.

Promotion of the Klan was initially amateurish, as evidenced by this 1917 brochure created by Imperial Wizard Simmons. (From the collections of the Manuscript, Archives, and Rare Book Library, Emory University.)

fund."[8] In late 1909 or early 1910, Frost was suspended by the Eminent Council of the Woodmen on "charges of mismanagement of the affairs of the order."[9] The case was appealed to the Georgia Supreme Court which confirmed his ouster. In September of that year, Frost was indicted by a Gwinnett County, Georgia grand jury on multiple charges, including selling stock in a "salted" gold mine and the theft of stock certificates. Reports of his indictment described him as "a well-known Atlanta capitalist and until recently head of a fraternal insurance order."[10] By 1913, the "capitalist" was publishing a magazine, and was now described as a "*littérateur.*"[11] This endeavor apparently failed as well. Even after his association with the Klan, Frost's financial troubles continued. While he was acting as the Klan's recruiter in Alabama, a series of legal notices in the spring of 1916 advertised a Receiver's Sale on behalf of the McKenzie Trust Company for a hotel and related property owned by Jonathan B. Frost in Marietta, Cobb County, Georgia.[12]

Birmingham proved to be fertile ground for the Klan's message, and after a few weeks of Frost's recruiting "the new members piled in." In need of money, Simmons took the train to Birmingham to "settle up with Frost," only to find that his recruiter had "skipped" with the funds, leaving Simmons and his new Klan "heavily in debt."[13] Simmons sued, with the matter lingering in court for several months. In October, newspaper reports indicated that Frost was fighting extradition to Alabama and had requested a hearing in front of the Governor of Georgia.[14]

Following his break with the Knights of the Ku Klux Klan, Frost attempted to organize a similar fraternal order in Kentucky and Tennessee. Simmons sought a restraining order and Frost once again settled, signing an agreement "never to attempt the organization [of a

[8] *New Orleans Times-Picayune,* 29 March 1910
[9] Ibid.
[10] *Tampa Tribune,* 15 September 1910.
[11] *Columbus (GA) Ledger,* 23 March 1913.
[12] *Marietta (GA) Journal,* 31 March 1916.
[13] Shepherd, "How I Put over the Klan," 35.
[14] *Macon Telegraph,* 5 October 1916.

Klan] at any time or place."[15] In spite of this settlement, he was apparently not one to allow a small setback or legal issue to deter him.

By mid-1917, Frost was living in Nashville, Tennessee, having founded the Soveren Klan of the World in July of that year. Newspaper reports described him as the Majestic Soveren of the group and "one of the most prominent fraternal order men in the United States."[16] This new fraternal organization, while not identifying itself as the Ku Klux Klan was, for practical purposes, a carbon copy of Simmons's. Its ritual and stated aims were essentially the same, not to mention its regalia, which was "almost identical to that worn by the Ku Klux."[17] Its literature (copyrighted by Frost in September 1918) made it clear that *this* Klan was the true inheritor of the spirit of the original Invisible Empire whose deeds continued to thrill audiences in movie theaters across America. Its membership—if the numbers were to be believed—dwarfed that of Simmons's Klan. There were more than a thousand Soveren Klansmen in Nashville alone. Lodges were being formed in Georgia, Arkansas, Louisiana, Oklahoma, Mississippi, the Carolinas, and Florida as well as the District of Columbia. Its members were being recruited from the "leading men" of their communities.

Meanwhile, Simmons's Knights of the Ku Klux Klan were far slower in efforts to recruit members, even in their home state of Georgia. Based on newspaper accounts, a Klavern was active in Athens in the late spring of 1918.[18] In November, Colonel Simmons was reported to be in Columbus "looking toward the establishment of the clan (*sic*) in this city."[19] The news item provided an address that prospective members could contact. A Macon unit of the Klan was apparently not formed until 1920.[20]

Recruitment should have been easier. Based largely on the ongoing success of *The Birth of a Nation*, the Ku Klux Klan had come to be

---

[15] *Atlanta Constitution*, 15 August 1920.
[16] *Columbus (GA) Ledger*, 15 May 1918.
[17] *New Orleans Times–Picayune*, 7 September 1918.
[18] *Macon Telegraph*, 1 June 1918.
[19] *Columbus (GA) Enquirer-Sun*, 17 November 1918.
[20] *Macon Telegraph*, 3 August 1920; 18 November 1920. See also Hux, "The Ku Klux Klan in Macon, 1919-1925," 155-56.

synonymous with patriotism and fearless loyalty. At least three "photoplays," the alternative name for the silent motion pictures of the day, featured the Klan in prominent and often novel roles. In *Those Without Sin* set in the 1860s, masked midnight raiders of the Klan tarred and feathered the villain.[21] *The Mormon Maid*, an "exposé of Mormonism," featured "Mormons wearing [Ku Klux Klan garb] when making raids upon enemies of the faith."[22] Capturing the espionage hysteria of the war years, the revived Klan takes "drastic measures" against German spies in the 1918 *Daughter Angele*.[23]

Confederate veterans' organizations and the United Daughters of the Confederacy took full advantage of the Klan's positive image. Across the South, essays on the Klan of the Reconstruction Era won student literary contests sponsored by the groups, ensuring that the proper legends were passed on to the next generation. After seeing *The Birth of a Nation*, the UDC's Helen Plane, the moving force behind plans to carve a Confederate monument on the face of Stone Mountain, wrote the sculptor Gutzon Borglum: "Since seeing this wonderful and beautiful picture of Reconstruction in the South, I feel that it is due to the Ku Klux Klan which saved us from Negro domination and carpet-bag rule, that it be immortalized on Stone Mountain. Why not represent a small group of them in their nightly uniform approaching in the distance?" Borglum responded by including a Klan altar in his plans for the memorial. He would later become a member of the Klan's inner circle.[24]

Adulation of the Klan was not limited to the motion picture screen. At the 1916 International Convention of Rotary Clubs held in Cincinnati, Nashville Rotarians proudly dressed in "Ku Klux garb" while playfully initiating about fifty other Rotarians into the "secret order."[25] The 1917 Senior Class of the all-female Wesleyan College in Macon adopted the nickname "the Ku Klux Klan," displaying its "class banner of red and white satin with its skull and cross bones" at functions given in

---

[21] *Evening Star (Washington DC)*, 1 March 1917.
[22] *Oregonian (Portland, OR)*, 13 January 1918.
[23] *Winston-Salem (NC), Journal*, 8 December 1918.
[24] Freeman, 61-2.
[25] *Cincinnati Post*, 20 July 1916.

their honor.[26] Other college campuses organized Ku Klux Klan secret societies, being a member of which was significant enough to warrant attention on one's engagement announcement.[27] In Indiana, Colonial Dames, Mexican Bandits, and Klan sheets were acceptable disguises on Society Page accounts of Halloween balls.[28]

While the publicity and positive image generated by *The Birth of a Nation* were important in the revitalization of the Klan, other, greater forces were in play. As the movie adequately demonstrated, these fearless men had braved all to save their civilization and way of life. The winds of war that were then sweeping Europe and much of the rest of the world were soon to buffet America, heralding the call once again for men of action, courage, and patriotism.

---

[26] *Macon Telegraph*, 27 February 1916; 24 May 1917.
[27] *Richmond (VA) Times Dispatch*, 10 December 1916; *Rockford (IL) Republican*, 29 July 1918.
[28] *Elkhart (IN) Truth*, 1 November 1919.

Chapter 10

Secret Agent Men

From history's perspective it is often difficult to appreciate that prior to the era of The Great War of 1914-18, America was primarily a rural, agrarian nation with a foreign policy that was at least inward-looking, if not isolationist. With notable local and regional exceptions, the lives of many Americans were in some way directly or indirectly tied to the land, especially in the South. Patriotism was unswerving, unabashed, and unquestioned. The wounds, if not the memory, of the Civil War had for the most part healed. While many were quick to identify themselves as Northerners or Southerners, all swore loyalty to the same flag.

The events that began nominally with the June 1914 assassination of Archduke Ferdinand in an obscure Balkan county were merely one more step toward the inevitable collision of social and political forces that traced their origins to decades earlier. While it would be nearly three years before America's formal entry into the conflict, its influence was felt immediately. War-related commerce spurred the growth of Northern manufacturing and Southern agriculture alike. Loosened credit and increased demand for goods and services fueled inflation. Perhaps most importantly, many young men fresh off the farm were thrust into the horrors of the European battlefields, forever changing their lives and worldview.

America's formal tenure in World War I was relatively brief, only about nineteen months. Despite the nation's neutrality during the early years of the war, many of her citizens had developed strong opinions as to whether or not intervention should be considered. For many, perhaps most, the feeling at the outset of the conflict was one of national patriotism and support of those perceived to be America's natural allies. At the same time, most opposed direct involvement by the nation's troops, including, most prominently, the President. Woodrow Wilson had pursued his 1916 presidential campaign under the slogan, "He Kept

Us Out of the War." Moreover, there were large numbers of Americans who opposed the war on ethnic or ideological grounds, or alternatively, supported those who fought against the Western Allies. Many cities, especially in the North, had large communities of German immigrant stock. Various trade unionist movements, typified by the International Workers of the World (IWW), were led by committed socialists who opposed the war as a struggle between capitalists. There were pacifists and those whose anti-war sentiments were grounded in religious belief.

The attitudes of 1914 slowly began to erode under the steady trickle of war news from Europe. The German invasion of neutral Belgium in August at the outset of the conflict brought stories of rape, pillage, summary executions of women and children, and other atrocities that horrified most Americans.[1] The May 1915 sinking by a German submarine of the RMS *Lusitania*, an unarmed luxury passenger cruise liner, caused 128 American deaths among some twelve hundred total casualties.

Rumored, then documented, evidence of domestic networks of German spies, together with sabotage directed at interfering with American aid to Allied forces, engendered a wave of patriotism and calls for intervention in the war. New York City harbor's Black Tom Island explosion of munitions bound for Europe in July 1916, a fire at the Kingsland, New York, munitions factory in January 1917, and a munitions barge explosion at a California Naval Yard two months later were German attempts to intimidate America and forestall her entry into the war. They had the opposite effect. In the South, there were rumors that German agents were attempting to enlist Negroes in their covert attempts to weaken American resolve.

The one event most closely associated with the United States' decision to declare war on Germany was the interception by British

---

[1] To quote a 1919 account of the events: "The whole truth will never be known, but more than 100,000 citizens of Belgium and France were put to death on various pretexts; thousands of women made the sport of violent beasts who wore the Kaiser's uniform; thousands of little children maimed and tortured and every conceivable barbarity and infamy committed upon them." (Hough, *The Web*, 476.) Newspaper reports of the day were more specific, at times bordering on the sensational.

intelligence of the infamous Zimmermann Telegram. Intended for the German ambassador in Mexico City, the coded message detailed plans to induce Mexico to declare war against the United States if America entered the war on the side of the Allies. Germany proposed a military alliance that would allow Mexico to reclaim lands in Arizona, Texas, and New Mexico that had been lost to the United States in the mid-nineteenth century. Sent in January 1917, its veracity was questioned until publically admitted in early March by the German Foreign Secretary, Arthur Zimmermann. This plot, plus Germany's decision to pursue unrestricted submarine warfare, pushed President Wilson to call for a war resolution, declaring that, "The world must be made safe for democracy." His request was granted by Congress on April 6, 1917.

Shortly after Wilson's call for war, the newspapers were full of news, "confirmed by federal agents," of a campaign on behalf of the German government to incite a Negro revolt in "the tobacco and cotton belts of Georgia, Alabama, the Carolinas, and parts of Florida."[2] Foreign agents were said to be behind the migration of black workers to industrial centers in the North, as well as a plot "to induce the negroes to migrate to Mexico with a view to crippling industries in the South which depend on negro labor." In parts of Mississippi and Louisiana "an organized German movement" was afoot to incite the Negroes, promising them "complete franchise freedom and sociality equality" in exchange for their aid against the United States.[3] It was rumored that "farmers in some agricultural districts have formed Ku Klux Klans to meet possible uprisings."[4]

Meanwhile, in East St. Louis, Illinois, "business and professional men" were organizing "a society similar to the Ku Klux Klan...to rid the city of undesirable blacks."[5] In October 1917, Herbert Bigelow, a well-known socialist and pacifist, was kidnapped and flogged by a group of men dressed in robes and hoods "similar to those...worn by the Ku Klux Klan."[6] His punishment was said to be inflicted "in the name of the

[2] *State* (Columbia, SC), 14 April 1917.
[3] Ibid.
[4] *Augusta Chronicle*, 5 April 1917.
[5] *Belleville (IL) News Democrat*, 2 June 1917.
[6] *Miami (OK) District Daily News*, 8 November 1917.

women and children of Belgium." In November a band of men "masked like the Ku Klux Klan" seized seventeen IWW men, took them to a remote location and "administered lashes and a coat of tar and feathers." It was reported that in Kentucky, "an organized band of 800 Ku Klux Klan members" had declared war on traitors and pacifists.[7] In Ada, Oklahoma, a hundred men were said to have formed a "home guard" "similar to that of the old Ku Klux Klan" in response to railway bridge burnings designed to wreck troop trains. "WCU and IWW agitators" were the suspected culprits.[8] Throughout 1917 and well into 1918, newspapers nationwide reported the formation of "Ku Klux Klans" and similar vigilance organizations whose end goals were support of the war effort, oftentimes by intimidation and extra-legal means.

Despite these reports' reference to the Klan, none of these groups or incidents were associated with Simmons's Knights of the Ku Klux Klan, Frost's Soveren Klan of the World, or any other national or regional organization. They were local grass-roots responses to the perceived troubles of the day, perhaps in some aspects influenced by the still wildly popular movie, *The Birth of a Nation*. Their occurrence underscored a belief that democracy and the status quo were under threat, that positive action was needed. For the first time in the memory of most, America faced many powerful enemies, both foreign and domestic. It was a time of intense patriotism coupled with war-fed paranoia against foreign spies as well as those citizens and immigrants who opposed, or at the least failed to support, the conflict.

While the various "Klans" and related organizations formed during the war years were private, there was one that had official sanction: The American Protective League (APL). Founded in early 1917 as the brainchild of A. M. Briggs, a wealthy Chicago businessman, it became "a vast, silent, volunteer army organized with the approval and operated under the direction of the United States Department of Justice, Bureau

---

[7] *San Diego Union*, 31 October 1917.

[8] *Tulsa (OK) World*, 8 November 1917. WCU stands for "Working Class Union," an anti-capitalist labor union with a basic socialist philosophy. The WCU was known for its use of violence and extra-legal actions in pursuit of its goals.

of Investigation."[9] Sent out with the semi-official blessing of the Federal Government, the APL boasted a quarter-million badge-carrying secret members with chapters in every state and major city. Working closely with the Military Intelligence Division and civilian enforcement agencies, it referred more than three million cases for investigation during its brief existence of less than two years. Under the provisions of the Espionage Act of 1917 and its amendments, known as the Sedition Act of 1918, almost anyone who did or said anything that might remotely be constructed as not supportive of the war effort was subject to arrest, trial, and imprisonment. Despite its semi-official status, the private operatives of the APL were not bound by the niceties of the Constitution. Covert spying, summary civilian arrests, and unlawful searches were its stock-in-trade. Mass sweeps looking for slackers, draft-dodgers, and others whose papers were not in order resulted in the detention of hundreds of men, most of whom were guilty of no crime. A few harsh words uttered in a bar after a drink or two could result in an unexpected visit from agents of the Bureau of Investigation.[10] Those who served in the APL during the war thought themselves heroes; others saw its legacy as that of trampled civil liberties and state-sanctioned vigilantism.

For men like Simmons, the social and political turmoil of the war offered opportunity, something to be exploited. By the time of America's entry into the hostilities in the spring of 1917, Simmons's Klan was still in its infancy, having established only a few Klaverns in Georgia and Alabama. Per its charter, it was "to have been a public order, like other orders, with members carrying benefit insurance and openly wearing their lodge buttons."[11] The near-hysteria of the day regarding spies and saboteurs changed that. Simmons realized the Klan could operate as its own investigative bureau, providing not only a sense of purpose, but also fulfilling its role as a patriotic institution. And like the Klan of the 1860s, its ability to spy and intimidate would be augmented immensely through anonymity, not unlike that of the American Protective League. Simmons

---

[9] Hough, 3.
[10] The Bureau of Investigation was the predecessor of the FBI.
[11] Shepherd, "Ku Klux Koin," 9.

established a "secret service" within the Klan, a clandestine network of spies in support of the war effort. To further this end, he converted the Klan into a secret organization. In an interview some years later, Simmons told a reporter, "I issued a decree during the war submerging membership in the Klan. Our secret service work made this imperative." Explaining further, "I ordered members to keep their membership in the Klan a secret from everybody except each other. I told them not to admit publically that they belonged to the Klan."[12]

Simmons himself belonged to the "Citizens' Bureau of Investigation" in Atlanta, a minor organization whose members worked under individual members of the American Protective League. As head of his own "secret service" within the Klan, Simmons served as liaison with "federal judges, federal attorneys, and federal secret service officials and operatives." It was in large part this lure of the Klan's "secret service," the opportunity to materially help the nation and its military, which accounted for its initial growth and success.[13]

By early 1918, local and often spontaneous action continued across the nation against those who were perceived to not be in full support of the war. In Ohio, an Austrian immigrant who refused to buy a Liberty Bond was smeared with yellow paint, dunked in cylinder oil and then rolled in sand.[14] In Wyoming, the One Hundred Percent American Society called for an application of yellow paint for "Kaiser lovers."[15] In Salinas, California, members of the "Committee on Traitors" paraded in "the white robes of the old Ku Klux Klan."[16] The general reaction of the news media seemed to be one of quiet approval.

Meanwhile in the South, Simmons's Klan had taken on an activist role. In early May, a group of some 150 masked Klansmen silently rode through the streets of Birmingham led by an American flag and a fiery cross. Printed cards were distributed, warning idlers to "Go to Work."[17] A few weeks later, Columbus, Georgia, was host to a similar

---

[12] Ibid.
[13] Ibid.
[14] *Cleveland Plain Dealer*, 13 April 1918.
[15] *(Cheyenne) Wyoming State Tribune*, 31 January 1918.
[16] *San Jose (CA) Evening News*, 27 April 1918.
[17] *Miami (OH) District Daily News*, 7 May 1918.

demonstration, this time with banners reading, "Loafers, Go to Work," "Tightwads, Loosen Up," "Pro-Germans, Get Right," and "No Yellow Dogs Tolerated." A "satisfied red-blooded American" who watched the spectacle exclaimed, "Bully!!"[18]

In Athens, Georgia, the Klan took more direct action. Forty year-old J. T. Norris was seized by eighteen masked Klansmen for having been heard to say that "he hoped every pound of flour that is being sent to Europe would be sunk before reaching its destination, and that he hoped that every bushel of wheat would be burned before it ripened." [19] In a ceremony on the steps of the Athens City Hall before a crowd estimated to number a thousand, Norris was forced to apologize, sign a loyalty oath, and kiss the American flag. The proceedings were explained to the crowd by a Professor Giles of the State College of Agriculture, indicating some degree of official endorsement. In an editorial comment, the *Savannah News* expressed approval, their only reservation being that the Klan members had no real need to disguise themselves.[20] By mid-year, Klan activity was reported in several agricultural communities around the state, warning "slackers of every description."[21]

In Alabama, the actions of the Klan took on a more aggressive and threatening nature. In June, parades were held in Mobile and Dothan as "a warning to slackers, loafers, and gamblers, to IWW and labor agitators, and to all German sympathizers."[22] A few days later in Birmingham, a Negro named Hale who had been appealing to the black community "to throw off the shackles of their corporation masters" was "stripped, tarred and feathered" in a rural graveyard.[23] In mid-June, a "well known negro labor leader," the president of the Negro Longshoreman's Union, was kidnapped in Mobile from police custody by armed men in Ku Klux Klan robes. His offenses were related to being "ring leader" of the union, as well as his attempts to organize "negro cooks...and washerwomen with the view of having them fix exorbitant

---

[18] *Columbus (GA) Ledger*, 26 May 1918.
[19] *Augusta Chronicle*, 1 June 1918.
[20] Quoted in the *Miami (FL) Herald*, 7 June 1918.
[21] *Columbus (GA) Ledger*, 18 June 1918.
[22] *Gulfport (MS) Daily Herald*, 3 June 1918.
[23] *Gulfport (MS) Daily Herald*, 8 June 1918.

prices for their services."[24] He surfaced several days later in New Orleans after having been strongly advised to leave town.[25] In Montgomery, the Klan issued warnings to "women of the streets and hotel-strumpets," as well as "men that hang around pool rooms."[26] In Gadsden, masked Klan members placed a "slacker cage" on the courthouse square as a "warning that loafers must go to work and every person must do their part to help win the war or suffer the penalty of the cage, accompanied by a coat of tar and feathers."[27]

By early fall, the Klan was "much in evidence" in Columbus, Georgia, working with the Muscogee County Fuel Administrator to enforce "gasless Sundays." Klan members "in full regalia" were on the streets the entire day, "silent and mysterious-looking," making notes of the tag numbers of vehicles on the road. "Automobile traffic was reduced to a minimum," the *Macon Telegraph* reported, while the *Columbus Enquirer-Sun* opined somewhat approvingly that "this organization usually can be counted upon to do its full duty, as it sees it, in any emergency." [28]

The war had allowed the Klan to find its public niche as a patriotic organization that not only spoke the words but was willing to back them up with deeds. It was during these early days that the order adopted the role of a secret society bent on protecting American values, often by unconventional means. It was a society true Americans should respect and malefactors should fear, a society whose wrath was to be avoided. For many in this time of uncertainty, the concept seemed to be a good one.

---

[24] *Montgomery (AL) Advertiser*, 17 June 1918.

[25] *New Orleans Times-Picayune*, 18 June 1918.

[26] *Montgomery (AL) Advertiser*, 2 July 1918.

[27] *Charlotte Observer*, 10 July 1918.

[28] *Macon Telegraph*, 23 September 1918; *Columbus (GA) Enquirer-Sun*, 23 September 1918.

Chapter 11

Militants, Bolsheviks, and the Gentlemanly Gorilla

The hostilities of World War I came to a practical end in November 1918, effectively eliminating the threat of German spies and saboteurs. Three months later in Kansas City, the local division of the American Protective League held a farewell dinner at one of the city's finer hotels prior to its formal demobilization. Described by a local paper as "The Modern Ku Klux Klan," members pledged to maintain the bonds of friendship and turn their energies toward "cleaning the city politically."[1]

Several hundred miles to the southeast, the end of the conflict would seem to have weakened the prime *raison d'être* for Simmons's Knights of the Ku Klux Klan. He need not have worried. The year 1919 would turn out to be one in which domestic turmoil replaced the perceived foreign threat of the war years. Despite her growing industrial might, America had been ill-prepared militarily for her 1917 entry into the war. The nation was even less prepared to deal with the flood of veterans returning from overseas duty, often to discover that in their brief absence the world they once knew had changed. The year following the end of the war would turn out to be one of race riots and labor strife, with the former threat of German *Kultur*[2] now replaced by the perceived menace of Bolshevism.

Beginning in the spring and continuing into the summer and fall of 1919, the nation was wracked by racial discord rooted in post-war social change. The Northern industrial labor shortage resulting from the military call-up was in part filled by blacks emigrating from the South. The number of black migrants was estimated to be some 500,000 during the war years, drastically changing the demographics of many urban

---

[1] *Kansas City (MO) Star*, 6 February 1919.
[2] *Kultur* (German: *culture*) A term commonly used in the World War I era (and subsequently) to refer to the supposed superiority of Germanic culture. It is often associated with militarism and used in an ironic context.

areas. In Detroit, for example, it was estimated that in 1914 there were less than 1,000 Negroes in the city. By late 1919, some 12,000 to 15,000 were thought to be working in the automobile industry alone, challenging returning veterans for what was once considered certain employment. The same trend held true in the steel mills of Pittsburgh and the garment industry of New York City.[3]

American blacks had served with distinction in Europe, the majority in supportive roles, but with a significant number fighting side-by-side with French troops. For the first time in the lives of many, they were treated as social equals. It was feared that "the valiant deeds of Negro soldiers in Europe" would lead to their being "chesty" on their return,[4] or that they would "come back from the war with a 'swelled head' and be inclined to strut about."[5] In what some saw as a validation of this, many of the racial disturbances of 1919 involved returning soldiers and sailors. Others attributed the newly revived demands of blacks for social and employment equality to a new generation of "militant leaders," a group of "radials and revolutionaries...spreading Bolshevist propaganda."[6] In these uncertain times, the ill-defined fear of Bolshevik revolution seemed to become a catch-all cause for any threat to the status quo.

A *New York Times* editorial in early October 1919 was telling.[7] Referring primarily to a "new negro problem," it documented more than three dozen race riots and clashes in the first nine months of the year. The month of July saw major disturbances in Washington, Chicago, Norfolk, and Charleston with dozens killed and many others injured. There would be more by the end of the year. Racial clashes were not limited to urban areas. In Georgia, for example, the *Times* reported six incidents between February and August of the year, all in rural areas. The greatest loss of life took place in Millen in April, with seven said to have been killed. The paper called for a Congressional investigation, but offered little else in terms of concrete solutions.

---

[3] *New York Times*, 5 October 1919.
[4] *Topeka Plain Dealer*, 9 May 1919.
[5] *Springfield (MA) Republican*, 5 March 1919.
[6] *New York Times*, 5 October 1919.
[7] Ibid.

If race issues were not enough to frighten the public, a terrorist bombing campaign by anarchists that begun during the war years added another reason. In one especially bold effort, approximately three dozen bombs bearing a fictitious New York return address were mailed in late April 1919 to prominent businessmen and political leaders around the country. Designed to arrive on International Workers' Day, May 1, they were the sent by the followers of Luigi Galleani, an Italian immigrant, well-known anarcho-communist and revolutionary activist. One such "infernal machine" was sent to the address of then-former Georgia Senator Thomas W. Hardwick in Sandersville, Georgia. Hardwick had been one of the sponsors of the Immigration Act of 1918 that allowed near-immediate deportation of socialists, Bolsheviks, and others whose philosophies were deemed anti-American. [8] Unknown to the bombers, Hardwick had moved to Atlanta, where he was living in a temporary apartment on Peachtree Street while he established a law practice. The package was forwarded there. The shrapnel-packed bomb exploded as Hardwick's black maid, twenty-three year old Ethel Williams, opened it, tearing off both of her hands and putting out one eye. Hardwick's wife was less severely injured.[9] Senator Hardwick attributed the attack to "Bolshevik cussedness."[10] The *Macon Telegraph* and *Columbus Ledger* called for "deal[ing] with this cowardly gang in a firm and more drastic way," including the prohibition of immigration, and the use of "force" against Bolshevism and the IWW.[11]

With federal and state authorities seemingly powerless to stop what appeared to be a breakdown of society, the Klan's message found fertile ground. In Georgia and Alabama, Simmons's Knights of the Ku Klux Klan continued to attract members, although apparently in limited numbers. In contrast, his former associate's competing organization, Jonathan Frost's Soveren Klan of the World, appeared to be thriving. By

---

[8] Also known as the Dillingham-Hardwick Act.

[9] The maid's wounds were significant, with initial newspaper reports indicating that she was not expected to live. She did survive, however, and until her death decades later received a monthly check, initially from Hardwick and subsequently his daughter after his death in 1944.

[10] *State (Columbia SC)*, 1 May 1919.

[11] *Columbus (GA) Ledger*, 5 May 1919.

late 1918, branches were being established throughout the states of the former Confederacy. Frost himself was also apparently enjoying personal success. A June 1919 social item announced the New York wedding of his daughter, (said to be "a widely known Shakespearean actress") to Roy Lowndes Bull, an "overseas hero" and recipient of the Distinguished Service Cross.[12] The bride's father was described an "an author of note" for his works on Shakespeare as well as "head of the big fraternal order which has members throughout the county."

During the same month his daughter was getting married, Frost was establishing a branch of the Soveren Klan in Richmond, Virginia. The initial number of 213 members was said to have grown "to upward of 1,000" by the first of August. Members of the new branch were quick to deny news reports that they had armed themselves and stood "ready to ride forth and strike terror into the hearts of any member of the negro population which (*sic*) may furnish occasion for such action." The denial in itself was clearly a warning.[13]

As if at least two well-organized competing Klans were not enough, a third was established in the spring of 1919 by former Vaudeville performer A. B. ("Texas") Ritchie. Touring extensively in the West and Midwest during the war years under the moniker "The Gentlemanly Gorilla," Ritchie billed himself "the strongest man in the world." His usual routine consisted of such feats as towing a string of ten to fifteen vehicles attached to a rope around his neck. A typical pitch promised, "He will bend iron bars across his muscles, break board planks across his chest, chew iron pipes like gum, bite in two double stacks of playing cards as if they were biscuits."[14] Occasionally he was accompanied by his "sparring partner," twenty year-old Gladys Moon, said to be "the most

---

[12] *Columbus (GA) Ledger*, 8 June 1919.

[13] *Baltimore Sun*, 1 August 1919. Although membership in the Soveren Klan of the World was said to be secret, it was also noted that each member had been provided with a red, white, and blue triangular badge with a star in the triangle. This was to clearly differentiate them from other Richmond men wearing a button with the letters "K.K.K." The latter designated members of the "Keep Klean Klub," a local group organized by prominent local "banker and capitalist" John Kerr Branch "whose hobby is to keep the city clean."

[14] *New Orleans Times-Picayune*, 17 March 1915.

perfect athletic girl" in the country.[15] Apparently having realized the potential profit in starting one's own Klan, Ritchie quit the tour circuit to do just that in his native North Carolina.

Ritchie's Klan was christened the Loyal Order of Klansmen (LOOK), seeking as the ideal member "the Lover of Law and Order." He reported that he held an option on a 5,000 acre tract of land near Charlotte on which he intended to start a colony of like-minded people. A "Military Department" was being set up to train men between twenty-one and thirty-eight to be ready to respond to calls from the authorities for aid "to suppress riots and such violence."[16]

Ritchie's solicitation of members was more direct than that of Simmons or Frost. Advertising heavily in North Carolina newspapers, his logo featured a skull and crossbones emblazoned with "Ku Klux Klan" on a background of a shield bearing the Cross of Lorraine—certain to appeal to veterans of the Great War. Initial entreaties to those in power seemed to produce some interest. The governor of Mississippi gave his tentative endorsement when advised that the new order stood for the "protection of the white man's womanhood and civilization in the South."[17] Governor Bickett of North Carolina was not so impressed, blasting LOOK as "silly" and "a wicked appeal to race prejudice."[18] After some negotiation with the Governor, Ritchie agreed completely drop the Ku Klux Klan theme. The Loyal Order of Klansmen disappeared from news reports thereafter, an apparent failure.

Despite Ritchie's setback, the close of the year of 1919 still found America uncertain of her new-found role in the greater world at large, and struggling to cope with the emerging social, demographic, economic, and technological changes that accompanied and followed the war era. No one could have predicted what the following year would bring, but the events to follow would have a major influence on the future of the Knights of the Ku Klux Klan and its evolving role in American life.

---

[15] *Tucson (AZ) Daily Citizen*, 27 August 1916.
[16] *Charlotte Observer*, 22 June 1919.
[17] *New Orleans Times-Picayune*, 3 July 1919.
[18] *Greensboro (NC) Daily News*, 30 June 1919; *Charlotte Observer*, 30 June 1919.

Chapter 12

The End of the Beginning

After five years of existence and the occasional positive attention in the press, Simmons's Knights of the Ku Klux Klan had achieved only modest success. New members were most often recruited by word of mouth or newspaper ads similar to the one that appeared in the *Atlanta Constitution* in October 1919. Partially typewritten and crudely drawn, it appealed to "REAL MEN" who were "of dependable character, serious thought and manly motives" while excluding "Rough-necks," "Rowdies," and "Yellow-streaks." Those interested were invited to contact "Ti-Bo-Tim" at an Atlanta post office box. The Klan remained at best a regional organization with essentially all of its 2,000 to 3,000 members in Georgia and Alabama. Simmons was perennially short of money, managing his organization from a small non-descript office in downtown Atlanta. Meanwhile, competing organizations such as Frost's Soveren Klan of the World appeared to be thriving. An objective observer of the day might have considered the prognosis for the long-term success of Simmons's Klan to be a grim one.

For many reasons, 1920 was a pivotal year in American history. Even though the Great War had ended abruptly more than a year earlier, the social, demographic, and economic changes that accompanied the era were slower to manifest themselves. January 1920 marked the start of the so-called Great Recession, a severe economic downturn that heralded the practical end of the war-fueled expansion that began with the conflict in Europe more than five years earlier. The years 1916 through 1920 saw the greatest bout of inflation in American history. Based on the then-new Consumer Price Index, the value of a dollar in 1920 was only half that of its value in 1916. If the race riots and anarchist bombings of the previous year were not enough, now events seemingly beyond anyone's control were threatening the economic security of average Americans.

The eighteen months of recession that began in 1920 were characterized by severe deflation whose total approximated that of the entire decade of the Great Depression of the 1930s. The segment of the economy most severely affected was agriculture, the lifeblood of the South. Cotton prices, which had soared more than 500 percent between mid-1914 and mid-1920 in a classic economic bubble, plummeted. Across the South, farms were abandoned as sharecroppers, unable to make a living, fled to mill towns and cities. The migration of blacks to the North resumed with a vengeance, radically changing the population and racial makeup of both cities and farming areas. As farm foreclosures rose, merchants who depended on credit sales declared bankruptcy. Banks, uninsured and loosely regulated, failed. In Georgia, for example, some forty-five percent of banks operating in the state in 1916 had failed or otherwise gone out of business by 1925.

1920 also marked the first year in which the decennial census found the majority of Americans living in cities, some attracted there by industrial growth, others forced there by economic failure elsewhere. The perceived threat of Bolshevik revolution continued as city-dwellers looked with suspicion on the increasing numbers of blacks and immigrants who competed for jobs. Among the young, there was a new sense of independence, perhaps influenced by motion pictures, the freedom of mobility afford by automobiles, and later in the decade, the ubiquitous presence of radio.

Throughout the nation, and especially across the South, there was social and economic uneasiness, an uncertainty as to the country's direction. Many had reached the conclusion that America had entered a period of moral decline. The challenges of the day presented opportunities to those willing to exploit them, a fact that would by year's end benefit the Knights of the Ku Klux Klan. This role would fall to a man named Edward Young Clarke, Jr. who, with his business partner Elizabeth Tyler, was the proprietor of a small Atlanta advertising agency named the Southern Publicity Association.

The person who claimed credit for introducing William Simmons to Edward Clarke was John Quincy Jett, "a professional fund-raiser and self-styled bootlegger" who answered an ad for the Klan he saw in an Atlanta newspaper in 1919. Jett was Elizabeth Tyler's son-in-law and at

The Klan under Imperial Wizard Simmons's leadership initially struggled in its recruitment of new members, primarily due to poor marketing. This crudely designed ad appeared in October 1919 in an Atlanta newspaper. (*Atlanta Constitution*, 8 October 1919.)

Edward Young Clarke, an Atlanta advertising executive, took over recruitment of new Klan members in June 1920, later taking over day-to-day management of the organization in 1922. His marketing skills saved the struggling Klan from almost certain failure in the early 1920s. (*The World's Work*, May 1923.)

the time was employed by the Southern Publicity Association. He was thus well aware of Clarke and Tyler's marketing skills. After joining the Nathan Bedford Forrest Klan No. 1 and hearing Simmons speak a few times, Jett recounted, "I decided that the only thing that would save America and the white people of the world would be the Ku Klux Klan. I knew it would sell to the American people on sight if E. Y. Clarke would tell the people about it, and with Mrs. Tyler looking after the business end of it I knew it would be a money maker."[1]

The passage of time allows one to make two reasonable statements: First, were it not for Clarke and Tyler, it is probable that Simmons's Knights of the Ku Klux Klan would have faded into obscurity in the early 1920s, a fate suffered by many other fraternal orders of the era. Second, it was Clarke and Tyler's marketing genius that in an amazingly brief period of time took the Klan from a small regional fraternal order to a national organizational colossus wielding vast political and economic power.

Edward Y. Clarke, Jr. was born in Atlanta in 1877 to a prominent family, son of a former owner of the *Atlanta Constitution*.[2] Described as "a short slender man with a thick mop of black hair that grew low on his forehead," he favored round spectacles and "walked with a bouncy gait." While historians have referred to him as "a disciple of P. T. Barnum," all agree that he was a skilled promoter with both vision and the necessary ability to follow through. He initially planned to enter the ministry, but ended up working as a reporter for the *Constitution* shortly after the turn

---

[1]Shotwell, "Crystalizing Public Hatred: Ku Klux Klan Public Relations in the Early 1920s," 11; *Georgia Free Lance (Dublin, GA)*, 29 October 1925. Jett's rambling account of his association with the Ku Klux Klan was published in a series of 8 articles in the *Georgia Free Lance* between October 29 and December 17, 1925. The newspaper, which existed for less than six months in late 1925 and early 1926 was published by then ex-governor and Klan opponent Thomas W. Hardwick. It appears that the primary purpose of this short-lived publication was to serve as a public vehicle for Hardwick's anti-Klan views.

[2] E. Y. Clarke, Sr. was, among other things, author in the 1870s and 1880s of several editions of *Atlanta Illustrated*, a history of the city accompanied by demographic data and lithographic prints.

of the century.[3] After seven years as a reporter and subsequently a period of other jobs, Clarke began working for the Georgia Chamber of Commerce in 1914. There he was given the responsibility of organizing the Georgia Harvest Festival, scheduled to be held in November 1915. In spite of J. Q. Jett's assertion that he introduced W. J. Simmons to Clarke, the two probably met through activities related to the Festival. Eleven fraternal societies in Atlanta were to participate in a "mammoth parade" with "at least 10,000 secret order men."[4] Simmons was to act as Deputy Grand Marshall of the parade, an office that would likely have introduced him to Clarke, who served as the festival's General Manager. The week-long event was a spectacular success, cementing Clarke's reputation as a skilled organizer.

It was through the Georgia Harvest Festival that Clarke in turn met his future business partner, Elizabeth ("Bessie") Tyler. Her background is less well known. She was said to be widowed with a child by age fifteen. While lacking formal education, by the time she met Clarke she had become "a down-to-earth business woman, a pragmatist with a tendency toward ruthlessness."[5] The two entered into a business alliance, Clarke serving as the public face of the Southern Publicity Association while Tyler attended to the realities of everyday affairs. A tall, heavy-set woman, Tyler was often said to have been the real intellect behind the Klan's national expansion in the years that followed.

During the war years, the Southern Publicity Association conducted advertising and fund-raising drives for a number of clients including the Anti-Saloon League, the YMCA, the Theodore Roosevelt Memorial Fund, and the Salvation Army, among others. Clarke was innovative, going so far as to hire an airplane to drop leaflets from the sky as part of one fund raising campaign.[6]

---

[3] It is of note that E.Y. Clarke, Jr.'s brother Francis also worked there, eventually working his way up to managing editor, a post held during the early 1920s and the Klan's heyday in Atlanta.

[4] *Atlanta Constitution*, 14 October 1915.

[5] Shotwell, 18. Tyler was said to have run a house of ill-repute prior to joining forces with Clarke. There is little doubt that their relationship was—at times—more than a simple business one.

[6] Ibid., 19.

Elizabeth Tyler, E. Y. Clarke's partner in the advertising agency, was said by many to be the intellect behind the Ku Klux Klan's initial success under Clarke's leadership. As a woman, she was ineligible to be a Klan member, so she worked as an employee of the Propagation Department. Having made a small fortune in a few short months working with the Klan, she resigned her position in early 1922, later moving to California. (*The World's Work*, May 1923.)

Simmons's relationship with Clarke was one born out of both necessity and desperation. By the late spring of 1920, the Klan, like the national economy, was struggling. At Jett's suggestion, the two men met, Simmons willing to overcome his aversion of publicity in hopes of recruiting new members, Clarke with the mind of a businessman, always eager to earn another dollar. Initially, it appears that Simmons's plan was to hire Clarke to conduct a membership drive. Clarke was quite reluctant, however, telling Simmons, "Why I have lots of friends among the Jews and Catholics. They have helped me in Red Cross drives and all the other drives for various purposes here in the South, and I don't see how I can afford to break away from them." To associate himself with the Klan meant that Clarke "would have to drop his Southern Publicity Association entirely and give up all his drives." [7] The two men eventually struck a bargain, one that would change the future of the Klan.

Since its beginning, new inductees into the Klan had paid a $10 "Klectoken" as a membership fee. This was described as a "donation" which exempted it from being taxed as income. On June 7, 1920, Simmons and Clarke signed an agreement that allowed Clarke to hire organizers ("Kleagles") and recruit new members for the Klan. Of the $10 Klectoken, Clarke was to retain $8 and pass the remaining $2 on to Simmons and the Klan. From his $8 cut, Clarke agreed to pay all expenses. It was a high price to pay, but it brought almost immediate results. On a practical basis, the Southern Publicity Association ceased to function independently, instead becoming the in-house "Propagation Department" of the Klan. Clarke was made Simmons's chief of staff and given the title of Imperial Kleagle. As a woman, Elizabeth Tyler was not eligible for Klan membership. A vital partner to Clarke, she was subsequently described simply as an employee of the organization. The two began work immediately and within months had hundreds of recruiters in the field, thus beginning an intense period of expansion.

In addition to the recruitment of new members, one of Clarke's first tasks was to create a favorable public image for the Klan. Both in the South and nationwide during the war years, various acts of lawlessness had been attributed to "the Klan," or those who purported to represent it.

---

[7] Shepherd, "Ku Klux Koin," 39.

In those days, Simmons's organization was still quite small and regional. Clearly many—perhaps most—of the deeds for which it was blamed were wrongly attributed. On the other hand, the Knights of the Ku Klux Klan had been willing to threaten, and sometimes commit, extra-legal acts of violence and intimidation against draft dodgers, slackers, and others of similar ilk. Even if the Klan were innocent in many cases, its rhetoric alone was sufficient to raise doubts as to its culpability. As Imperial Wizard, Simmons had been publicity-shy, preferring marches and displays designed to provoke curiosity, and raising more questions than answers as to the exact nature of the secret order. Typical was a parade of "hundreds" of robed and masked Klansmen, members of Atlanta Klavern No. 1, who "marched and countermarched up and down Whitehall and Peachtree" Streets in May 1920, a month before Clarke's contract was signed. The *Atlanta Constitution* carried a somewhat tongue-in-cheek account of the event, referring to the marchers as "ghosts, phantomlike spooks, wearing white flowing robes, grotesque headgear with peaked tops, and full white masks." As if to downplay the significance of things, the reporter noted, "No one knew their mission, few asked." [8]

Prior to mid-1920, news reports of activities involving the Knights of the Ku Klux Klan had been infrequent. Under Clarke's direction, that all changed as the Klan aggressively expanded its horizons and public persona. [9] In mid-August, more than a hundred Klansmen marched in Macon, Georgia, following the formation of a new Klavern there. The news item noted branches of the Klan were "being formed throughout the country." [10] Two weeks later, Simmons attended the initiation of some two hundred new members in the Sunday School room of the Grace Methodist Church in Atlanta. [11] In September, Simmons was fêted at the Elks' Club in Savannah where he had participated in the formation of a Klan chapter of "several hundred" members. [12]

---

[8] *Atlanta Constitution*, 7 May 1920.
[9] See *Appendix for an illustrative graph of newspaper coverage of the Ku Klux Klan between 1910 and 1940.*
[10] *Atlanta Constitution*, 14 August 1920.
[11] *Atlanta Constitution*, 28 August 1920.
[12] *Atlanta Constitution*, 28 September 1920.

As new recruits flocked to join the Klan, the economy at large seemed to be in a downward spiral, especially in the agricultural South. Cotton prices, which had hovered near forty cents per pound in late 1919 and through mid-1920, were in freefall, eventually bottoming out at less than ten cents a pound in 1921. Even this figure was deceptive, as the inflation-devaluated dollar was worth only half what it had been a few short years earlier. Across the cotton belt, there were calls to withhold cotton from the market in hopes that a short supply of the commodity would increase prices. But for many farmers, this was not an option. The agricultural system ran on credit; money borrowed in the spring planting season was to be repaid with the fall harvest. Failure to pay could lead to bankruptcy, so even with sharply diminished prices, many were forced to sell their cotton for less than it cost to produce.

Some chose more radical means to keep cotton off the market. In a number of areas written warnings were posted on rural gins, allegedly from the Ku Klux Klan and demanding that the owners not gin and bale cotton. Some who refused found their gins torched. Simmons, now the public face of the Klan, was quick to deny any involvement of his organization, calling the allegations "outrageous slander."[13] As Imperial Wizard he decreed "that every member of the Klan is commanded to use all the influence within his power to suppress operations of the so-called night riders, and to assist officers of the law in the apprehension of the terrorists."[14]

It was becoming evident to Clarke that a majority of citizens did not understand the Klan, what it stood for, its goals, or its actions. He was determined to remedy that. In November, a series of anticipatory newspaper notices invited the public to hear Imperial Wizard Simmons speak at the Atlanta Theatre on "The Ku Klux Klan, Yesterday, Today, and Forever." The address was to show how the Klan "not only saved the South, but the entire nation," in the years following the Civil War. "Especial attention" was to be paid to the "insinuations emanating from

---

[13] From a historical perspective, Simmons was likely being truthful.
[14] *Atlanta Constitution*, 31 October 1920.

certain sections of the country that the Ku Klux Klan is involved in the operations of night riders, gin burners and others."[15]

On November 7, Simmons spoke for more than three hours to a standing-room-only crowd in the theater. Recounting how the ideals of the Klan dated to the dawn of human history, he cited examples of the "Klan spirit," such as the Cromwell Revolution in England and the Boston Tea Party in America. His address was punctuated by "numerous witty sallies, entirely extemporaneous" which "moved the audience to gales of laughter." The Klan, Simmons said, had no part in the "campaign of terrorism in the cotton districts." Summarizing the purpose of the event, he declared, "We are not here for advertising ourselves. The Klan needs no advertising. We are not here for applause, although it makes us happy to know that you feel we deserve it. We are here to correct the mistaken ideas about the Klan, to give you an insight into its true aims and operations." [16]

The *Constitution's* reporter, evidently quite impressed, wrote "So loud and frequent was the cheering and hand clapping that a casual observer might have mistaken the lecture for a popular entertainment act on a theater program, rather than a serious and dramatic explanatory address by the head of a secret order of world renown."[17] It would be some years before the ironic nature of his statement was to become evident. Later in the month, Simmons repeated his address in front of large audiences in New Orleans and Houston, the latter delivered in the "packed to capacity" auditorium of the First Christian Church. Later that evening he presented the charter to the newly organized Houston Klan with its initial membership of more than a thousand men.[18]

By early December, the spate of gin burnings appeared to have waned. Even though Simmons had denied any connection with these "terrorist" events, he was quick to take credit for stopping them. The Klan issued a statement alleging Simmons had "received letters from nearly every section the southern states in which the night riders were

---

[15] *Atlanta Constitution,* 5 November 1920.
[16] *Atlanta Constitution,* 8 November 1920.
[17] Ibid.
[18] *Atlanta Constitution,* 28 November 1920.

active commending the Imperial Wizard and members of the Klan for the prompt action…in suppressing the activities of the night riders."[19] It would have been impossible to verify that the Klan's actions had anything at all to do with this outcome, but there was nothing to be lost by claiming success.

As the recruitment and publicity drives shifted into full gear, other events were playing out that would remove one other major barrier to the Klan's spread, the issue of Jonathan B. Frost's Soveren Klan of the World. This completing organization was apparently thriving outside of Georgia. Once more attempting to halt what he considered infringement on his Klan's charter and copyright, Simmons had filed a supplemental lawsuit in 1919 in Fulton County (Atlanta) Superior Court seeking to enjoin Frost from the use of any Klan-related themes. For whatever reason, the action had become mired in the legal system; by mid-1920 Frost had not even been served with notice of the suit.

With Clarke now in charge and acting as Simmons's chief of staff, things changed. Frost was served notice of the suit in July 1920. He immediately sought to have the case transferred to Federal District Court. On August 18th, Judge Samuel H. Sibley denied Federal jurisdiction in the case, transferring it back to the Georgia Superior Court. The case was heard in late September. In the interim, Frost had begun using a different name for his Klan, hoping to avoid an injunction. His tactic failed, heralding the end of the Soveren Klan of the World and at the same time removing potential competition for would-be "Klan" members in a number of states.[20]

---

[19] *Atlanta Constitution*, 5 December 1920.

[20] While Simmons may have benefited from the legal actions to remove Frost's Klan from competition, others were not so fortunate. Atlanta Attorney W. H. Terrell served as the Klan's Klonsel (general counsel) from 1916 and had filed the actions against Frost. On November 1, 1920, shortly after the legal victory, he resigned his position, apparently continuing private practice and his position on the City Board of Education. On October 10, 1921, he filed suit against the Knights of the Ku Klux Klan seeking $100,000 in legal fees for work in the Frost matter. He stated, "I was successful in defeating this organization (Frost's Soveren Klan) and made it possible for the Klan to reap millions. I have filed suit in a small amount compared to the huge sums the Klan has been able to gather because of my services." (*Macon Telegraph*, 11 October 1921.)

Imperial Wizard Simmons closed out the year with a cynical gesture designed to soften his (and the Klan's) image of unyielding racism. For some years prominent members of the black community had sponsored an annual "Old Slave" Christmas entertainment event to honor the dwindling number of former slaves. In late 1920, in the midst of the recession, funds were far short of their goal. Simmons summoned Rev. B. R. Holmes, a well-known black minister, to Klan headquarters and presented him with a check for $125. The amount was sufficient to ensure that the celebration would take place, with distribution of gifts and money to the former slaves and a memorial service for those deceased. The gift was duly reported in the *Constitution*, the sum representing a relatively small investment in image building.

As the fall of 1920 merged into winter the Knights of the Ku Klux Klan were ascendant, the outlook bright and the future seemingly unlimited. But just as the Klan hierarchy was celebrating their victory over Jonathan Frost, a man named Julian LaRose Harris was returning from a several-year stint in Europe, where he had been most recently editor and general manager of the *Paris (France) Herald*. Julian, a newspaperman and son of the beloved Southern writer Joel Chandler Harris, wanted to run his own paper. As fate would have it, an interest in the *Columbus (GA) Enquirer-Sun* was available and for sale. Harris saw it as the perfect opportunity. Little could he have realized that this decision would set him on a collision course with the Knights of the Ku Klux Klan.

Part IV

The Rise to Power

Despite...sporadic and generally favorable publicity, the Invisible Empire remained confined to Alabama and Georgia and as late as 1920 could best be described as just another indolent southern fraternal group. With a total membership of less than two thousand, there was no indication that the Knights of the Ku Klux Klan, from among hundreds of secret societies and patriotic fraternities, would vault to national prominence.

Kenneth T. Jackson
The Ku Klux Klan in the City 1915-1930
Published 1967

There can be little doubt that the purely commercial motive had much to do with the successful promotion of the Klan....But it must not be forgotten that the commercial motive alone can never explain [its] marvelous spread....

Even granting, however, that Clarke and his assistants were merely commercializing hates and prejudices, it is well to remember that men joined the Klan because it appealed to their patriotism and their moral idealism more than to their hates and prejudices. The baser motives were present, but they alone can never account for the spread of the Klan.

John Moffatt Mecklin, PhD
The Ku Klux Klan: A Study of the
American Mind
Published 1924

Chapter 13

Ku Klux Koin: The Spread of the Klan[1]

While the Klan of the 1920s may have presented itself as a patriotic organization bent upon preserving and promoting the true values that made America great, there is little doubt that the motivations of its leaders were far more base. Perhaps on some levels it did succeed in one aspect of the American dream, albeit briefly and only for a select few. Under the guidance of Edward Y. Clarke the organization became a finely honed machine that annually generated tens of millions of dollars in an era when the average American earned less than $1,000 per year. As such, it was and remains one of the great American success stories in the world of marketing and publicity.

Despite all his high-toned rhetoric, one of—if not *the*—prime motivations for W. J. Simmons's founding of the Knights of the Ku Klux Klan was the opportunity it presented for financial reward. The empiric problem was that Simmons lacked the skills and abilities to realize this aspect of his goal. For the first years of its existence, the Klan sputtered along, attracting relatively few members in a limited geographic area, chronically short of money and tottering on the edge of bankruptcy. Under the Clarke regime (with the able assistance of Elizabeth Tyler) all of this changed. Membership numbers zoomed from the hundreds to the hundreds of thousands in a remarkably short period of time, eventually exceeding several million. The task was not an easy one. Legitimate opposition to the Klan's message and methods was formidable. This aspect will be addressed in more detail in later chapters. For the moment, however, the story of the Klan's propagation is a fascinating one in and of itself.

---

[1] "Ku Klux Koin" was the title of one of a series of three articles on the Klan written by William G. Shepherd and published in *Collier's* magazine in July 1928.

Historically, the legacy of the Ku Klux Klan was inextricably associated with the South and the Civil War, carrying with it an anti-black, anti-Northern bias. The revived Klan was founded in the city Sherman burned, its name, regalia, ritual, and worldview in many ways supposedly lifted from the Klan of the 1860s (with more than a little assistance from the silver-screen blockbuster, *The Birth of a Nation*). Simmons's original marketing plan, if he had one, was to capitalize on the revived popularity of the Klan as the visible motif for a fraternal, beneficial order. Prior to mid-1920, its spread was contiguous, with essentially all of its members in Georgia and Alabama. Simmons eschewed publicity, preferring instead to maintain a veil of secrecy and exclusivity designed to attract both curiosity and potential members. While his literature and rare public statements focused on what the Klan stood *for*, the overwhelming public perception centered on what it was *against*. News reports often blamed "the Klan" for acts of lawlessness, irrespective of any concrete proof. The secretive nature of the order made such allegations difficult to deny. Clarke set out to change all this.

Clarke's plan was simple in concept, but challenging in its execution. Having cut a deal with Simmons to retain eight out of every ten dollars paid by new members, his primary concern was expanding the order's membership. To accomplish this he needed to change—or at least soften—the public image of the Klan. He believed, apparently correctly, that membership expansion would be self-inductive; basically, the larger and more powerful the Klan became, the more who would want to join it. Hand-in-hand with an increasing membership, other income producing opportunities would arise including, for example, sales of regalia, insurance products, and the like. The Klan's literature may have promoted one-hundred percent Americanism, but its new management saw it as a potential font of near-unlimited income.

Any expansion needed operating capital. One of Clarke's first moves was to put some $7,000 of his own cash into an operating fund and sell $26,000 of general obligation notes backed by the Knights of the Ku Klux Klan, Inc.[2] With the immediate financial crisis stemmed, he set out to develop a national recruitment strategy. The nation was divided into

---

[2] Wade, *The Fiery Cross*, 155.

"Domains," each ruled over by a "Grand Goblin." Initially, New York State and Washington, DC had their own Domain, while the others were made up of "Realms" corresponding to individual states, which were in turn subdivided into districts.[2] Under Clarke's organization a "King Kleagle" presided over a Realm. Within that Realm individual recruiters ("Kleagles") were dispatched to found new provisional Klaverns. Kleagles, representing the front line of Klan, were well compensated. Of the $10 Klectoken paid by each new member, $4.00 was retained by the Kleagle, $1.00 by the King Kleagle, and 50¢ by the Grand Goblin. Of the remaining $4.50, Clarke and Tyler kept $2.50, with $2.00 going into the Klan's Imperial Treasury. This was, in essence, an early variant on a multi-level marketing scheme made popular in decades hence by such household names as Avon and Tupperware. On a practical basis, each King Kleagle served as a district sales manager under a Grand Goblin who occupied the position of regional sales director. Within months, Clarke had 200 Kleagles in the field; the number would eventually exceed a thousand.[4]

Individual Kleagles came from a broad background. Most had in common a good working knowledge of fraternal orders and many were active members of the Masons, Shriners, Odd Fellows, the Knights of Pythias, and others. Exactly how to recruit new members was left to each individual, but with guidance and support from those above them in the hierarchy. Each area of the country was different, as was each town or city. A number of techniques were used effectively. Kleagles were advised to attempt to recruit high profile members of each community, particularly members of law enforcement, politicians, prominent businessmen, and ministers. To lawmen, the Kleagle pitched the Klan's firm stance on law and order; to the politician, the offer of block voting and monetary support; to the businessmen, the opportunity to garner the exclusive trade of other Klan members; to ministers, the Klan's avowed focus on charity, morality, and chastity, not to mention its firm support

---

[3] Fry, *The Modern Ku Klux Klan*, 45. Only Florida, in 1920-21 a relative backwater, was not included in a Domain. The Imperial Kleagle did have a post office box address in Jacksonville, however, for those who wished to join.

[4] Cutlip, *The Unseen Power: Public Relations. A History*, 332. See also Part IV of the *New York World's* series on the Klan, 9 September 1921.

of Prohibition.[5] Ministers were often offered the position of "Kludd" (chaplain) in newly formed Klaverns—without paying the usual $10 donation, of course. A few positive words from the Sunday pulpit in support of the Klan could work wonders for recruitment.

The strategy used to attract new members varied widely by region. In the cotton-producing areas of the South where blacks made up a significant proportion of the population and played an integral part in economic life, appeals focused less on race than on the issues of morality, bootlegging and the enforcement of the law. At the other extreme in such cities as Detroit and Philadelphia, the Klan's avowed anti-immigrant stance and its belief in white supremacy were used to attract those who perceived foreigners and blacks as threats to their jobs, livelihoods, and way of life. In California, Orientals became the scapegoats, as did Mexicans in the Southwestern border states. In the heavily Catholic cities of the northeast, an appeal to religious bias came in the form of papist conspiracy theories seeking to undermine the fundamental American principle of separation of church and state. For those men interested in "doing something" about America's threats and perceived imminent decline, joining offered a chance for action. In short, Klan recruiters seemed to have something for everyone. Even in states whose population was predominantly white and Protestant, the simple flag-waving theme of American patriotism alone was sufficient to attract thousands of members.

In some towns and small cities, the Klan would announce its arrival by the burning of a cross in a prominent site sure to be seen by all, but only after inviting the local press and quietly spreading the word that a major event—the exact nature of which was left to the public's imagination—was to take place at a certain location and time. In others, more subtle means were employed. A prospective candidate for membership might receive a letter advising him that "a friend"—always

---

[5] An example of one of the advantages of being a Klansman can be found in the *TWK Monthly*, the "Official State Publication" of the Alabama Knights of the Ku Klux Klan. TWK was understood to mean "Trade with a Klansman," a movement that was common at the time. The October 1924 issue contained a wide variety of paid ads ranging from insurance sales, to furniture dealers, to beauty shops, to auto supply stores, and to printers and tailors.

unnamed—had suggested that he was "100 PER CENT AMERICAN" and therefore the sort of man the Klan needed. A series of such form letters—with slight variations in the pitches—were tested by Clarke in early 1921.[6]

While much of the actual recruitment of members was done on a semi-covert basis, Clarke set up a speakers' bureau of lecturers (Klokards) ready to present the Klan's message to curious audiences. Often addressing civic clubs, fraternal organization meetings, and political rallies, the Klokards, a number of whom were ministers, rallied supporters and encouraged sympathizers. Employing Chautauqua-style oratory, their messages played on the fears and prejudices of their audiences. Simply put: Organized groups of Catholics, Jews, aliens, and Negroes represent threats to the American way of life. Morals in the United States are deteriorating as evidenced by bootlegging, sexual vice, gambling, and the like. These forces have insinuated themselves at all levels of American society and government. "The sole weapon against such sin and degradation is a Protestant alliance though the Ku Klux Klan; therefore if you are on the side of God and the heavenly hosts, join the Klan."[7]

Perhaps the best known of the Klan orators was the Rev. Caleb A. Ridley, who served as pastor of Atlanta's Central Baptist Church while at the same time holding the office of Imperial Kludd (national chaplain) of the Klan. Ridley's message was one of unabashed Anglo-Saxon supremacy delivered with sermon-like oration. An account of one of his July 1922 speeches at the Macon City Auditorium attended by some 300 people described his talents: "(He) gave his audience an exhibition of his versatility as a tragedian, comedian, contortionist and an acrobat. Several times he clasped an American flag in his hands to illustrate some remark, and each time the audience generously applauded." Cards were handed out inviting listeners to fill out and return if they wished to apply for Klan membership.[8]

---

[6] Monteval, 19. Wording and capitalization are those of the letter's author.
[7] Cutlip, 337.
[8] *Macon Telegraph*, 7 July 1922.

The Rev. Ridley also had a fondness for strong drink, a habit that on occasion caused him to miss speaking engagements. In June 1923, the Atlanta Baptist Ministers' Conference went on the record citing "the continuance of Dr. C. A. Ridley in the Baptist ministry as injury to the cause of Christ and a reflection upon the honor of Baptists."[9] He was expelled and subsequently resigned his pastorate to lecture full time for the Klan. In October of that year, Ridley's automobile was observed by an Atlanta motorcycle officer to "be zigzagging on Peachtree Street" resulting in his arrest on the charge of "being drunk and operating an automobile."[10] His explanation was that "he had driven out into the country where he was accosted by a man" who apparently forced him to drink whiskey. After his release from jail he denied that he was drunk and that he was found with two bottles of illegal whiskey in his vehicle.

In areas with large Catholic populations, Klan speakers included "escaped nuns" and "converted priests" who related lurid tales of sadistic cruelty and sinful debauchery hidden behind cloistered walls. Helen Jackson, author of *Convent Cruelties or My Life in the Convent: Awful Revelations*, was one of the more notable speakers.[11] Often touring with L. J. King, an "ex-Romanist" and alleged former priest, she regaled sex-segregated audiences with horrors experienced during her ten years as a novice and nun. According to one historian, "She claimed to have firsthand knowledge of infanticides and abortions forced on nuns by the priests who fathered their babies. Displaying little leather bags, Jackson told her riveted audience that these were used to dispose of the convents'

---

[9] *Macon Telegraph*, 13 June 1923.

[10] *Seattle Daily Times*, 18 October 1923.

[11] The frontispiece of the book further described its contents as recounting "A providential delivery from Rome's Convent Slave Pens." Sales were apparently quite brisk at speaking events. The author's copy, available in an exact copy as a PDF download from the internet, was the 13th edition, published in 1926. Each copy was numbered and signed. If the numbering system is to be believed, more than 160,000 copies had been printed. According to Wade (p. 180, 481), Jackson's maiden name was Barnowska, and her prime contact with a Catholic institution occurred when she was committed by her sister to a Catholic reformatory in Detroit in 1895. Her anti-Roman lecture series appears to have been motivated by a desire for revenge, not to mention an excellent income from book sales.

A GREAT
MASS MEETING FOR MEN

A MASS MEETING FOR
MEN will be held at the
Court House, Sunday afternoon,
May 13th, 1917, at 3:00 o'clock, to
which every man is urged to show
his patriotism by his presence.
The meeting will be addressed by
Rev. S. J. Winchester.

SUBJECT:

AMERICA'S
GREATEST MENACE

ADMISSION FREE

(145/362)

From the outset, one of the ways the Klan's message was presented to the public were lectures given by speakers (Klokards) who extolled the values of the order, usually while encouraging eligible men to join. (From the collections of the Manuscript, Archives, and Rare Book Library, Emory University.)

murdered newborns and aborted fetuses."[12] If this alone was not enough to raise fear of the Catholic menace, it was alleged that organizations such as the Knights of Columbus were secretly stockpiling arms in their meeting halls, awaiting the Pope's call for armed insurrection.

Throughout the1920s, the increasingly popular medium of the motion picture remained a useful recruiting tool. In many ways, Klan philosophy maintained a love-hate relationship with the movie industry. A 1924 editorial in a Klan publication was typical. Titled "How Movies Are Undermining Religion," it accused the industry of being "engaged in a systematic propaganda which, if not checked, will eventually destroy civilization and pull down the republic." [13] Accusing movies of trying to "win the public to the cause of immorality" and "making a systematic attack on Protestant Christianity," the author alleged moviegoers were driven to crime, divorce, and worse through "the tremendous power of suggestion." With this said, *The Birth of the Nation* was widely used as a recruiting tool, as was the 1920 film *The Face at Your Window*, an anti-Bolshevik work revolving around a plot by foreign agitators to overthrow the United States government.

The direct recruiting work of the Kleagles in 1920 and 1921 was supported to some degree by advertising and positive reviews about the Klan, many planted as news stories in the general press. There were billboards touting the Klan's message in select cities which, with other publicity, sought to neutralize negative images of the organization while promoting its message of "one hundred percent Americanism." Clarke signed contracts with advertising agencies in New York and Chicago, and in the summer of 1921 purchased half and full-page ads in the daily newspapers of New York, Chicago, Milwaukee, and other cities.[14] A typical full-page ad in the *Fort Worth Star-Telegram* in August 1921 took the form of a proclamation from William Joseph Simmons as Imperial

---

[12] Blee, *Women of the Klan: Racism and Gender in the 1920s*, 89.

[13] *TWK Monthly*, October 1924. It is interesting for a current-day observer to the read the article while substituting the phrase "video game industry" for "motion picture industry." As such, the 1924 article suddenly seems quite current and quite possibly written by those who believe video games contribute to crime and immorality.

[14] Cutlip, 340.

Wizard of the Knights of the Ku Klux Klan. Addressed to "All Lovers of Law, Order, Peace and Justice, and to All the People of the United States," it reiterated that the Klan was a "law-abiding, legally chartered, standard fraternal Order, designed to teach and inculcate the purest ideals of American citizenship, with malice toward none and justice to every citizen regardless of race, color or creed." [15]

By 1920, visual media had become a prime method of advertising and publicity. Major news stories of the day displayed photos whenever possible, and illustrated magazines dominated the newsstands. In contrast to Simmons, Clarke understood this, and early in his tenure as Imperial Kleagle commissioned a series of photos of the Klan to be distributed as publicity photos when the occasion arose. Most depicted a white-robed Klavern in some sylvan setting paying homage to the standard props of a cross and American flag, labeled with such captions as "God is our refuge and strength." One showed Simmons seated at his desk, studiously reading what appears to be a Bible. A large photo of a group of Klansmen surrounding a burning cross is propped to his left, while on the wall above the desk are photos of a woman, presumably his wife, and a framed advertising poster from *The Birth of a Nation*. In the background, a large American flag leans against the wall, its triangular shape forming a steeple above the head of the Imperial Wizard.

Clarke's experience as a newspaper reporter—not to mention the fact that his brother was the managing editor of the *Atlanta Constitution*—resulted in wide press coverage, much of it positive. Ready-for-press stories were delivered to newsrooms, making composition easier for the paper's reporters, while at the same time assuring that the Klan's message would be properly rendered in print. [16] Sometimes an extra incentive was offered to be sure the story was given good coverage. As one of Clarke's former Klan employees sarcastically noted after breaking with the group, "The average man don't know what can be put in the daily papers for $100." [17]

---

[15] *Fort Worth Star-Telegram*, 15 August 1921.
[16] Cutlip, 341.
[17] *Georgia Free Lance (Dublin, GA)*, 29 October 1925.

On taking over publicity for the Klan, E. Y. Clarke immediately set out to improve its public image. This staged photo shows Imperial Wizard Simmons in his office studiously reading what appears to be a Bible under the backdrop of the American flag, with a painting of a mounted Klansman holding a burning cross on the wall above him. (John Shotwell.)

Well aware of the growing power of the illustrated media, one of E. Y. Clarke's first acts as head of the Propagation Department of the Klan was the production of a series of staged publicity photos of Klan rituals incorporating the themes of the Christian Cross and American Flag. (John Shotwell.)

Both to counter the overly secret nature of the Klan and give the public a hint of its power, in late January 1921, Clarke arranged to induct some 528 candidates into membership in Birmingham, Alabama.[18] Calling on his experience in organizing Atlanta's Harvest Festival, the ceremony was designed to be both spectacular and intimidating. The night was bitterly cold, with temperatures hovering at 25 degrees and a biting wind blowing out of the northwest. It had rained heavily, leaving the Alabama State Fair Grounds, the site of the induction, knee-deep in water. The events were open only to Klan members and inductees, but were staged in such a way that they could be observed by the public from a distance. Newspaper reporters were given a closer look and allowed to stand on a housetop within the grounds where they were watched closely by Klansmen-guards.

The ceremony began at 8:30 PM as the initiates were ushered into a great square formed by "hoards" of white-robed, hooded and masked figures, guarded on the periphery by mounted horsemen, also in Klan regalia. In the center of the fairground's racetrack, white-clad Klansmen formed a large cross as two searchlights played upon them to the accompaniment of "weird whistling and calls from the dark corners of the grounds and from nearby hills." In front of it all was the throne of Imperial Wizard Simmons, "surrounded by a thousand Klansmen," where inductees took the oath of loyalty in front of 'the living emblem" of the cross.

The show was successful. The Associated Press gushed, "This was the first time in history the public has been permitted to witness a Ku Klux Klan conclave, even from a distance," noting that the initiates "now sit among the gods of the empire invisible." After the event, Simmons issued a statement to reporters saying the "new order" stood for "one hundred per cent Americanism and reconsecration to [the] bedrock principles" of white supremacy, separation of church and state, and

---

[18] Accounts of the event were published widely in the press. Representative newspaper reports can be found in 28 January 1921 issues of the *Miami* (FL) *Herald*, the *Macon Telegraph*, and the *Colorado Springs Gazette*, among others. In reading newspaper accounts of the event, one cannot help but be reminded of the Nazi Party's stage-managed Nuremberg rallies of the 1930s, but on a far smaller scale.

"protection of woman's honor and the sanctity of the home." Its goals were positive ones, not negatives, he assured. As to membership, he boasted "The order has 30,000 members above the Mason and Dixon line; it has 7,000 in Chicago." The press dutifully reported these numbers, but to an objective observer, they could only have been swallowed with a grain of salt. The Klan's membership had grown indeed, but early in 1921 it remained primarily centered in the southern and southwestern states. Like any good advertising executive, Clarke understood that a "fact," though quite dubious, takes on an air of authority when repeated often enough.

By early fall, however, the Klan's membership had expanded to approximately 100,000 nationwide. Its explosive growth and seeming success as an organization attracted scrutiny from both the curious press and suspicious governmental officials throughout the county. Back in Atlanta, Simmons, Clarke, and other members of the order's hierarchy were quietly basking in the glow of success as the cash continued to flow in. On May 6, 1921, a "grateful" Klan presented Imperial Wizard Simmons with a house on Atlanta's prestigious Peachtree Road, alleged to have cost $25,500, plus a sedan and $25,000 in back pay to compensate him for the order's lean early years. The presentation of the house, as with most events engineered by Clarke, was expertly done. The popular ex-Senator Thomas Hardwick, now Governor-elect, gave a brief speech to mark the event.[19] The house, partially obscured from the street by a thick stand of trees, was prominently marked by a large pole placed at the roadside and topped by an American flag. At the bottom of the pole a shield adorned with stars and stripes announced the home's name, "Klankrest," above which was a large Christian cross, all designed to promote the religious, patriotic nature of the Klan. In July, Clarke announced that Klan offices, which had been located in a series of mid-city buildings, would soon move to new quarters further out Peachtree Road. By September, the huge four-columned Greek revival mansion of

---

[19] Hardwick would later become one of the Klan's staunchest opponents, but in these early days had been heard to say positive things about the order. In his gubernatorial reelection bid in 1922, only a year and a half later, he would be handed one of the largest electoral defeats in Georgia history courtesy of his stance against the Klan.

This group photo of the Klan leadership was taken on the veranda of the Imperial Palace, probably in late 1921 or early 1922. W. J. Simmons is seated in the middle front row holding a cane, with E. Y. Clarke immediately to his right. (John Shotwell.)

Under the leadership of W. J. Simmons, the Ku Klux Klan maintained a low public profile. When he took over publicity in 1920, E. Y. Clarke sought to change this. By mid-1921 Klan headquarters were moved to a huge columned mansion on Atlanta's famed Peachtree Street, a public display of the success and wealth of the hooded order.

E. M. Durant had been purchased and converted to the Imperial Palace.[20] Clarke made extensive modifications to the house and its five-acre grounds, allegedly spending approximately $100,000 in the process.

In addition to money to be made directly from Klan membership "donations," there were other sources of income that Simmons had failed to tap during the first years of the order's existence. Unlike Klan disguises of the 1860s Klan, modern Klansmen were forbidden from making their own robes. Simmons had outsourced this production; given the membership numbers it scarcely would have been worthwhile for him to do otherwise. Clarke contracted with the newly established Gate City Manufacturing Company to be the exclusive provider of robes and related regalia. It had been incorporated by C. B. and Lottie Davis, "who were undoubtedly Clarke and Tyler," according to one author.[21] Tyler owned the Searchlight Publishing Company, which took care of all the Klan's printing.[22] Both Clarke and Tyler were incorporators of the Clarke Realty Company, which was in charge of land purchases for the Klan.

---

[20] It is of note that both Klankrest and the Imperial Palace were purchased in the name of Edward Y. Clarke, and remained titled as such for a number of months prior to being transferred to the Klan as a result of public scrutiny resulting from the *New York World*'s exposé and the Congressional hearings in September and October 1921. The initial base cost of the Imperial Palace was said to be $35,000. Much of the work of the Propagation Department remained at the Klan's former downtown offices, while most other affairs moved to the Palace. The building was owned by the Klan from 1921 to the late 1920s when it was sold, eventually becoming the property of the Catholic Church. The Cathedral of Christ the King was completed there in 1939, an ironic touch given the Klan's virulent opposition to Catholicism. Atlanta's street numbering system was changed in the mid-1920s. The current address of the former site of the Imperial Palace is 2699 Peachtree Street NE, on the southeast corner of Peachtree Street and East Wesley Road. All evidence of the Palace has long since disappeared. The amounts paid for the Simmons home and the Imperial Palace were revealed in the October 1921 hearings.

[21] Cutlip, 350. See also *New York Times*, 17 July 1922.

[22] A 1925 catalogue of Klan robes and banners shows the combined sewing and printing production facilities located in Buckhead, Atlanta, Georgia. This was apparently quite a significant business enterprise. More than eighty employees pose in front of a large three-story building, with a smaller one-story building to its side.

One can only speculate as to how much money flowed into Klan coffers in the first year after Clarke and Tyler assumed responsibility for membership recruitment. One historian estimates that in the first fifteen months, Clarke and Tyler received $212,000 while Simmons garnered $170,000 for doing essentially nothing.[23] This was to be just a start.

In an interview with a journalist several years later,[24] Simmons estimated that in 1922 the Imperial Treasury in Atlanta was raking in some $35,000 a day—more than $12,000,000 a year—from dues, new initiates, robe sales, etc. This was only about a quarter of the total income generated by the Klan; the rest remained with local Klaverns, producing sudden wealth for many of their leaders. In these heady days of seemingly endless money the Imperial Wizard had no idea that by late 1922 he would be deposed, having had control of the Klan's money machine wrested from him by those intent on grabbing the power and the spoils for themselves. Simmons, bitterly resentful of his ouster, estimated that with "only" one million members the Klan could have generated some $58,000,000 a year in dues and fees for "advanced" degrees of membership. As events were to play out, however, he was to be thrust back into relative obscurity while others would take the revived Knights of the Ku Klux Klan to new levels.

---

[23] Wade, 157.
[24] Shepherd, "Ku Klux Koin," 9.

KING KLEAGLE

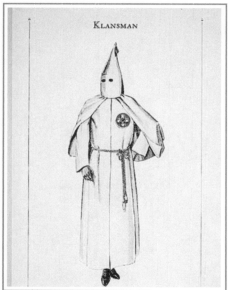

KLANSMAN

One of the significant sources of income for the Knights of the Ku Klux Klan, Inc. was the sale of regalia, jewelry and the like. Klan uniforms varied in color, ornamentation and price depending on rank. The regalia of a King Kleagle (a state-level officer) is more adorned than that on an ordinary Klansman. (*Klan Regalia Catalogue*, 1925.)

Chapter 14

A Standard Fraternal Order: The Klan in Action

The Ku Klux Klan of the 1920s was structured and operated as a fraternal order, not unlike hundreds of others in the day. Given its philosophy and deeds over the years, however, it is not surprising that this fact is often forgotten. At its peak in mid-decade, the Klan counted millions of members in its ranks, raising the fundamental question of the motivations of men who joined, and what happened after they did so. As noted in the previous chapter, it is reasonable to believe that much of the Klan's expansion was based on the fact that it was a lucrative enterprise, cleverly advertised and adroitly marketed. But what of those individuals behind the masks, those who made up its membership? As summarized by Shotwell,

> (T)here were no "typical" Klansmen and no single reason for belonging to the Ku Klux Klan. E. Y. Clarke and his associates organized a highly flexible public relations campaign with appeals and propaganda that could be easily adapted to suit the distinctive moods, fears, and desires of individuals and communities of the 1920s. They recognized the vague suspicions and frustrations of white Protestant Americans and articulated them into a concrete package of hatreds and objections. In so doing, Clarke and his aides mobilized public disaffection, created irreparable cleavages, and left an indelible stain on American society.[1]

Despite efforts to do so by a number of historians, there is no simple way to characterize Klansmen of the 1920s. As the order spread throughout the North American continent during the decade, various strategies attracted varied groups of joiners. While all members nominally subscribed to a stated set of values, Klan membership, like politics, was quintessentially local. A 1921 recruitment card offered to prospective members, read, "Your friends state you are a "Native Born"

---

[1] Shotwell, 72.

American Citizen, having the best interest of your Community, City, State, and Nation at heart, owing no allegiance to any foreign Government, political party, sect, creed or ruler, and engaged in a Legitimate occupation, and believe in:

The Tenets of the Christian Religion
White Supremacy
Just Laws and Liberty
Closer Relationship with Pure Americanism
The upholding of the Constitution of these United States
The Sovereignty of our State Rights
Freedom of the Speech and Press
Closer relationship between Capital and American Labor
Preventing the causes of mob violence and lynchings
Preventing unwarranted strikes by foreign labor agitators
Prevention of fires and destruction of property by lawless elements
The limitation of foreign immigration
The much needed local reforms
Law and Order[2]

It was the sort list that might have appealed to any true American. The card instructed the bearer to "present this card at the door for admittance," the key to the "opportunity to become a member of the most powerful secret, non-political organization in existence." How could one refuse? In theory, new members were to be inducted in an elaborate ceremony in which the "alien" applicant was "naturalized" as a citizen of Invisible Empire, swearing *Obedience* to the Imperial Wizard, *Secrecy* as to all "matters and knowledge of the Knights of the Ku Klux Klan," *Fidelity* to other Klansmen and the organization (which specifically included the vow to "pay promptly" one's dues) and *Klanishness*, which was defined as the practical application of the beliefs listed above. In practice, however, things were often far different.

In the Klan's initial expansion, most members were recruited by Kleagles working on a commission basis. The more members recruited,

---

[2] Klan form P-214, dated 29 July 1921.

Form P-217

"NON SILBA SED ANTHAR"

Your friends state you are a "Native Born" American Citizen, having the best interest of your Community, City, State and Nation at heart, owing no allegiance to any foreign Government, political party, sect, creed or ruler, and engaged in a Legitimate occupation, and believe in:—viz.

The Tenets of the Christian Religion.
White Supremacy.
Protection of our pure womanhood.
Just Laws and Liberty.
Closer relationship of Pure Americanism.
The upholding of the Constitution of these United States.
The Sovereignty of our State Rights.
The Separation of Church and State.
Freedom of Speech and Press.

Closer relationship between Capital and American Labor.
Preventing the causes of mob violence and lynchings.
Preventing unwarranted strikes by foreign labor agitaters.
Prevention of fires and destruction of property by lawless elements.
The limitation of foreign immigration.
The much needed local reforms.
Law and Order.

REAL MEN whose oaths are inviolate are needed.

Upon these beliefs and the recommendation of your friends you are given an opportunity to become a member of the most powerful secret, non-political organization in existence, one that has the "Most Sublime Lineage in History," one that was "Here Yesterday," "Here Today," "Here Forever." Present this card at door for admittance, with your name, occupation and address.

Name ....

Occupation ....

Address ....

Discuss this with no one. If you wish to learn more, address Ti-Be-Tim ....
"DUTY WITHOUT FEAR AND WITHOUT REPROACH."

The Klan application form with its nonsensical "Latinish" motto of *Non Silba Sed Anthar* ("translated" as "Not for Self But for Others") detailed the stated philosophy of the organization, an agenda of "One-Hundred Percent Americanism." (Kenan Research Center at the Atlanta History Center.)

the greater the Kleagle's income. As Henry P. Fry, a former Kleagle who broke with the Klan, recounted in 1922:

> In the present mad scramble for commissions on the "donations," the Kleagles administer the obligation (oath of membership) at any time and place that suits the convenience of the "alien" with ten dollars, and Ku Kluxes are manufactured on the "pay-as-you-go" style in stores, factories, banks, physicians' office, and any other place where there is freedom from intrusion. One enthusiastic Kleagle wrote to the home office that he had arisen from his bed one night after midnight, and clad in his pajamas had administered the obligation to a "worthy alien," whose ten dollars burned so badly in his pocket that he could not wait until daylight to be separated from his money.[3]

As the Klan's power and influence grew, there was much contemporary discussion as to the type of man who would join the order or, if not a member, support its philosophy and actions. The subject was widely covered in the press, in magazine articles, and in several books. In 1924, for example, John Moffatt Mecklin PhD, a Professor of Sociology at Dartmouth College, published *The Ku Klux Klan: A Study of the American Mind*. Referring to "The rise of the modern Klan as the most spectacular of all the social movements in American society since the close of the World War,"[4] he concluded that "The Klan makes a powerful appeal to the petty impotence of the small-town mind,"[5] serving as "a refuge for mediocre men, if not weaklings, for obvious reasons."[6] "Almost without exception," Mecklin wrote, "the leaders in the various professions and in business are not in sympathy with the Klan. The strength of the Klan lies in that large, well-meaning, but more or less ignorant and unthinking middle class, whose inflexible loyalty has preserved with uncritical fidelity the traditions of the original American stock."[7]

---

[3] Fry, 67.
[4] Mecklin, *The Ku Klux Klan: A Study of the American Mind*, 3.
[5] Ibid., 107.
[6] Ibid., 109.
[7] Ibid., 102.

Mecklin was simply wrong. Klansmen were not so easily classified. The demographics of Klan members varied from region to region, from state to state and from town to town. Klan membership was secret; there were no public records and most Klan rosters were lost or destroyed during the period of the order's decline. Many joined during its period of ascendancy in the early 1920s, but in later years a history of Klan membership represented both an embarrassment and liability, especially to those in public life. Despite this, several historians have correlated existing Klavern rosters with contemporary occupation and economic status to provide a glimpse of who became citizens of the Invisible Empire. As a general statement, many Klansmen were familiar with fraternal orders; it was not unusual to belong to more than one. Kleagles recruited heavily from the Masonic orders, despite the fact that the Masons were on record as opposing the Klan. Ministers frequently found the Klan's stance on morality in keeping with their worldview and were well represented in the order's early days. In 1924, the Klan was said to claim "as members three-quarters of the 6,000 delegates to the Southeastern Baptist Convention," a number that most likely represented both wishful thinking and a gross exaggeration. [8]

More specific examples are cited by Jackson in his seminal work on the urban Klan in the early 1920s. Of the membership of Klan No. 14 in Knox County, Tennessee, approximately 29% came from white-collar occupations, and 71% from blue-collar trades. Businessmen, salesmen, ministers, and clerks made up the majority of the former, while railroad employees, unskilled laborers, carpenters, and textile workers were most heavily represented in the latter category. In sharp contrast, Klansmen from the Aurora, Illinois, Klavern in 1922 were predominantly from white-collar occupations, representing nearly two-thirds of the membership. Dentists were the largest single group, but of some 73 members, only one was a minister. [9]

---

[8] MacLean, *Behind the Mask of Chivalry: The Making of the Second Ku Klux Klan*, 8.

[9] Jackson, K. T., *The Ku Klux Klan in the City 1915–1930*, 62, 119. Aurora is located in what is today the greater Chicago area. The Chicago Klan had a similar occupational distribution in the same era.

The records of the Athens, Georgia, Klan No. 5, one of the first established outside of Atlanta, revealed the order had a broad appeal across social and economic boundaries, enrolling "approximately one in ten of the native-born, Protestant white men eligible for membership."[10] The average Klansman was a married, middle-aged father of between three and four children.[11] Nearly a third belonged to other fraternal orders including the Masons, Odd Fellows, Woodmen of the World, Elks, and Knights of Pythias.[12] Professionals such as physicians, attorneys, ministers, pharmacists, and the like made up 8% of the total 364 members on the roster. Managers, petty-proprietors, public employees, and clerks were among the largest groups, totaling 58% of all members. Skilled tradesmen made up 19% and unskilled workers 15%.[13]

The name of the Ku Klux Klan is traditionally associated with the rural South. Surprisingly to many, however, at its peak in the mid-1920s the order's center of gravity was in the Northern Mid-west, with the largest Klaverns in major cities. From its 1915-1920 roots in Georgia and Alabama, the spread was at first primarily westward. By 1922, 61% of all members were in the Southwest, with 22.2% in the South. In the following two years the Klan's growth was explosive in the states of Indiana, Ohio, and Illinois; by 1924 their members accounted for four out of every ten Klansmen (40.2%). At the same time, fewer than one out of six (16.1%) Klan members were found in the South.[14] During the nearly three decades of existence of the Knights of the Ku Klux Klan, the largest concentrations of members were recorded in the cities of Chicago, Indianapolis, Detroit, and Philadelphia.[15]

It is impossible to estimate with any real accuracy the total membership of the Klan at or near its peak. The order's leadership

---

[10] MacLean, 9.

[11] Ibid., 10.

[12] Ibid., 7.

[13] Ibid., 55.

[14] Jackson, K. T., 15. The Southwest is defined here as the states of Texas, Oklahoma, Arkansas, Louisiana, New Mexico, and Arizona. The South refers to southern states east of the Mississippi, as well as West Virginia and Kentucky.

[15] Ibid., 239.

routinely exaggerated the number of Klansmen to make the order seem all the more powerful. With a policy of a secret membership sworn to silence on all things Klanish, there was little fear that such deception would be revealed. Many joined by paying their Klectoken, but for a variety of reasons quietly withdrew after attending a few meetings. According to J. Q. Jett, the average Klan recruit attended only about four meetings before dropping out.[16] Many did so when they realized the disparity between the Klan's rhetoric and its actions. Shotwell quotes a former Georgia state senator who joined in 1922 but did so only after discovering that a number of other prominent politicians were Klansmen. "He agreed to go through with the initiation and was greatly impressed by the solemnity of the ritual and the apparent purity of motives. After the ceremony, however, he overheard several of his fellow Klansmen, including the sheriff (who had recruited him), conspiring to ride out and flog a local citizen who was suspected of bootlegging."[17] The senator never attended another meeting. Jett alleged the policy of overstating the Klan's membership originated with Clarke who considered such deception to be just another form of positive publicity.[18]

Like the apocryphal debate about the number of angels that can dance on the head of a pin, many scholars have cited widely divergent figures for Klan membership in its 1924-1925 heyday. Estimates range from a million, which, based on all objective evidence, is clearly low, to as high as 8,904,871 in 1925, the latter remarkably precise figure cited in a *Washington Post* article relying on data from "an authoritative source."[19] All such figures are based on speculation, and frequently derived by manipulating the most fragmentary local or regional data through uncertain extrapolations to yield national figures. Estimates often make

---

[16] *Georgia Free Lance (Dublin, GA)*, 29 October 1925. Jett was Elizabeth Tyler's son-in-law and the man who took credit for introducing William Simmons to Edward Y. Clarke.

[17] Shotwell, 66.

[18] *Georgia Free Lance (Dublin, GA)*, 29 October 1925. Jett's exact quote: "The leaders [of the Klan] will tell you they have from ten to twenty million members. Clarke started this. I have heard him tell a press man that they had a million in one state when the fact was they did not have five thousand. He was only wishing he could get the million."

[19] *Macon Telegraph*, 20 November 1930; 1 December 1930.

no differentiation between members who were active, and those who may have dropped out but remained on the Klan's rolls. Some may include members of Klan auxiliaries, such as Women of the Ku Klux Klan and the youth-based Junior Klan. In his definitive history of the Klan, Chalmers cites a figure of "more than three million" in the mid-1920s.[20] Jackson estimated a total figure of just above two million for the Klan's total enrollment during its existence between 1915 and 1944, with about 1.5 million active members at its apex.[21] Hiram W. Evans, the Imperial Wizard between 1922 and 1939, cited a figure of five million-plus for the Klan's peak membership.

From one perspective, the precise membership of the Knights of the Ku Klux Klan is of less importance than its influence on American society and thought, both in the era and the years that followed. History is replete with bold examples of far-reaching social, political, and economic turmoil wrought by the actions of individuals and small groups in pursuit of an agenda in support of or at odds with the status quo. Certainly, it can be argued that the series of events that led to the creation of the 1860s Ku Klux Klan were sparked by John Wilkes Booth's bullet. Whether the Klan boasted of one or nine million members is less important than the corrosive effect of its philosophy and deeds on American life.

In examining some of the fragmentary records of Klaverns of the 1920s, one cannot help but be struck by the seeming mundaneness of the Klan's day-to-day activities. Presided over by an Exalted Cyclops, and assisted by a bewildering array of officers whose titles played on the "kl" alliteration (Klaliff, Klokard, Kludd, Kligrapp, Klabee, Kladd, Klarogo, etc.), meetings were opened with a prayer and singing, and for the most part dealt with local issues important to that Klan. At the end, the group stood and sang the Closing Klode to the tune of the traditional eighteenth century Baptist hymn "Blest Be the Tie That Binds:"

---

[20] Chalmers, *Hooded Americanism*, 291.
[21] Jackson, K. T., 235-237. This figure included both male and female persons (the latter in Klan auxiliaries). One-half were said to live in metropolitan areas of 50,000 or greater in population.

Blest be the Klansman's tie
Of real fraternal love
That binds us in a fellowship
Akin to that above

On a quarterly basis, the local Klan's Kligrapp (secretary) was required to submit a report to the headquarters of their individual Realms detailing the number of active members, those who had joined or been suspended, the number of meetings held, and their attendance. Klans were "taxed" on the number of active members, with a portion going to the Imperial Treasury and a smaller amount to the Realm.

Surviving Klan correspondence often concerns minutiae: In April 1926, John C. Swope, a member of the Lexington, Kentucky, Klan No. 97 was involved in an automobile accident in east Tennessee. In response to Swope's request, the Grand Dragon of the Tennessee Klan sent out a letter to the Knoxville Klan requesting that local Klansmen "use your influence in behalf of Kl. Swope to see that he is given a fair trial." In October 1926, Ben A. Ray, who represented himself as a member of the Asheville, North Carolina, Klan, skipped out of his Knoxville, Tennessee, boarding house, leaving the proprietress, Mrs. P.O. Wilford, with an unpaid $15.00 bill. She wrote the Klan, seeking payment. The Klan's Department of Investigation and Intelligence tracked down Ray and discovered he was not a Klan member. They paid the bill to Mrs. Wilford after receiving promises from Ray that he would reimburse them.[22]

In many areas, especially the upper mid-West, local Klan organizations served as a focus for social activities. An August 1924 invitation from the East St. Louis, Illinois, Klans invited other Klansmen to a three-day meeting to be held at the nearby Monks Mound park, featuring national Klan speakers and a naturalization ceremony, as well as a flying circus with wing walking, trapeze acts, a parachute jump, and "a gorgeous display of fireworks with streamers and phosphorus rays." Later that fall, the Bloomington, Illinois, Klan announced an upcoming

---

[22] The Klavern documents and correspondence cited in this section are from the collection of the Emory University Manuscript and Rare Book Library.

As the Klan became an increasingly powerful force in American social and political life in the early 1920s, print media attitudes were generally those of skepticism. Photos of Klan ceremonies were commonly reproduced in magazines of the day, including these from a 1923 four-part series on the order appearing in *The World's Work*. (*The World's Work*, September 1923.)

THE KKK
IS WATCHING
YOU

In many sections of the nation and particularly in the South, the Klan of the 1920s adopted the role of an extra-legal regulatory organization, often threatening and punishing those deemed to have violated some moral code, e.g., drunkenness or marital infidelity. So great was fear of the Klan that often only a warning was needed. A card like this, delivered anonymously, frequently served as a warning to miscreants. (From the collections of the Manuscript, Archives, and Rare Book Library, Emory University.)

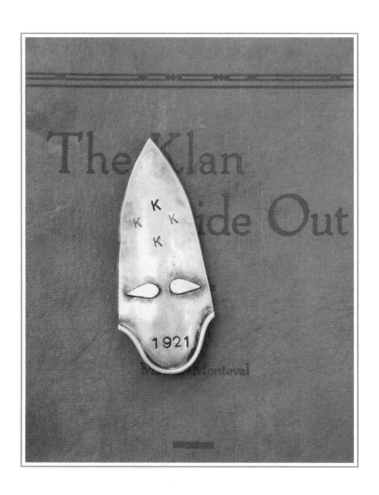

This pin, likely locally made in east-central Georgia, commemorates a 1921 Klan event. (Private Collection.)

This Hero Cross of The Knights of the Ku Klux Klan was awarded in the 1920s to a Klansman from east-central Georgia for outstanding service to the order. The medal was originally suspended from a red, white and blue ribbon. (Private Collection.)

Part of the appeal of the Ku Klux Klan was its nature as a fraternal order. In the 1920s, a number of musical works were composed that reflected this aspect. These labels are from 78 rpm records: "Wake up America and Kluck, Kluck, Kluck," and "Daddy Swiped Our Last Clean Sheet and Joined the Ku Klux Klan." (From the collections of the Center for Popular Music, Middle Tennessee State University.)

"naturalization as well as a weinner (*sic*) roast," to be followed a few days later by "a pork roast."

Such surface banality often masked the Klan's more sinister side. In spite of the order's avowed respect for law and order, its stated belief in the tenets of the Christian religion, and its goal of upholding the Constitution of the United States, all too often Klan members themselves violated both moral and legal codes in their self-appointed roles as enforcers of their own views of right and wrong. This type of extra-legal activity would be a major factor in the Klan's eventual decline and failure. Though the reasons for joining the Klan varied, for some it was the opportunity to attempt to "clean-up" their communities, to deal in an active way with the perceived problems of postwar America. At times, the Klan acted in ways that assisted law enforcement; for example, Klan-led raids against Georgia bootleggers in the early 1920s were neither illegal nor discouraged in some areas. At other times, the Klan's righteous vengeance was visited upon those perceived to have violated some moral code. Adulterers, drunkards, and wife-beaters were common targets, especially in the South. In some sections of the nation, immigrants felt the Klan's wrath. In others, it was persons of color who suffered, especially blacks who fraternized with whites (or vice versa). In an oft-repeated scenario, the offender would be warned, either by a mysteriously delivered written note, an anonymous phone call, or occasionally with a visit from masked Klansmen. Failure to comply could result in flogging, tar and feathering, or worse, including mutilation and murder.

Such acts of extra-legal violence did not escape the eyes of law enforcement or the press. In many communities, however, the Klansmen were lawmen themselves. Newspapers that relied on ad revenue for their existence were often easily persuaded to turn a blind eye to the Klan's activities, or else risk losing valuable accounts from merchants who were members of or supported the Klan. Even in those cases that came to trial, a friendly judge or a Klan-packed jury would assure that many deeds went unpunished.

Written history is replete with detailed accounts of Klan-sponsored violence in the early 1920s and the failure (or inability) of government and law enforcement to adequately prevent or punish it. Many—some might venture most—such events went unreported to the authorities. Some incidents spawned relatively minor local or regional news.[23] Others, such as the Klan-related murders of two young men near Bastrop, Louisiana, in August 1922, produced national headlines.[24] More will be said on this incident in a later chapter. For the moment, however, it is instructive to focus on the actions of a single Klavern in a moderately-sized Georgia city during this era. The events there, while unique to the persons and circumstances, provide a typical example of the Klan's self-assumed vigilante[25] actions.

The Macon, Georgia, Dixie Klan No. 33 was organized in August 1920 with "over forty" initial members receiving the provisional charter. The order grew rapidly, and by November of that year, the local Klavern was comprised of some 125 members, a sufficient number to warrant a permanent charter.[26] The Klavern initially positioned itself as a positive force in the community. In March 1922, for example, two robed Klansmen silently "invaded" a luncheon of Community Chest workers to contribute $25 "to be distributed among the welfare organizations represented by the campaign." In June 1923, "thousands" lined the sidewalks of Mulberry and Cherry Streets (two of the city's main thoroughfares) to watch as several hundred uniformed Klansmen paraded to Central City Park to initiate more than 400 new members. The masked marchers carried banners reading "Duty Without Reproach," and "We are the Soldiers of the Cross, the New Militia of Christ."[27] The Klansmen's auto tags were covered to prevent identification; lawmen present to direct the crowd did not object.

The Macon Klan's public persona hid its private one. The Dixie Klan No. 33, like others, had a Vigilance Committee that received and responded to reports of legal and moral infractions. Many were sent by

---

[23] E.g., the J. C. Thomas murder case of January 1921. See Greene, 240.

[24] See Duffus, "How the Ku Klux Klan Sells Hate," 240-243.

[25] The word "vigilante" is from Spanish, meaning watchman or guard. As used in English, it generally refers to a person who takes extra-legal action, most commonly against a person or persons in punishment for a perceived crime.

[26] *Macon Telegraph*, 3 August 1920; 18 November 1920. See also Hux, 155-156.

[27] *Macon Telegraph*, 20 June 1922.

aggrieved spouses and lovers, others by those self-righteously reporting some moral infraction that did not rise to the level of criminality.[28] This committee, or members of it, issued warnings and often dispensed punishment to those deemed to have violated some tenet of the social order. Most commonly in Macon, the punishment came in the form of beating or flogging. Most victims had been accused of such behaviors as marital infidelity or drunkenness, or of violating laxly enforced laws such as the distribution of illegal liquor. A warning from or action by the Klan induced extreme fear in its recipient, often hindering legitimate attempts by law enforcement to investigate the incidents. As summarized by Chalmers, contrary to popular belief "the Georgia Klan seldom directed its violence toward Jew, Roman Catholic, and Negro. They were the objects of its semantics, but its direct action was visited primarily upon its fellow white, native-born Protestants."[29]

Publicly known kidnappings, floggings, beatings, and similar outrages attributed to the Macon Klan apparently began in January 1922 with the abduction of Dr. Robert F. Mills, a chiropodist,[30] who was kidnapped at gunpoint on College Street near Mercer University after been lured out on the pretext of seeing a patient. His twelve year-old son, who had accompanied Mills, was taken as well. The pair were taken to a rural cemetery where the doctor was whipped by masked assailants for the alleged offense of marital infidelity. The boy was forced to watch as his father was beaten. Afterwards, Mills was left to walk home, while his son was dropped off a block from their home on Appleton Avenue. Out of fear and intimidation, Mills did not report the incident to the authorities.

A few months later in June 1922, Dr. Eugene Schreiber, a 33 year-old physician who recently moved to Macon from Boston was kidnapped at gunpoint near his home, driven to the country, threatened, and strongly advised to leave town. Schreiber was estranged from his wife and

---

[28] Contacting the Klan to report someone was quite simple. Many newspapers had small notices in the Classified section, of which one appearing regularly in the *Columbus (GA) Ledger* in September 1921 was typical. It read, "If you wish to communicate with the Ku Klux Klan, address P. O. Box 735."

[29] Chalmers, 71.

[30] Chiropodist is the alternate name for a podiatrist.

had recently filed for divorce. It was revealed that his office nurse, Mrs. Vera Bergenheim, whom he had represented as his sister-in-law, was in fact his lover. He departed the city within days.[31]

Dr. Mills's ordeal was not over. In the months that followed his flogging, the Klan continued to watch him, going so far as to follow him to Florida to spy on his activities.[32] His wife received threating letters stating that if her husband failed to return home, "you will know that we have gotten him."[33] Fearful for his life, in late October Mills contacted his attorney who sent a letter then-Governor Hardwick appealing for protection. Within days Mills was visited by a man named Payne who represented himself as an investigator dispatched by the Governor. Assurances were given that the matter was being looked into and that protection would be provided.[34]

A few days later, Dr. Mills was kidnapped a second time near his home when his car was forced against the curb by a large Cadillac touring car. His two sons, aged twelve and four, were abandoned in Mills's vehicle as their father was carried away. Mills had taken to carrying a pistol for protection. He tried to use it to defend himself, but the weapon misfired as he tried to shoot at his assailants. They took his gun, severely beat him with it, and advised him to leave town. He recognized several of his kidnappers as sheriff's deputies. This time the police were contacted, with the incident receiving extensive coverage in the local newspaper.

In April 1923, Lynwood L. Bright of Macon, and his lover, the wealthy Mrs. Frederica Pace of New York, were abducted from a downtown Macon street. They were driven to the country where Bright was beaten as Mrs. Pace was forced to watch. This occurred just after Bright's sensational divorce trial during which Bright and Pace were accused of adultery.[35]

The summer of 1923 saw multiple similar incidents. Despite the seeming well-intentioned efforts of law enforcement, no progress was

---

[31] *Macon Telegraph*, 25 June 1923; 26 June 1923; 28 June 1923.
[32] *Macon Telegraph*, 5 November 1922.
[33] *Macon Telegraph*, 7 November 1922
[34] *Macon Telegraph*, 11 September 1923.
[35] *Winston-Salem Journal*, 5 April 1923.

made in solving the crimes. The police were hampered by the reluctance of the victims to talk, and the possible knowledge that some of the kidnappers may have been members of law enforcement. In July, an alcoholic house painter was kidnapped and "told to change his ways."[36] A few days later a carpenter was taken and flogged for "moral issues". He knew his kidnappers but refused to divulge their names.[37] August 9th saw "a night of wholesale kidnapping."[38] A small store owner (apparently black), was taken and severely whipped for having "talked 'rough' to a white woman."[39] Three other men were seized and beaten the same night, reportedly by the same gang.

The spate of abductions and the powerlessness of law enforcement to stop them produced local alarm. "Failure of the victims to give the police more information to work upon makes the work of the police department difficult," one city councilman announced.[40] Bibb County Sheriff J. R. Hicks suggested a substantial reward might make a difference, and the Macon City Council voted to contribute to a fund established for that purpose. Within days, both Governor Clifford Walker, supported vigorously by the Klan in the 1922 elections, and the Dixie Klan No. 33 had contributed to the fund, with the local Klavern issuing a proclamation condemning the violence. Both actions were most likely cynical moves designed to divert attention from the Klan's culpability.

In mid-August 1923, Sheriff Hicks established a special motorcycle squad, available to respond on a moment's notice to a call of another kidnapping.[41] The same day, Governor Walker announced the possibility of imposing martial law in Macon if order could not be restored.[42] The following day, Saturday, August 18, the "flogging gang" was almost apprehended when bystanders heard cries for help coming from an automobile just in front of Macon's Terminal Station. The apparent

---

[36] *Macon Telegraph*, 11 July 1923.
[37] *Macon Telegraph*, 17 July 1923.
[38] *Macon Telegraph*, 11 August 1923.
[39] *Macon Telegraph*, 10 August 1923.
[40] *Macon Telegraph*, 15 August 1923.
[41] *Macon Telegraph*, 18 August 1923.
[42] *Macon Telegraph*, 19 August 1923.

victim was described as "a white man" who was being beaten in the rear of the vehicle as he tried to cry for assistance. A group of men responded but were driven back by a volley of gunshots from the car. A nearby patrolman rushed over and was also fired upon. He returned fire as the kidnappers sped away with their victim. The policeman commandeered another vehicle and gave chase, exchanging gunfire as the pursuit led to the east of the city. The fleeing vehicle was eventually bottled up in a dead end street. After a brief stand-off, it turned and "dashed through" the police line, making good its escape. The apparent victim, who was never identified, did not report the incident to the police.[43]

Despite this initial setback, law enforcement's efforts to apprehend the floggers were successful. Within a few days, three brothers, all Klansmen, were arrested in the process of beating a Negro man.[44] Two weeks passed without further kidnappings. In early September, a total of seven arrests had been made in connection with the incidents over the summer. All were Klan members and all would plead innocence before the court. Charles H. Garrett, Solicitor General of the Bibb Judicial Circuit, publically announced "the Ku Klux Klan of Macon is deeply involved in the floggings," citing "evidence of organized activity of [its] members."[45]

The most notable of those arrested was Dr. C. A. Yarbrough, a prominent local dentist. A 1912 graduate of the Southern Dental College, Yarbrough had established a "lucrative" practice in Macon and was well known in the community, living "in one of the best homes in the city, a colonial mansion at 438 Vineville Avenue."[46] The dentist was known to be a Klan member. His office displayed "photographs of men wearing Klan regalia" on the walls, and its rooms had been used for "classes of instructions in the creed of the Klan." Yarbrough had been under suspicion for some time. Informants had referred to him as the "whipping boss."

---

[43] *Tampa Tribune*, 19 August 1923
[44] *Macon Telegraph*, 22 August 1923.
[45] *Macon Telegraph*, 7 September 1923.
[46] *Macon Telegraph*, 5 September 1923.

The situation had reached crisis proportions in terms of negative publicity for the Klan. The Atlanta headquarters of the Klan dispatched a team of investigators to assist local law enforcement in finding and convicting the responsible parties. In what appeared to be an unusual breach of Klan protocol, the Imperial Palace provided lists of local members and seemed open to providing assistance in the conviction of the accused, whom they acknowledged as Klansmen.

The Klansman-dentist's trial began on September 10. The evidence to confirm the accusations appeared overwhelming, with a number of witnesses identifying him as the leader of the "lash gang." In one interesting turn, the letter that Dr. Robert Mills supposedly sent to Governor Hardwick had ended up in the possession of Yarbrough. It turned out that Mills's attorney, through whom he had written the letter, was close to the Klan. Word was delivered to the Imperial Palace in Atlanta. The letter to Governor Hardwick "disappeared before finding its way into the state house mail sack." The man Payne, who visited Mills as Hardwick's representative, was identified in fact as being J. P. Durkee, the local Klan's Kleagle. Two mail clerks and one post office inspector were said to have been commended by the Klan for their "faithfulness." A telephone call to Hardwick confirmed that he had neither received the letter nor dispatched an investigator.[47]

After several days of testimony, the case went to the jury, the prosecutors sure of a conviction. The panel declared Yarbrough innocent after just three hours of deliberation. Within two weeks, Yarbrough was placed on trial a second time. Again, despite strong evidence against him, the judge was forced to declare a mistrial due to a hung jury. The defendant was brought up for a third trial in October. Once again the result was a mistrial due to the jury's inability to reach a verdict. The divided jurors were deadlocked eight to four in favor of acquittal after fifty hours of deliberation.[48] A fourth and final trial in December resulted in a second acquittal, effectively ending the State's attempt to convict Yarbrough of the crimes for which he had been charged.[49] His name

[47] *Macon Telegraph*, 25 September 1923; 11 September 1923.
[48] *Macon Telegraph*, 26 October 1923.
[49] *Macon Telegraph*, 6 December 1923.

cleared by the court, Yarbrough remained active in Klan affairs for several years thereafter.

During the course of the trials several sheriff's deputies known to be Klan members or supporters were dismissed from their positions, citing a "lack of flogging cooperation."[50] According to one insider, the somewhat inexplicable assistance of the Klan's Imperial Palace had more to do with a political dispute within the Klan organization at the time than with a desire to see the floggers punished.[51]

Frank Alexander, a local merchant and Klansman, was not so fortunate in court. He was convicted in December 1923 of floggings based on evidence not dissimilar to that against Yarbrough.[52] After losing on appeal, he began serving his sentence on the chain gang in September 1924. Less than two months later, Governor Clifford Walker commuted his sentence and reduced his fine. The circumstances were unusual in that Walker did not consult with the State Prison Commission, instead acting alone in his capacity as Governor. It was speculated that Walker was "merely fulfilling his promise to the Klan to pardon any Klansman convicted of a crime in Georgia."[53]

The Knights of the Ku Klux Klan was undeniably a fraternal order. A 1924 *Klansman's Manual* urged members to study the text "so as to become proficient in knowledge of the mechanism and purposes of the order."[54] The last paragraph of the book, in a section devoted to procedures regarding the conduction of a Klonklave (meeting), suggests that leaders be supplied with a copy of "Roberts Rules of Order or some standard Manual of Parliamentary Law." It is doubtful that such a reference would have given guidance as to the proper procedure for kidnappings and floggings.

[50] *Macon Telegraph*, 2 October 1923.
[51] *Georgia Free Lance (Dublin, GA)*, 26 October 1925.
[52] *Macon Telegraph*, 8 December 1923.
[53] Hux, 161.
[54] Knights of the Ku Klux Klan, Inc., *Klansman's Manual*, 86.

Chapter 15

Opposition: The Klan Under Siege

The twentieth century order known as the Knights of the Ku Klux Klan was not conceived in a vacuum, and neither did it operate in one. Opposition to its formation and its continued existence was real and often quite intense. For the first few years it remained more of a subject of derision than of overt disdain. Its rapid spread after mid-1920 changed the equation. The odd Southern institution with its secrecy and strange costumes burst onto the national scene, spreading like an upstart religion from town to town, state to state, and region to region. Suddenly its philosophy, however right or wrong it may have sounded to ordinary Americans, became a topic of national interest and concern. Was the Klan a potentially positive force, or was it a pernicious movement concealed by the purloined flags of Christianity and American nationalism?

The positive images of the Klan generated by Lost Cause movement and *The Birth of a Nation* did not allay the concerns of such groups as the NAACP, various segments of the American labor movement, and religious leaders of all stripes. From the outset they expressed their opposition, or at the very least their concern, as to the Klan's motives and plans. Letters to the editor, the occasional editorial column, or items carried in newspapers served by the Associated Negro Press were the most likely public venues for such apprehensions. [1] During the war and the years that immediately followed, the Klan's espoused role of Americanism and opposition to Bolshevism was not far from the mainstream. Most newspapers of the day, especially in the South where the Klan was active, were fairly neutral or gave their grudging support. It

---

[1] The Associated Negro Press was a news wire service founded in 1919 serving mainly newspapers written for African-American readers.

was only in 1921 and thereafter that the revived Klan became a true national issue and a common topic in the press of the day.

The debate raged for years in both private and public circles, around kitchen tables, in general stores, and in academia. In May 1923, for example, *The Reference Shelf*, a resource publication designed for high school and collegiate debating societies, produced an issue on the topic, "*Resolved: The Ku Klux Klan should be condemned by all right thinking Americans.*"[2] The long list of "Affirmatives" supporting the premise included the Klan's bigotry, violence, commercialism, and potential abuse of its growing power. The "Negatives," however, focused on the Klan's "exalted ideals," including its patriotism, Christianity, and its efforts to deal with "the negro problem." In this era of rapid change in America's national character and self-image, few were precisely sure where the Klan stood in the general scheme of things.

Surprisingly, the most virulent opposition to the Klan came not from outsiders but from the ranks of those who understood it best— former Klan members. It was one of these, at the time a fortyish former newspaper reporter named Henry P. Fry, whose efforts to expose the true nature of the order paradoxically contributed to its explosive growth. His desire to share his knowledge led to the *New York World's* exposé of the Klan in September 1921. That in turn produced calls for a Congressional investigation, which took the form of hearings in front of the House Committee on Rules the following month. Originally, it was assumed that these public airings would expose the Klan as an entity driven by money and hate. The actual outcome was far different.

Rumors of the *World's* forthcoming series on the Klan began to circulate in mid-summer 1921, causing some who had previously kept silent to go public with their concerns. On August 5, the front page of the *Greensboro (NC) Daily News* bore the headline "Grand Dragon Craven Disbands Ku Klux in This State." Major Bruce Craven, head of the Realm of North Carolina as well as a "lawyer, financier, and writer," publically resigned from the Klan, calling it an "organization exclusively engaged in the collection of initiation fees," and "a failure and a fraud." Apologetically admitting that he joined the Klan based on what he

---

[2] Johnson, "Ku Klux Klan," 9.

thought were its high ideals, he bitterly denounced the order and its leaders and expressed regret to those whose membership he had solicited. In a move more symbolic than real, Craven "disbanded" the North Carolina Klan. The Imperial Palace immediately filled his position. He expressed his belief that Imperial Wizard Simmons was "personally sincere," but "not competent to head the organization." The Klan had been usurped by "strong-minded men without sincerity or dreams, [who] took charge of it, control it, and laugh at the poor fools who fall for it." Craven decried the Klan's focus on money, its willingness to engage in or ignore criminality, and its exaggeration and lies, especially as to membership. Instead of the touted 60,000 Klansmen in North Carolina, he said, "there are at the present time perhaps 5,000 in the state who have paid their initiation fees..., most of whom as soon as they got in and saw who was there, kissed their money good-bye and quit."[3]

In the summer heat of 1921, Craven's denunciation of the Klan seemed all but ignored by the national press, who appeared to view it as a more of a local issue. In Atlanta, however, Simmons, Clarke, and Tyler were girding themselves for the rumored series of articles that would dominate the national news for most of the month of September. It was Henry Fry's four-month membership in the Klan—during three of which he served as a Kleagle—that would form the basis of the *World's* articles.

Fry was born and reared in east Tennessee and was living in Chattanooga at the time he joined the Klan. Well educated, he was a graduate of the Virginia Military Institute and had served with distinction during the Great War, joining as a private before rising to the rank of captain at the time his discharge. He had broad career experience, working over the years as a newspaper reporter, publicity man, and salesman. Like William Simmons, he was attracted to fraternal orders. Prior to the Klan, Fry had joined the Masons, the Knights of Pythias, the Odd Fellows, the Red Men, the Junior Order United American Mechanics, the Royal Arcanum, the Woodmen of the World, the Elks, the Eagles, the Owls, and the Theatrical Mechanics Association. With admitted Southern naivety, he reasoned "I could see no reason why a fraternal order

---

[3] *Greensboro (NC) Daily News*, 5 August 1921.

commemorating the deeds of the original Klansmen should not fill a
need in the country today."[4] Most importantly, he was evidently quite
insightful; the more he learned of the Klan, the more concerned he
became that it was a corrupt organization representing a threat to the
American way of life. In his letter of resignation to Imperial Wizard
Simmons, Fry said,

> I have reached the conclusion that [the Klan] is a historical fraud, that it
> is a money making scheme run for the benefit of a few insiders; that it is
> engaged in an evil propaganda in promoting unwarranted religious and
> racial hatred against the Jews, Roman Catholics, negroes, and foreign-
> born American citizens; that your entire scheme is a dangerous public
> menace that will inevitably lead to bloodshed and if successful, must
> result in revolution; and that, in the interest of decent Americanism, it
> should be suppressed by the federal and state authorities.[5]

Fry approached the Pulitzer family-owned *New York World*, known
for its sensationalism and the standard-bearer of the day for so-called
"yellow journalism." The *World* eagerly embraced the concept of doing an
exposé on the Klan, immediately launching a team of investigative
reporters to dig up what could be found. With much advertisement and
fanfare, the series of articles began on September 6th, running
consecutively for twenty-one days. Under often-blaring headlines and
richly illustrated with photos and reproductions of "secret" Klan
documents, the *World* publicized its findings as a public service to all
Americans stating:

> For all its trumpery features, Ku Kluxism, incorporated by William
> Joseph Simmons and propagated by Imperial Kleagle Clarke, is a menace
> to American life and institutions because it spreads though the formation
> of religious and racial suspicions and hatreds, because it drags in its train
> a crop of lawlessness and outrage and arrogation of supra-legal powers as
> an inevitable outgrowth of the traditions which it revives, and because,
> being secret, masked and oath-bound, it is largely irresponsible in its
> censorship of public standards and private conduct. To keep this menace,

---

[4] Fry, 2-3.
[5] Ibid., 26.

which so far is more potential than actual, from being translated into life
is why the World has undertaken this exposure.[6]

Given its history and reputation for ginning up circulation through
journalistic overstatement, the *World's* exposé proved remarkably accurate. At times assuming a tone of gleeful sarcasm while at others presenting a litany of facts and fact-based conclusions, the articles were for
the most part well-researched, well-documented, and accurate.[7] Perhaps
the biggest error was the estimate of the then-current size of the Klan as
between 500,000 and 650,000 members when, in fact, the Klan's
membership at the time was less than 100,000, predominantly in the
South and Southwest. These figures were, however, qualified as being
based on the "boasts of its leaders."

The paper's editors seemed to take particular joy in exposing the so-
called "secrets" of the order. The Kloran, the forbidden bible of occult
ritual, was available for all to see in the reading room of the Library of
Congress. The initiation rite was said to be a parody of Christian
baptism. William Simmons was portrayed as a dangerous fool and
plagiarist. One article pointed out how an integral part of a Klansman's
initiation was based on a poem stolen by Simmons from a long dead
poet. The order's "Latin" motto, *Non Silba Sed Anthar*, supposedly
translated "Not for Self, But for Others," made little sense in any known
language; it had apparently been created by Simmons to sound Latinish.[8] Even the Klan's lore was attacked: Simmons's initial lighting of the

---

[6] The *World's* series was carried by a number of dailies nationwide,
although the exact publication dates varied slightly. The quotes in this section
are taken from the series but are not directly attributed to an individual
newspaper or assigned an individual date.

[7] From the viewpoint of historians, many of the "facts" on the early days of
the Klan find their sources in this series. The *World* also received assistance from
the NAACP, and members of the Masonic order, both Klan opponents.

[8] Although historians of the Klan have been harsh in their criticism of the
motto, there are hints as to where Simmons might have seen the phrase. "Not
for Self, but for Others" is properly expressed in Latin as *Non sibi sed aliis*. This
motto was found on the seal of the Trustees of the Colony of Georgia (and
currently adorns the seal of the Georgia Historical Society). It is possible that
Simmons took some inspiration from this source and simply misspelled the

Fiery Cross on Stone Mountain while enduring "surging blasts of wintery winds…and a temperature far below freezing" was shown to be false. The *World's* reporter found the official Weather Bureau figures listed the temperatures for the day in question as falling between a high of 68 degrees, and a low of 48. One article listed dozens upon dozens of "outrages" such as kidnappings, floggings, and tar-and-featherings in states where the Klan was strong.

The series' most severe criticism was reserved for Edward Clarke and Elizabeth Tyler, earning them the sobriquet, "Salesmen of Hate." Described as the moving force behind the Klan's expansion in 1920-21, in the *World's* opinion they represented individuals whose prime concern was raking in cash from new and existing members. Reporters unearthed previously undisclosed evidence that shortly before signing on with the Klan in 1920, Clarke had been accused of embezzling from the Roosevelt Memorial Association, one of his clients. It was implied that the matter had not been brought to trial due to interference from Klan members in the Atlanta solicitor's office. Even years earlier, according to further investigation sparked by the exposé, Clarke had been expelled from Atlanta's First Congregational Methodist Church where he had been secretary and business manager. He was accused of "lying, extortion, fraudulent and unjust dealings, improper handling of funds, false and malicious slander, inordinate ambition, hypocrisy, and treachery."[9]

Most damaging, however, was information on Clarke's and Tyler's personal relationship. The *World's* reporter found that in October 1919 the two had been arrested in a police raid on "a notorious underworld resort" at 185 South Pryor Street in Atlanta "run by Mrs. Tyler," implying it was a house of ill-repute.[10] The two were arrested "in their nightclothes" after the police had been tipped off by Clarke's estranged wife. She had recently filed for divorce and was apparently present when the two were taken into custody. Clarke and Tyler were charged with disorderly conduct and paid a small fine at a later court hearing. An

---

Klan's motto. In a 1928 interview he alleged the motto was "part Latin and part Saxon." (Shepherd, "How I Put Over the Klan," 32.)

[9] Shotwell, 62.

[10] *Columbus (GA) Enquirer-Sun*, 21 September 1921.

additional charge of the possession of illegal liquor was dismissed when Tyler's son-in-law, J. Q. Jett, volunteered that the liquor had been his and paid a twenty-five dollar fine. Clarke tried to explain the circumstances by stating he and Tyler were merely business partners and that she had taken him in because he was ill with influenza. Tyler responding by simply stating that the report was "a malicious lie."[11]

The lure of personal scandal affecting two controversial figures caused an immediate stir in the news services. Reporters attempting to confirm the details were surprised to find that both the police arrest records as well as the court records had disappeared completely from the files. The Clerk of Court and the local Solicitor, the latter a known member of the Klan, promised to investigate and punish the guilty parties. Nothing was ever done.

The *World's* exposé was carried initially by nineteen newspapers in widely scattered cities across the United States, ranging from Seattle to New Orleans to New York. With a combined circulation of nearly 1.8 million, the issue of the Klan was transformed overnight from a regional to a national issue. In Georgia, the *Columbus Enquirer-Sun*, owned at the time by Tom Loyless and Julian Harris, was the only newspaper to print the series initially, although the Hearst-owned *Atlanta Georgian* picked up the articles later in the month.[12] The response of the state's other papers was surprisingly muted, perhaps due to sympathy with the Klan, or fear of its influence. The *Macon Telegraph's* editorial writer opined weakly that the order's future was yet to be determined, despite the *World's* revelations of hatred, bigotry, and lawlessness.[13] The *Marietta Journal* was more supportive, implying that there could be some good to come out of the Klan.[14] The state's premier paper, the *Atlanta Constitution*, was largely silent, perhaps because Edward Clarke's brother was the managing editor.

The *World* saw an immediate surge in its circulation, leading its competitor, the Hearst-owned *American*, to start its own series of articles

---

[11] *Macon Telegraph*, 21 September 1921.

[12] According to the *Macon Telegraph*, (31 August 1930), the *Georgian's* circulation dropped by 20,000 as a result of the articles.

[13] *Macon Telegraph*, 2 September 1921.

[14] *Marietta (GA) Journal*, 13 October 1921.

written by C. Anderson Wright, a New York King Kleagle and organizer of a proposed air arm of the Klan, the Knights of the Air. Wright's articles were syndicated by a number of papers nationwide, but failed to draw the attention or success of the *World's* exposé.

In a matter of weeks, the Ku Klux Klan had become a truly national topic. Across the broad reaches of America, politicians, editorial writers, and common citizens alike were calling for action against the Klan. The Department of Justice announced it would soon begin a "sweeping investigation" of the order's activities. The Post Office Department had already begun looking into the Klan's use of the mails.[15] The *World* polled the nation's governors via telegram, asking for their opinion on the Klan and the value of the paper's exposé. Most responses were measured and equivocal; only Governor Thomas Hardwick of Georgia gave a modicum of public support, confirming the Klan's right to secrecy and exclusivity, and stating "there is no complaint against it in this state."[16]

The Klan's initial response to this overwhelming onslaught of negative publicity was to announce that it had retained "200 of the leading attorneys of the United States" to sue the *World* and any other newspaper that carried the series for an aggregate of $10 million in damages.[17] While doing this, the Imperial Place also dispatched Elizabeth Tyler to New York. She checked into an exclusive hotel, stating she was in town for a shopping trip and a bit of recreation, but willing to meet with reporters while there. The press generally found her quite charming; she opined that the *World* had been "misled" by its informants, but thanked the paper for the publicity and the increasing number of membership applications it had generated.[18]

Some two weeks into the series, the Imperial Kloncilium of Klan met in Atlanta to decide what next steps should be taken. Its first order of business was dealing with the unexpected announcement by Edward Clarke that he would be tendering his resignation to Imperial Wizard

---

[15] *New Orleans Times-Picayune*, 9 September 1921.
[16] *Columbus (GA) Enquirer-Sun*, 16 September 1921. In his response Hardwick purposely noted, "I do not belong to the order."
[17] *Columbus (GA) Ledger*, 8 September 1921.
[18] Shotwell, 149.

Simmons as a result of the revelations of his past made by the *New York World*. Tyler, apparently uninformed in advance of the decision, was livid, castigating Clarke for his inability to stand up to criticism. Within hours, the announcement had been spun to say that Clarke and Tyler had informed Colonel Simmons "that they would consider it an honor to step down and out for the good of the Ku Klux Klan if their connection with it should be come embarrassing to him or the order at any time."[19] Within days the proffered resignations had been declined.

Unexpectedly, the Klan's attitude changed. On September 28, two days after the last article in the *World's* exposé was published and three weeks after its threats to sue the newspapers, Imperial Wizard Simmons announced that the Knights of the Ku Klux Klan were calling for "a sweeping government investigation" of the order, pledging cooperation and "full assistance" in every aspect in the proposed inquiry. Letters had been sent to President Harding and Attorney General Harry M. Daugherty with this request. The same day, Congressmen T. J. Ryan of New York and Peter F. Teague of Massachusetts introduced resolutions in the House of Representatives calling for Congressional investigation of the Klan.[20] Two days later, Simmons sent telegrams to each member of the House "asking his vote in favor of an investigating bill."[21] The requests for investigation may have seemed foolhardy, but they were perhaps the best of several alternatives. The veil of secrecy that surrounded the Klan for years had been unceremoniously jerked away by the press. Any further attempt to hide the organization's activities would have been fruitless. To the surprise of the Klan hierarchy, the *World's* exposé had brought a flood of new membership applications. The order's message, however dangerous and out of the American mainstream it may have appeared to some, appealed to others. Publicity, even potentially damaging publicity, could be twisted in a positive way if properly addressed. Clarke and Tyler, promoters *extraordinaire*, were back. It was a risky gambit, but one that might succeed. The Klan was willing to take that risk.

---

[19] *Columbus (GA) Ledger*, 22 September 1921.
[20] *Columbus (GA) Ledger*, 28 September 1921.
[21] *Macon Telegraph*, 1 October 1921.

The Congressional Hearings on the Ku Klux Klan began on October 11, 1921, in the large Caucus Room of the House of Representatives. They were based on resolutions proposed by several representatives and were held under the aegis of the Committee on Rules. The first witness was Roland Thomas, an editor of the *New York World.* Thomas outlined the basis of his paper's investigation, and reviewed its findings in broad detail. His testimony was followed immediately by that of C. Anderson Wright, author of the Hearst paper's series on the Klan. Both men's testimony served to raise questions about the Klan's motives and methods, and whether or not the order was responsible for illegal acts including tax evasion, mail fraud, and various incidents of violence. Wright, in particular, criticized Elizabeth Tyler, accusing her of being the real power behind Simmons and Clarke.

Late in the day, O. B. Williamson, a "post-office inspector," was called to testify. He said he had spent several days at the Imperial Headquarters in Atlanta investigating the Klan and interviewing Simmons, Clarke, and Tyler. Clarke in particular had been most helpful, and "very freely gave me all the information I asked for."[22] Williamson introduced multiple exhibits detailing the Klan's finances and other operations. Nothing appeared amiss. Next came William J. Burns, Director of the Department of Justice's Bureau of Investigation.[23] In a very brief statement, Burns testified that the Bureau had been investigating the Klan, but the inquiry had been put on hold pending the outcome of the Congressional investigation.

On the evening of the first day of the Klan hearings, an attempt was made to assassinate Elizabeth Tyler at her home in Atlanta. Or so was the public led to believe. Five .32-caliber steel-jacketed rounds were fired into Tyler's bedroom, whizzing over her head as she leaned over the bed of her daughter, who was ill. Shortly thereafter the *Atlanta Constitution* received a message from an anonymous caller stating, "I just want to say that we got Mrs. Tyler tonight and we will get Simmons tomorrow." The police found few clues at the scene. Simmons, contacted regarding

---

[22] Committee on Rules, 28.
[23] Burns's successor was J. Edgar Hoover.

the threat, seemed unconcerned.[24] It would later be established that the attempted assassination had been staged by the Klan, presumably as a move to arouse sympathy.

Despite the events of the night before, the hearing resumed the following morning with testimony from several witnesses representing the African-American community. Representatives of The National Equal Rights League of Colored Americans and three ministers expressed fear and disdain for the Klan's avowed racial stance. They were followed by Paul E. Etheridge, the Klan's attorney, whose brief testimony sought to impeach several points made by earlier witnesses.

Imperial Wizard William J. Simmons, the hearing's star witness, began his testimony on the afternoon of October 12. The Wizard was introduced by William D. ("Willie") Upshaw, congressman from Georgia's 5th District who heaped praise upon "my long-time personal friend and constituent." Immaculately dressed in a vested suit with a high-collared shirt and a gold watch chain adorned with fraternal keys, Simmons delivered his testimony while reading through pince-nez glasses—appearing for all the world like the high-moraled Methodist minister he had portrayed earlier in his career. In measured words, he explained that the goal of the Klan was to promote Christian American ideals, with loyalty to God and country. It stressed positive values, not negative ones. No law-abiding citizen need fear the Klan. It was not racist. As to its rejection of blacks, Jews, Catholics, and others, Simmons pointed out that groups such as the Knights of Columbus were open only to those of the Catholic faith. The Klan, like many other existing organizations, had the right to limit its membership eligibility. In regard to the tales of violence documented by the *New York World*, Simmons explained that such actions were antithetical to the moral code of the Klan, therefore these excesses—if they in fact happened—were the responsibly of those seeking to damage the Klan's reputation, or by renegade members acting on their own. Simmons wrapped up his testimony for the day by stating, "Standing here in the presence of God, before this committee of one of the greatest law making and deliberative bodies in the world, and standing in the shadow of the Capitol of our

---

[24] *Macon Telegraph*, 12 October 21.

great Nation, I say to you gentlemen, that if the Ku Klux Klan was guilty of a hundredth part of the charges that have been made against us, I would from this room send a telegram calling together the grand concilium (*sic*) for the purpose of forever disbanding the Klan in every section of the United States."[25]

Testimony resumed the following morning.[26] Simmons laid out his practical interpretation of the Klan's philosophy, skillfully parrying each question or doubt with adroit deflection, often answering questions with questions, and resembling to his supporters a modern-day reprise of Jesus before the Pharisees.[27] With regard to Craven, Fry, and Wright, the ex-Klan members whose revelations had led to the extensive negative coverage in the press, Simmons explained, "Julius Caesar had his Brutus, Jesus Christ had his Judas, and our great and illustrious Washington had his Benedict Arnold. Sir, I can state to you that I can enter the fellowship of all three of those because I have suffered in my soul as a result of the treasonous and treacherous conduct of traitors."

By the end of the day, the committee members seemed mollified. Simmons summed up his testimony by stating,

Again I want to express to you, Mr. Chairman, my deep gratitude and thanks for the courtesies you have extended to me. I want to say to all those men and women who have given assurance, with your permission, of their belief in me that they have my thanks, and I want to say to my persecutors and the persecutors of this organization in all honesty and sincerity, no matter to what creed or race you may belong in your persecutions, through the medium of the press or otherwise, that you do not know what you are doing. You are ignorant of the principles as were those who were ignorant of the character and work of the Christ. I can not better express myself than by saying to you who are persecutors of the

---

[25] Committee on Rules, 77.

[26] In an interesting development, Thomas E. Watson, now a Senator from Georgia, appeared uninvited at the hearing. In a breach of protocol, he demanded to be allowed to ask "the witness" (Simmons) a question. Deferring to his status as a Senator, the chairman allowed Watson to make a brief statement, during which he said Simmons was his constituent with whom he was "very slightly acquainted," that he (i.e., Watson) did not belong to the Ku Klux Klan but intended to defend it "from any unjust attacks from anybody."

[27] See the Book of John, Chapter 8, and others.

William Joseph Simmons was the founder, Imperial Wizard of The Knights of the Ku Klux Klan, Inc. and Emperor of the Invisible Empire. A poor manager, the organization struggled under his leadership. He was pushed from his position of power in a 1922 Imperial Palace coup led by Hiram W. Evans. (*The World's Work*, May 1923.)

Klan and myself, "Father, forgive them, for you know not what you do," and "Father, forgive them, for they know not what they do."[28]

With that, Simmons collapsed, unconscious, as the room was filled with spontaneous applause. Assistant Attorney General Crim was heard to say, "For cheap theatrical effect, damn such a fakir, I've been suspecting this for many minutes," before consulting privately with the chairman of the committee. The parties allegedly involved in this exchange later denied that it took place.[29]

The hearings scheduled for Friday, the 14, were cancelled. On the following Monday, Simmons, now returned to reasonable health, underwent a day-long grilling by members of the committee. Once again, the Wizard effectively countered potentially hostile questioning with essentially nothing new revealed. Late in the afternoon the committee went into executive session for ten minutes, returning to announce the unanimous vote to call no further witnesses and to bring an end to the hearings. The Associated Press reported the following morning, "The proposed investigation of the Ku Klux Klan by Congress blew up today."[30]

The strategy had worked. Even before the hearing's official end, news reports began to swing to the side of the Klan. "It is evident that the Ku Klux Klan has more friends in Congress today than prior to the beginning of the investigation at the hand of the Rules Committee of the House," one account began.[31] While the possibility of further investigation could not be excluded, "the Klan is receiving daily advertising the value of which could not be estimated in money." What had begun as an attempt to expose a corrupt and evil organization had unexpectedly become a boon for recruitment. As the hearings had revealed, there were perhaps 100,000 active Klansmen in October 1921.

---

[28] Here Simmons paraphrases Jesus's words on the cross from The New Testament Book of Luke 23, Verse 34 (KJV): "Then said Jesus, Father, forgive them; for they know not what they do. And they parted his raiment, and cast lots."

[29] Committee on Rules, 142.

[30] *Montgomery Advertiser*, 18 October 1921.

[31] *Macon Telegraph*, 17 October 1921.

Within the next year, the order would induct some 1,100,000 new members.[32]

While the Klan's most intimate mysteries may have been laid bare, events in the following weeks took a strange twist. In early November it was discovered that the Library of Congress's copy of the Kloran, the repository of the occult rituals of the Klan, had disappeared from the reading room. It was, as one reporter described it, "as lost as the proverbial tribes of Israel."[33]

---

[32] Shepherd "The Fiery Double-Cross," 8.
[33] *Macon Telegraph*, 3 November 1921.

Part V

The Seeds of Destruction

Not a single solitary sound reason has yet been advanced for putting the Ku Klux Klan out of business. If the Klan is against the Catholics, so are the Masons. If the Klan is against the Jews, so are half of the good hotels of the Republic and three-quarters of the good clubs. If the Klan is against the foreign-born or hyphenated citizen, so is the National Institute of Arts and Letters. If the Klan is against the negro, so are all of the States south of the Mason-Dixon line. If the Klan is for damnation and persecution, so is the Methodist Church. If the Klan is bent upon political control, so are the American Legion and Tammany Hall. If the Klan wears grotesque uniforms, so do the Knights of Pythias and the Mystic Shriners. If the Klan holds its meetings in the dead of night, so do the Elks. If the Klan conducts its business in secret, so do all of the college Greek letter fraternities and the Department of State. If the Klan holds idiotic parades in the public streets, so do the police, the letter-carriers and the fire men. If the Klan's officers bear ridiculous names, so do the officers of the Lambs' Club. If the Klan uses the mails for shaking down suckers, so does the Red Cross. If the Klan constitutes itself a censor of private morals, so does the Congress of the United States. If the Klan lynches a Moor for raping someone's daughter, so would you or I.

"The Face in the Diaper" (Editorial)
H. L. Mencken and George Jean Nathan
The Smart Set, Vol. 70, No. 3, March 1923, p. 49

When the dreamer clashes with "practical" men, he usually comes off second best. Col. William Joseph Simmons, founder of the modern Ku Klux Klan, was no exception. He built up his hooded order to a point where $35,000 was being collected every day. Then, suddenly, he found himself on the outside looking in.

William G. Shepherd, "The Fiery Double-Cross"
Collier's, Vol.82, No. 4, July 1928, p. 8

Chapter 16

Toys for Tots—Floggings for Floozies

A wagering man in the late summer and early fall of 1921 would likely have given odds against the long-term survival of the Knights of the Ku Klux Klan. The *World's* exposé could only be characterized as an avalanche of bad news, and the Congressional hearings—not to mention the ongoing investigations by the Post Office Department and the Bureau of Justice—were fully expected to be the final blow. But things turned out differently. The Klan had survived a near-death experience, emerging stronger and more aggressive. The order was now a bona fide national topic, its philosophy and inner workings exposed, the subject of seemingly endless debate in both public and private circles. The fact that Congress had chosen to do nothing, putting an end to further hearings and investigations, imbuing the Klan with the tacit aura of governmental approval. Yes, its philosophy might be repugnant to some, but this was America, founded on the principles of Free Speech and the Right of Association.

It could no longer be argued that those who joined the Klan did not realize what they were getting into. It may well indeed have been a patriotic order advocating One Hundred Percent Americanism, but there was abundant evidence of its intimidation of those who disagreed with it, its self-righteous vigilantism, and its violence. The Klan may have sought as members the "finest" men of the community, yet in many circles, association with it became a professional liability. For others, however, naturalization as a citizen of the Invisible Empire offered other benefits: Votes for the politician, customers for the tradesman, an opportunity for bullies to heap abuse upon those whose moral code differed from their own.[1] The Klan may have survived yet another challenge, but continued to carry the seeds of its own destruction.

In the months that followed the Congressional hearings, the Klan was a near-daily topic in many newspapers across the country. The news fell into four broad categories. First were reports of evidence of the order's spread across broad expanses of the continental United States. Second was news of continued violence and intimidation attributed to, and routinely denied by, the Klan. Third—almost as a counterpoint—were fawning reports of the Klan's charity and largess to the downtrodden and those in need. Finally, were legal proceedings instituted by disgruntled members of the Klan attempting to oust Edward Clarke, a direct result of the *World's* exposure of immorality and probable financial malfeasance within the Imperial Palace.

Local papers often reported the arrival of the Invisible Empire with a mixture of fascination and inevitability. In Baltimore, for example, the Klan's first public appearance took the form of a midnight visit from six masked Klansmen, robed in their "spectacular regalia," to the home of a local professor of engineering who had committed suicide in the days following Christmas 1921. Silently, they knelt briefly beside the coffin, shook hands with the dead man's brother, and then swiftly departed. The following day at the cemetery, four Klansmen, again robed and masked, sat hidden in their car "with the curtains drawn" until near the end of the ceremony. Moving quickly, they briefly emerged from the vehicle, deposited a wreath on the grave and stood silently for a moment before "the machine sped away." The theater of the whole event was not lost on the correspondent: "The Klansmen followed the Ku Klux tradition of spectacular secrecy and swift movement in their efforts to pay final tribute to one who is assumed to have been a member of the order."[2]

Meanwhile, in countless cities and towns across the land, reports of presumed Klan-related kidnappings, whippings, and tar-and-featherings continued. Sometimes the necessity for action was removed by mere intimidation. Just before Christmas some seventy-five masked Klansmen

---

[1] *See Chapter Notes for a brief discussion of the political figures who joined, or were alleged to have joined, the Klan.*

[2] *Baltimore American*, 30 December 1921.

marched two-abreast through a section of Florence, South Carolina. The *Charleston Evening Post* reported, "Not a word was spoken. Not a house was entered. It is understood that the Ku Klux Klan never appears in public except in warning. Whether the organization intended its tour last night as a warning that the dozen or more houses of ill fame conducted by white women in the North Florence district must close or not is not known, of course, outside of the secret conclave. No notices were posted. It is understood that the Ku Klux do not consider it necessary to post notices. Their appearance is deemed sufficient notice that they are taking note of what is going on."[3] In Tulsa, Oklahoma, apparent home to a number of "roadhouses and moonshine stills," the county sheriff received a note on official Klan stationary demanding they be shut down. "This is no idle threat," the note read. "You must enforce the law or suffer the consequences."

Potential traitors were warned as well. In Millwood, South Carolina, just outside of Columbia, police found full-sized wax effigies of the turncoats Henry P. Fry, C. Anderson Wright, and Bruce Craven. The former two effigies were hanging from a tree, the latter lying in the road next to a note stating, "We would hang you, Bruce, but you are not worth the rope it would take to do it." Nearby was a fiery cross and a series of placards condemning the former Klansmen and issuing warnings to the public at large: "We are going to clean up this community. Thieves and thugs beware." Blacks in particular were instructed: "Law-abiding, hard-working and respectful negroes have nothing to fear from us." "Nigger women, get in the kitchen and over the wash tub." "Nigger men, get in the fields and shop. No loafing allowed anywhere."[4] One editorial writer commented, "Of course the Ku Klux organization will disclaim responsibility for the night's work, but the organization will get the credit for it, just the same."[5]

As offensive as such actions might seem to most, they stuck a chord in strange places. In Miami, several "colored boys" were arrested for forming a gang they called the "Ku Klux Klan" and beating up other

---

[3] *Charleston (SC) Evening Post*, 24 December 1921.
[4] *Greensboro (NC) Daily News*, 9 December 1921.
[5] *Charlotte Observer*, 21 November 1921.

boys.[6] In Tulsa, the Klan inspired a "Negro Ku Klux," a "band of blacks organized, according to their statement, to 'clean up the colored section of the city and run out all criminals found there.'" A spokesman revealed to reporters "that the negro vigilantes were organized to assist the county and city officials in eliminating crime in the negro district as far as possible."[7]

While the Klan intimidated and flogged, the Christmas season of 1921 seemed an especially propitious time for the order to display its charitable and benevolent side. In Whitesboro, Texas, robed Klansmen interrupted a school entertainment program to give a short talk on "what the Ku Klux Klan stood for," and to deliver Bibles and American flags for the school's teachers. After the brief presentation, "the white-robed figures silently filed out and disappeared in the darkness."[8] A week later and a hundred-odd miles to the South, "a white-robed figure" entered the First Baptist Church of Cleburne, Texas, during Sunday services. Without uttering a word, he handed the pastor an envelope containing $25 in cash with instructions on Klan stationary that it be sent to Buckner's Orphan Home in Dallas.[9] In Tulsa, the Klan made a similar gift of $50 to the girls of the Frances E. Willard Home.[10] Not all such institutions were eager to receive the Klan's assistance, however. The Waco, Texas, Methodist Orphanage diplomatically turned down the Klan's gift with the statement, "[T]he board of local control thinks it unwise to accept a gift from the Ku Klux Klan, whose membership, objects, and purposes are veiled in mystery and concerning which there is a wide diversity of opinion."[11]

In Mississippi, Klan No. 4 gave $42.50 to the local Doll and Toy fund "for the use in buying Santa Claus for the poor children of Biloxi."[12] The Henryetta, Oklahoma, Klan did even better. A news item in a regional paper noted, "Although the local Salvation Army will distribute

---

[6] *Miami (FL) Herald*, 18 November 1921.

[7] *Colorado Springs Gazette*, 19 December 1921.

[8] *Fort Worth Star-Telegram*, 20 December 1921.

[9] *Fort Worth Star-Telegram*, 27 December 1921.

[10] *Tulsa World*, 25 December 1921.

[11] *Dallas Morning News*, 24 December 1921.

[12] *Biloxi (MS) Daily Herald*, 23 December 1921.

many baskets of Christmas dinner, and the Red Cross is doing its good work in relieving the unfortunate, the Henryetta Ku Klux Klan is adding substantial donations to the Christmas cheer, while pursuing corrective tactics to the local derelicts of the city and surroundings." Their local acts of kindness included giving $50 to the widow of a day laborer who had been killed in a ditch landslide.[13] Likewise, the Birmingham Klan took advantage of the season to offer the assistance of "one thousand members...for policing the country districts of Jefferson County during the holiday season."[14] Again, in Texas, the Klan dispensed both "Christmas cheer" and worthy advice. To a widow with several children whose recently butchered whole hog had been stolen from her smokehouse, "the Klansmen took her another dressed hog, and admonished her to put a lock on the smokehouse."[15]

The charitable giving extended to the Klan's home state of Georgia. On Christmas Day the *Macon Telegraph* reported, "While nobody knows, or claims to know, just who there are, the members of Thomasville's Ku Klux Klan seem to be a generous body and have joined in the effort to relieve the poor and bring happiness to the hearts of those in need by a contribution to the Empty Stocking Fund and to other charities." Among their gifts was "an offering...to go to the relief of several old colored couples of the community."[16] Perhaps such "old colored" folk were fortunate to be living in Georgia. Only a day earlier, it had been reported that in Denison, Texas, "a band of robed and hooded" Klansmen had flogged three blacks accused of unknown offenses. One of them, a seventy-five year old man, was said to be seriously injured.[17]

While the public may have been confused as to what was happening within the clandestine Empire of the Klan, many insiders were not. The charges leveled by the *World* and the airing of former secrets before Congress had raised serious concerns among many rank and file members of the order. The Chicago Klan, for example, circulated a petition stating, "Klansmen, we cannot longer carry the burden laid upon

---

[13] *Tulsa World*, 24 December 1921.
[14] *Montgomery Advertiser*, 26 December 1921.
[15] *Fort Worth Star-Telegram*, 30 December 1921.
[16] *Macon Telegraph*, 25 December 1921.
[17] *Cleveland Gazette*, 24 December 1921.

the order by Edward Young Clarke and Mrs. Elizabeth Tyler. To attempt to do so means that the order will perish." The document went on to accuse them of "graft, mismanagement, and more especially of immorality."[18]

Publically, the Imperial Palace was silent, but turmoil reigned behind its columned façade. In early December, one newspaper reported:

> Internal disorders reached a head...and burst in a flood of charges revealing conditions which threaten the future life of the organization. Grand Goblins of four of the seven "Domains" of the Klan more than two weeks ago decided that important changes must be made to save the order from dissolution. They came to Atlanta, laid their charges before Colonel Simmons and the Imperial Kloncilium and demanded discharge at once of Clarke and Mrs. Tyler...The Kloncilium and Colonel Simmons exonerated Clarke and Mrs. Tyler and as a counter move the four Goblins were discharged.[19]

Meanwhile, Colonel Simmons was said to have departed for the North Carolina mountains "for his health" and was not expected to return until after Christmas. Edward Y. Clarke was left in charge.

The Goblins' demands regarding Clarke and Tyler set off a series of legal battles that would last well into the next year. Clarke swore out a warrant formally charging the Goblins with larceny after trust, resulting in arrest warrants being issued by the sheriff of Fulton County, himself a Klan member. In return, suits were filed against Clarke and the Klan alleging libel and slander, seeking an injunction against Klan officers, and the appointment of a receiver to manage the order's affairs. The most serious of the rebels' allegations were revealed in an affidavit given by Z. R. Upchurch, formerly an employee of the Klan's propagation department and close associate of Edward Y. Clarke. In addition to personal knowledge of the "immoral relations" between Clarke and Tyler, Upchurch charged that Imperial Wizard Simmons drank excessively and was often too drunk to effectively function as head of the

---

[18] *Columbus (GA) Enquirer-Sun*, 3 December 1921.
[19] Ibid.

order.[20] Various legal volleys continued into the spring, when the courts eventually ruled in favor of the Klan. Despite being wounded politically by the revelations, Clarke emerged as the clear victor in the challenge to his leadership. The infighting of the preceding months had given him the opportunity to rid himself of doubters and dissenters and to fill the Klan's hierarchy with his own supporters, men with morals as flexible as his. He would suffer the consequences in future struggles.

As the order spread, it should not be imagined that there was an absence of formal resistance to the Klan and all that it stood for. In some areas, this took the form of governmental opposition. The Governors of both Louisiana and Kansas, for example, were staunch opponents of the order, using the legal power of their states to thwart its social and political influence. In others, however, political support from the Klan (or alternatively, opposition to politicians who resisted or failed to support it) resulted in the election of both local and state-level officials. In Georgia, incumbent Governor Thomas Hardwick, an early supporter of the Klan, had turned against it and would be handed one of the largest electoral defeats in the state's history in his bid for re-election. In perhaps the most egregious example, by mid-decade the state of Indiana was nearly a Klan fiefdom politically, with both the Governor and over half of the elected members of the General Assembly members of the order.

In various local areas, Catholics, Jews, Negroes, and immigrants made up a sizable segment of the population when considered in aggregate. Oftentimes, however, *individual* groups represented either a real or practical minority, such as Jews in most cities, or politically disenfranchised blacks in the South. Divided both socially and politically, these groups often struggled in their expression of opposition to the Klan's bigotry and intimidation. To bring these socially, racially, and religiously diverse groups together in an effort to "curb the activities of the Ku Klux Klan," a group of concerned Chicago citizens formed the American Unity League (AUL) in June 1922. Described as "being made up of representative Protestant, Catholic, Jewish, and foreign-born

---

[20] *Columbus Enquirer-Sun*, 15 December 1921. The phrase used in the newspaper article was "unprintable charges concerning the past life of Mrs. Tyler and Clarke."

citizens," it was to be "non-political and non-sectarian."[21] The Honorary Chairman was the African-American Bishop Samuel Fellows of the Reformed Episcopal Church. Fellows described the League's purpose: "The Ku Klux Klan is a menace to religious freedom, a source of danger to the State, and its growing strength should be curbed through the united effort of all true Americans, regardless of creed, race or condition in life."[22]

Operating first in Chicago, the AUL's most effective weapon against the Klan was its weekly newspaper *Tolerance*, which began publication in September 1922. Drawing on the reports of its own investigators and from stolen membership lists supplied by disgruntled Klansmen, the paper began to publish the names, addresses, and occupations of members of the Chicago Klan. The effect on Klan members was immediate, cutting across social classes.[23] A grocer and a route salesman reported losing customers. A milkman reported "that several Negro-owned establishments broke off business relations with his firm." Augustus E. Olson, "one of the best known of the younger generation of south side businessmen" and president of the Washington Park Bank was fired by the bank's Board of Directors.[24] The AUL's secretary, Grady K. Rutledge, estimated that the Chicago Klan's membership had fallen from 55,000 to 10,000 in the first four months of the League's campaign, an allegation vigorously denied by the Klan.[25] By January 1923, the organization had published some four thousand names in twenty-one installments and was preparing to publish six thousand more. In case anyone might have missed any issues of the its weekly newspaper, the AUL reproduced the collected lists in a pamphlet titled *Is Your Neighbor a Kluxer?*, sold widely for fifty cents.

Offices of the American Unity League soon opened in other cities, hoping to duplicate their success in Chicago. In December 1922, the league announced the start of a campaign in New York City, to be headed by Neufield J. Jones, who had been appointed as regional director

---

[21] *Jewish Chronicle (Newark, NJ)*, 18 August 1922.
[22] *New York Times*, 12 August 1922.
[23] Jackson, K. T., 104.
[24] *New York Times*, 12 November 1922.
[25] Ibid.

for the Eastern and Southern States. Nationwide, the organization claimed a membership of 150,000.[26] Its success was not to last. Jones, the former head of the Federal Prohibition Enforcement Department for the State of Georgia, was a spy for the Ku Klux Klan.[27] He had served as an aide to William J. Simmons and been on the Klan's payroll since at least 1921.[28] His deception caused the AUL's campaign in his twenty-five-state district to end in miserable failure.

Meanwhile in the Midwest, the League and its newspaper came under increasing pressure from lawsuits levied by those wrongly accused of Klan membership. The most prominent of these was brought by William Wrigley, Jr., millionaire chewing gum magnate and owner of the Chicago Cubs baseball team.[29] It was eventually established that the Klan application said to be Wrigley's was a forgery. The Wrigley fiasco led to the resignation of AUL Secretary Grady Rutledge, who was also editor of the weekly *Tolerance*. He in turn defected to the side of the Klan and wrote a series of articles in *Dawn*, a competing Klan publication. The articles revealed the inner working of the American Unity League and gave the names and methods of the informers who had provided it with Klan membership lists.[30] By mid-1924, the American Unity League was bankrupt, its efforts to stop the Klan thwarted.

To some, perhaps many, it appeared in 1921 and 1922 that the increasing power and influence of the Knights of the Ku Klux Klan could not be stopped. Despite public airings of the order's dirty laundry and exposure of its bigotry and violence, its membership continued to grow. But others, perhaps more hopeful, recognized that the Klan would

---

[26] *New York Times*, 8 December 1922.

[27] *Columbus (GA) Enquirer-Sun*, 24 December 1922. According to a contemporary report in the *Macon Telegraph*, Jones was quite effective in stemming the flow of illicit alcohol. During the year he held the office, some 2,614 stills were destroyed in the state, along with 26,351 gallons of whisky, 2,300 gallons of wine, and 2,104,520 gallons of mash to be distilled into whisky. The reason for his leaving was that the new job paid better than the old one.

[28] Jackson, K. T., 116.

[29] The home field of the Cubs was known as Cubs Field between 1920 and 1926, becoming Wrigley Field in 1927.

[30] Jackson, K. T., 116.

eventually destroy itself. Yes, there had been and there would continue to be setbacks in their fight against it, but time, persistence, and exposure of the Klan's creed to the harsh light of public awareness would eventually prevail in bringing about its downfall. Among this group of believers was Julian LaRose Harris, owner of a small daily paper in a relatively small Georgia city. It would be his persistence at the risk of his life and of his livelihood that would help bring about the end of the Klan's rule in its home state of Georgia.

Chapter 17

The Son of Uncle Remus

Of the many iconic images associated with the South of the latter half of the nineteenth century, few are more familiar than those of the Ku Klux Klan of the 1860s, and of Joel Chandler Harris's *Tales of Uncle Remus*. Both were products of their time, the Klan a creature of Reconstruction, and Harris's writings a reflection of Southern nostalgia in the era of The Lost Cause. It is thus ironic that one of leading voices in opposition to the revived Ku Klux Klan in the early twentieth century was Julian Harris, the son of the man who created Uncle Remus. At a time when the Klan seemed ascendant, it was Julian Harris who was willing—even in the face of personal threats and financial failure—to take an early public stand against an organization he felt represented a menace to American society. As his biographers note, his newspaper, the *Columbus Enquirer-Sun*, became "the most strident and uncompromising editorial voice of its era throughout the state and most of the South" in the 1920s.[1]

Julian LaRose Harris was born in Savannah, Georgia, in 1874, the son of Joel Chandler Harris and Mary Esther LaRose, the daughter of a French-Canadian ship captain. He would not have a typical Southern upbringing. By the time of his teenage years, his father was a well-known and successful writer, folklorist, and editorialist for the *Atlanta Constitution*. Even as a child, Julian's worldview stretched far beyond the cotton fields of Georgia and would become more cosmopolitan in the years that followed. In the overwhelmingly Protestant South, he was raised by a mother who was devoutly Catholic. He often visited with his maternal relatives in Canada, spending nearly a year there between June 1890 and the spring of 1891, becoming fluently bilingual in French and English.

---

[1] Lisby and Mugleston, *Someone Had to Be Hated*, 4.

Following in his father's footsteps, at age eighteen Julian Harris took a job as a reporter for the *Constitution*. Over the next few years he advanced to progressively more responsible positions, becoming the paper's managing editor at age twenty-six.[2] Short—five feet, six inches in height—slender, bespectacled, and with a full head of dark hair, Harris maintained a certain formal demeanor in both his dress and interactions with colleagues. He was a man who took life seriously.

In 1897 Harris married Julia Collier, the daughter of Atlanta's mayor. Their marriage would last for some sixty-five years, though marked by both challenge and tragedy. Two children born in 1899 and 1901 would die in early childhood within a few months of each other. Facing bankruptcy, Julia's father died in 1900, a possible suicide.[3] It was perhaps these early twists of fate that drew Julian and Julia closer, as in the years that followed their individual careers in writing and the press were closely intertwined.

Tiring of administrative work at the *Constitution*, Harris moved briefly to the *Atlanta News* in 1904, before returning to his former employer the following year. Seeking bigger challenges, he resigned once again the following year to join with his father in launching a new publication, *Uncle Remus's Magazine*. An editorial in the June 1907 initial issue said:

> For all practical purposes, Uncle Remus's Magazine might well be called the Optimist: for it will preach a cheerful Philosophy and practice a seasonable toleration in all matters where opinions and beliefs are likely to clash. It will be a Southern Magazine by reason of its environment, as well as by reason of the fact that the South is a part — a very large and definite part of this great Republic of ours — but all its purposes and intentions, its motives and its politics will be broader than any section and higher than partisanship of any sort. It is purposed to issue a magazine that will be broadly and patriotically American, and genuinely representative of the best thought of the whole country.[4]

---

[2] A position that would be held in later years by Edward Young Clarke's brother.

[3] Lisby and Mugleston, 40.

[4] *Uncle Remus's Magazine*, 5.

It was this philosophy of toleration and national unity that would in many respects guide Harris's career in the years that followed. The magazine, too, would be struck by tragedy with the untimely death of Joel Chandler Harris on July 3, 1908, at the age of fifty-nine.

The absence of the man who embodied the magazine's values and viewpoint struck a cruel blow. Although Joel Chandler Harris left unpublished essays that appeared after his death, his son found it necessary to pen more of his own pieces to help fill the void. Now in his thirties, Julian Harris demonstrated his willingness to take stands on public topics that often conflicted with popular Southern thought of the day. In the years that followed, he wrote on convict leasing, mob violence, and most importantly, contentious political issues. His support of the Republican Party in the solidly Democratic South did little to win him friends or supporters while costing the magazine subscribers in the process.[5] After a number attempts at editorial change, *Uncle Remus's Magazine* failed in 1913, never achieving long-term profitability. On a personal basis, however, it did cement Julian Harris's reputation as a public voice willing to take a firm stand on controversial issues, even when he was clearly in the minority. He was a Republican in a sea of Democrats, a progressive in a region dominated by conservatives, an iconoclast amongst worshipers of the status quo.

Following the magazine's failure, Julian and Julia spent a few months in Europe before returning to New York in January 1914 to assume the position of Sunday Editor of the *New York Herald*. In late 1915, they moved to wartime Paris where Julian took over management of the *Paris Herald*, a position that would last until August 1916. After a brief stint in the military in 1917 and 1918, Harris became the *New York Herald's* chief European correspondent, witnessing the signing of the Treaty of Versailles in June 1919 and the birth pangs of the ill-fated League of Nations. Another brief tenure as managing editor of the *Paris Herald* followed, with the Harrises returning to America in October 1920. At forty-six years of age and with a vast experience working for others in all aspects of the newspaper business, Julian Harris wanted to

---

[5] Lisby and Mugleston, 57-62.

have his own newspaper. The opportunity would soon arise in the form of the *Columbus Enquirer-Sun.*

In April 1916, the financially struggling *Enquirer-Sun* had been purchased by a group of investors, including Thomas W. Loyless, a well-known Georgia newspaperman and at the time, majority owner of the *Augusta Chronicle.* Loyless readily admitted that his reason for buying into the *Enquirer-Sun* was "the sacrifice price at which the paper—after several years of unprofitable operation—was then offered." He saw it simply as an investment and did not initially take an active role in management. The *Enquirer-Sun* was one of Georgia's oldest newspapers, originally founded as a weekly (the *Columbus Enquirer*) in 1828 by Mirabeau B. Lamar.[6] In 1874, the paper merged with the *Daily Sun* to become the *Enquirer-Sun.* By the second decade of the twentieth century, the once-successful paper had fallen on hard times.

The city of Columbus had once been a thriving industrial center, but much of its manufacturing capacity was destroyed during the Civil War, replaced later by mills devoted to the processing of cotton. In the latter part of the nineteenth century and early part of the twentieth, the city experienced a period of increasingly rapid growth. Between 1880 and 1910, its population had doubled from approximately 10,000 to 20,000 and would more than double again by 1930. Camp Benning (later Fort Benning) was established nearby in October 1918 to provide basic training for troops serving in World War I. While an economic boon, this brought an influx of young single men to the area, often away from home for the first time and seeking entertainment. Many of the other newcomers to the city were former tenant farmers displaced by the boll weevil and the crash of the cotton-based economy in the 1920s. To those new to city life with its temptations and challenges, the Ku Klux Klan's mantra of traditional values, fervent Americanism, and law and order was appealing.

The Klan first appeared in Columbus on Saturday afternoon, May 25, 1918, when a squad of twenty-three robed and masked horsemen

---

[6] Lamar would leave Columbus in the 1830s, traveling to Texas where he eventually became the second president of the Republic of Texas.

Prior to being editorially managed by Tom Loyless and Julian Harris, the *Columbus Enquirer-Sun* displayed some approval of the Klan. This ad appeared in the paper in November 1918. (*Columbus Enquirer-Sun*, 15 November 1918.)

silently paraded in the downtown district for two hours.[7] The *Enquirer-Sun's* reaction was—like most newspapers of the day—generally positive. In doing so, the paper explained, they were there "to give silent, serious notice, which is the method of the Ku Klux Klan, visiting pool rooms and loitering places up and down First Avenue, then [making] a conspicuous stop in front of a well-known Broad Street place and continuing their ride, [visiting] localities, which, by the well informed, are known to be the habitat of men and women who do not enjoy the public confidence, either because of acts which are barely within the law, or because of indifferences to public opinion."[8] The account went on to say, "It was recalled that the Ku Klux Klan was always composed of courageous, fearless and conservative men, each one of whom was sworn to do his duty to his country and his neighborhood, and that the Ku Klux Klan was always the most dreaded of all organizations by evil doers, traitors, and unpatriotic people, and that by the same token they were the greatest comfort to all good citizens, and that no good citizen who was energetic and loyal need have any fear, no matter whether he be black or white." An accompanying editorial that day, and another the next, endorsed the actions of the Klan as a positive force in the community.

The *Enquirer-Sun's* approval of the Klan continued over the next two and half years. In September 1918, the order's assistance with the enforcement of wartime "gasless Sundays" brought praise. Two months later, a glowing review of William J. Simmons's visit to Columbus to promote the Klan was accompanied by display ads requesting "red-blooded MEN who are 100 percent American" and "seriously interested and prompted by purely unselfish motive" to contact Ti-Bo-Tim at a local post office box if they wished to join.[9] The race riots across the nation during the summer of 1919 prompted an editorial advising "the leaders of the negro race" that such disturbances in the South might

---

[7] *Columbus (GA) Enquirer-Sun*, 26 May 1918. There was some speculation that the twenty-three horsemen had something to do with the then-popular phase "twenty-three skidoo," suggesting that lawbreakers and other miscreants "skidoo."

[8] Ibid.

[9] *Columbus (GA) Enquirer-Sun*, 15 November 1918.

prompt the "Ku Klux Klan to take action."[10] In the summer of 1920, a series of fawning articles praised the newly revived Klan, culminating with the September 1 "spectacular parade" of robed Klansmen through downtown streets followed by an address by Imperial Wizard Simmons at the Muscogee County Courthouse.

The paper's seeming infatuation with the Klan was soon to change. Tom Loyless sold his interest in the *Augusta Chronicle* in late 1919, generating a significant profit. After being delayed by "certain personal and business reasons," he turned his attention to the *Enquirer-Sun* in the fall of 1920. Loyless traveled to Columbus, and after assessing the situation, was impressed with "the opportunity for the successful publication of a high-class morning newspaper" for the city, competing with its more staid rival, the evening *Columbus Ledger*.[11] He assumed personal editorial control of the paper while he sought out a partner to assist him in its management.

On November 7, 1920, the *Enquirer-Sun* carried an editorial deriding the Klan as "merely a sort of Halloween affair—a pumpkin with a lantern in it," something that the people of the South would not long tolerate if the order attempted "to set aside or overthrow the law of the land."[12] In response to the editor's statement, the *Philadelphia Public Ledger* produced an editorial averring "a secret political organization assuming the sinister name of the Ku Klux is liable to draw to itself the reckless, the intolerant and the bigoted, and hence becomes a menace to law and order. It is unsafe to overlook," the writer continued, "the possibilities of evil in such an organization."[13] The *Enquirer-Sun's* editorial writer—presumably Loyless—agreed. In a November 17 response titled "A Menace to Law and Order," he wrote in reference to the Klan: "[W]e want none of it hereabouts, and we do not believe that the great body of law-abiding, peace-loving citizens will countenance the secret activities of any body of men so masquerading in the sacred name of law and order."[14]

---

[10] *Columbus (GA) Enquirer-Sun*, 2 August 1919.
[11] *Columbus (GA) Enquirer-Sun*, 23 November 1920.
[12] *Columbus (GA) Enquirer-Sun*, 7 November 1920.
[13] *Columbus (GA) Enquirer-Sun*, 17 November 1920.
[14] Ibid.

Six days later in a signed editorial titled "A Personal Word," Loyless announced that he and Julian Harris had joined forces as co-owners to buy out the other owners of the *Enquirer-Sun*. Harris, Loyless said, was "known almost everywhere as one of the ablest newspaper men in the entire country."[15] Reflecting the change in management, the editorial page now featured a boxed statement reminding readers that the *Enquirer-Sun* was "dedicated to the service of the public." "In politics it is uncontrolled, with factions it has nothing in common, with the political feudist and demagogue no patience. Its position on public questions shall be contentiously taken, fairly presented and faithfully maintained." The paper had entered a new era.

With new ownership and editorial control, the *Enquirer-Sun's* coverage of the Klan changed. No longer willing to print the scripted news releases from the Imperial Palace, it restricted its coverage to facts, regularly printing items unflattering to the Invisible Empire. Initially, Tom Loyless was to guide the paper's editorial position while Julian Harris was to act as the *Enquirer-Sun's* general business manager. Notwithstanding his nominal title, Harris assumed a role that including active reporting and contribution to the paper's content, including its editorials. Both men stood together in firm opposition to the Klan, never hesitating to report news and events that they felt reflected the true character of the order.

By late 1920 and early 1921, the Columbus Klavern boasted an estimated four to five hundred members. Their regular meeting site was the armory above police headquarters, indicating support from city officials. A mimeographed statement released by the Klan circulated around this time read:

POLICE OFFICIALS, MAYORS AND OTHERS ENDORSE

KNIGHTS OF THE KU KLUX KLAN

From J. T. Moore, chief of police, and J. L. Couch mayor of Columbus, Ga.

---

[15] *Columbus (GA) Enquirer-Sun*, 23 November 1920.

"To whom it may concern: I take this method of endorsing the Ku Klux Klan. I am personally acquainted with many of the citizens of this city who are members of the local Klan, and I know them to be citizens whose integrity is above reproach and law-abiding in every respect. Seventeen members of the Klan volunteered their services and assisted the police department during a recent epidemic of burglaries. They did good work, and their services were appreciated by the police commissioners and myself. I think an organization like the Ku Klux Klan is a blessing in any community." --J. T. Moore, Chief of Police.

"I heartily endorse the above." -J. L. Couch, Mayor of Columbus, Georgia.[16]

Such overt support from leading political figures never deterred Loyless and Harris from printing news and events that reflected on what they saw as the corrupt and duplicitous nature of the Klan. In late January 1921, the paper carried the news that the Rev. Caleb Ridley, the Klan's Imperial Kludd, had been charged with making an inappropriate advance to a married woman. A few days later, the *Enquirer-Sun's* editorialist responded to an attack in the *Americus Times-Recorder* attributing the change in the paper's editorial stance to Julian Harris's Catholic heritage. The following weeks brought an avalanche of anti-Klan stories and editorials, some locally written and others reprinted from other papers across the nation. Although unsigned, the *Enquirer-Sun's* editorials undoubtedly reflected Harris's strong influence. The style was one of "in-your-face" defiance, derisively referring to the Klan as "Clucks-Clucks," William J. Simmons as "The Grand 'Wiz,'" and the order's "bumptious defense of the 'white Caucasian race.'"[17] Alleged Klan excesses now warranted front page news, such as the March 23, 1921, headline "More Revelation of Unscrupulous Ku Klux Methods." Changing course over a few short months, a leading daily newspaper in a major Georgia city had chosen to oppose the Ku Klux Klan, the first to do so with conviction and purpose.

---

[16] From original document in the J. L. Harris Papers, Emory University Library. See also Lisby and Mugleston, 114.

[17] *Columbus (GA) Enquirer-Sun*, 3 February 1921.

Perhaps in response to the headlines of the preceding day, on March 24, Loyless received a telegram from the *New York Herald* requesting information for a story on the Klan.[18] The telegram had been sent late in the day, and to his surprise on the morning of the 25, Loyless received an unsigned letter reading "Leave New York newspapers, troubles with KKK alone. 'DEAD MEN TELL NO TALES.'" The letter had been posted in Atlanta, and was composed on a typewriter "peculiarly like those used by Western Union." The facts suggested Loyless's telegram from the *Herald* had been intercepted. The matter was referred to the Post Office, but an Atlanta postal inspector issued an opinion that the United States mail had not been misused. Loyless and Harris then contacted the United States District Attorney, Hooper Alexander. Alexander gave an interview to the Atlanta papers in which he stated he had no basis to take action. Shortly thereafter Loyless received another threatening message, this time written on a Western Union Telegram blank:

> No, Hooper Alexander cannot help you. We uphold the law also. We have ears as well as eyes and can hear you over the phone as well as see your messages. The KKK has not harmed you yet. Why antagonize them? Better lay off.[19]

A few days later, a third message from the Klan arrived for Loyless:

> Some of your best friends belong to the KKK but we will be your friends no longer if you continue denouncing the KKK which you know nothing about. We see you every day, so take a tip from us. Lay off the KKK stuff.[20]

The *Enquirer-Sun's* campaign against the Klan continued over the months that followed, as did the threatening notes and interception of

---

[18] The account of these events is based largely on a 1921 interview with Loyless and Harris reported in *Leslie's* weekly newspaper. (Shepherd, "Fighting the K.K.K. on Its Home Grounds," 508-511, 526)

[19] Original in J. L. Harris papers, Emory University Library. Punctuation added for clarity.

[20] Original in J. L. Harris papers, Emory University Library. Spelling and punctuation corrected for clarity.

the paper's communications.[21] During the late summer of 1921, word spread that the *New York World* was planning a multi-part exposé of the Invisible Empire. Loyless and Harris wanted to carry the series, but initially declined to do so, thinking that one of the state's major papers would pick up the stories. None did so. The other consideration was financial. It was expensive to purchase the series from the *World*, and in a city where the Klan apparently had wide support, circulation could be severely hurt. In a later interview, the two owners said it was the Klan's threat of lawsuits against papers publishing the *World's* exposé that led them to change their minds. In Loyless's words, delivered with an appropriate bit of sarcasm, "We just couldn't help thinking what a shame it would be for Georgia, if newspapers in all the other States of the Union were sued for writing about the Ku Klux Klan and not a single newspaper in Georgia, where the Klan started, was called into court. Why, it would shut Georgia folks plumb out of the chance to hear the truth about the Ku Klux told in one of their own court rooms. No sir; we couldn't overlook the chance."[22] The threatened lawsuits were never filed, but the *Enquirer-Sun's* stand against the Klan cost it heavily in loss of subscriptions and political support. It was, more so than anything else, the principle of the issue, an editorial viewpoint that would continue for the remainder of the decade.

As the last few of the *World's* articles were published in the *Enquirer-Sun*, discreet ads appeared in the *Columbus Ledger*, the local rival paper, announcing a "Ku Klux Parade" scheduled for Friday evening, September 23. The *Ledger*, while not directly supporting the Klan, had not condemned it—an attitude taken by most Georgia papers of the day. On the morning of the scheduled day, the paper carried a full article announcing "elaborate plans" for a "spectacular pageant [to] be witnessed by throngs of Columbus people."[23] It was estimated that at least 350 Klansmen in full regalia would be marching. In counterpoint, the

---

[21] Shepherd, "Fighting the K.K.K. on Its Home Grounds," 508-511, 526. See also letter of 25 September 1921 from W. M. Houghton to Julian Harris. Original in J. L. Harris Papers, Emory University Library.

[22] Shepherd, "Fighting the K.K.K. on Its Home Grounds," 511.

[23] *Columbus (GA) Ledger*, 23 September 1921.

Enquirer-Sun the next day reported that "approximately 125 white-robed men, many from out of town," participated in the march.[24]

Prior to beginning their parade, the Klansmen initially gathered on the third floor of the municipal building, the headquarters of the Columbus police department. Led by two horsemen and an automobile emblazoned with "Ku Klux Klan," the group carried a fiery cross, two American flags, and signs reading "We were strong yesterday, we are stronger today and we will be stronger tomorrow," "Rome is busy while Protestantism sleeps," "America for Gentiles," "We stand for white supremacy," and the like. Deviating from their publicly announced route, the parading Klansmen marched back and forth in front of the offices of the *Enquirer-Sun*, a clear attempt at intimidation.[25] Having been advised in advance of the Klan's plan to parade in front of the paper's offices, Julian Harris opened the building's doors and windows, turned on all the lights and rushed out to stand on the sidewalk as the marchers passed, pretending to recognize individuals and scribbling notes on a piece of paper. According to his biographers, as he was "standing there, a stranger walked up behind Harris, pressed something hard in his back, and ordered him to stop writing or he would kill him then and there. Harris replied, 'Go ahead if you want to, but it would be pretty foolish to kill someone right out here in the open with all these witnesses.' The man hesitated for a moment and then walked on."[26]

The events of the day did nothing to weaken the *Enquirer-Sun's* stand against the perceived evils of the Invisible Empire. In the months that followed, the paper became embroiled in Columbus city politics, hoping that a new commission-based form of government with a city manager would lessen the Klan's influence. Instead, the change and resulting power struggle led to a series of violent attacks and the dynamite bombing of the mayor's home in the spring of 1922. Harris blamed the Klan, but no proof of the Klan's direct involvement was ever produced. The controversy became such an issue, however, that the

---

[24] *Columbus (GA) Enquirer-Sun*, 24 September 1921.
[25] Ibid.
[26] Lisby and Mugleston, 119.

Imperial Palace in Atlanta temporarily revoked the local Klavern's charter, only to reinstate it shortly thereafter with a new set of officers.

By late 1922, some two years after Loyless and Harris assumed joint ownership and editorial control of the *Enquirer-Sun*, the newspaper continued to struggle financially, often bested by its less-controversial rival, the *Ledger*. On November 13, 1922, Tom Loyless announced in an editorial that he was giving up his management position at the *Enquirer-Sun*. Julian Harris's role in the editorial policy of the paper had grown significantly; Loyless's stated reason for his resignation was "based upon the fact that Mr. Harris has written, or caused to be written, and published editorials to which I cannot subscribe." The exact topic of the dispute was never revealed, though it may have been Harris's skepticism over the enforcement of Prohibition.[27] Harris purchased Loyless's stock in the enterprise for $4,000, finally achieving his ambition of controlling his own newspaper. Over the remainder of the decade, he would continue his stand against the Ku Klux Klan and what he believed to be other threats to American society and democracy.

---

[27] Lisby and Mugleston, 129.

Chapter 18

New Characters and a Palace Coup

On Wednesday, January 4, 1922, Elizabeth Tyler announced her resignation from the Propagation Department of the Ku Klux Klan. By some accounts, her decision to get out was not unexpected. The Congressional investigation and *World's* exposé of her checkered past had taken their toll. She was physically and mentally exhausted. In a brief letter to the Klan, she gave the declining health of her adult daughter—suffering from advanced tuberculosis—as the reason for her resignation. "My physician, Dr. Henry McGhee, says I must rest or completely collapse," she said, indicating the stress she was under as a mother and caregiver.[1] But there were likely other reasons as well. While Edward Young Clarke was nominally the Imperial Kleagle, many said it was Bessie Tyler who represented the brains behind the operation. Perhaps she had come to the realization that the time had come to fold her cards and walk away. In only a year and a half with the Klan she had managed to amass a small fortune, including a columned mansion set in the midst of a fourteen-acre estate on Atlanta's Howell Mill Road. She could afford to live comfortably—and quietly—for the foreseeable future. As events would unfold over the coming months, she made a wise choice.

The same newspapers that reported the resignation of Tyler detailed the charges alleged in a lawsuit brought by a group of former Grand Goblins who had been fired in the wake of the alleged misconduct uncovered by the *World's* reporters. Citing purported financial irregularities and the "the dissemination and propagation of hatred and prejudice," the rebels demanded that Simmons, Clarke, and Tyler be removed and the Klan placed in receivership. Simmons summarily dismissed the allegations, referring to them as "a desperate attempt on

---

[1] *New York Times*, 5 January 1922.

the part of disgruntled and discharged employees."[2] By early March, the case had been effectively dismissed, with the court ruling in favor of the Klan on essential points and suggesting that any areas of contention be settled by and within the organization.[3] The Klan had won the victory, but its legal challenges were far from over.

On Sunday, March 19, Imperial Wizard Simmons published the first in a proposed series of ten articles "answering the attacks" made by the *New York World* the preceding autumn, while illuminating the purpose and philosophy of the modern Ku Klux Klan.[4] "The A-B-C of the Ku Klux Klan is," he explained, is quite simple: America first, Benevolence in thought, word and deed "based on justice practically applied to all," and Clannishness, the practical application of "real fraternity." The result of the attempted exposé and the subsequent Congressional hearings was the revelation of "a body of white Americans beneath the American flag with their hands upon the Bible and their eyes upon the fiery cross, which through all the ages has been the emblem of unselfishness and truth. Inevitably, the result of this disclosure was an immediate and tremendous inpouring of applications for membership." The first article of the series was the only one to be published; the same judge who had ruled in favor of the Klan a few days earlier enjoined the further publication of Simmons's one-sided defense.

With Elizabeth Tyler's resignation and Simmons's seeming disinterest in the day-to-day operations of the Klan, Clarke's position of control was strengthened. In the late summer of 1921, they had hired— with Simmons's approval—Fred L. Savage to fill the position of Imperial Night-hawk, the head of the Klan's Department of Investigation. Savage's main qualification was from his previous job as a strike-breaking detective on the docks of New York. On May 1, 1922, Clarke promoted him to the additional position of chief of staff, effectively taking over many of the previous duties of Tyler.

On June 9, Simmons announced he was taking a leave of absence, a "six-month vacation" needed "because of ill health." It was rumored that

---

[2] *Bay City (MI) Times*, 6 January 1922.
[3] *Oregonian (Portland, OR)*, 9 March 1922.
[4] *State (Columbia, SC)*, 19 March 1922.

he might go to Europe. In his absence, Edward Clarke was to assume the title of "Imperial Wizard *pro tempore*." Rumors swirled as to the true cause of Simmons's sabbatical, perhaps best expressed in a lawsuit filed later in the summer by disgruntled Tennessee Klansmen alleging he "had been for some time…on a prolonged debauch, during which time it is believed that he was under the effect of intoxicating liquors and drugs and hence not physically and mentally capable of transaction of business of the Klan."[5]

With the Imperial Wizard's departure, whatever obstacles might have stood in the way of Clarke's consolidation of power were removed. The fact that the Klan had been under attack from outside the walls of the Imperial Palace did not mean there was no dissention within. Louis D. Wade, Imperial Kligrapp (National Secretary), former cotton mill superintendent and Simmons's close associate, had become a thorn in Clarke's side. Within days of the start of Simmons's vacation, Clarke announced that Wade was being fired "as an economy step."[6] In truth, Wade had objected to Clarke and Tyler's handling of Klan funds, alleging they "have become suddenly enormously wealthy from ill-gotten gains collected from the ranks of Ku Klux men."[7] The Klan found a way to justify his dismissal while at the same time hoping to ensure his silence. According to J. Q. Jett:

> They wished to oust him but he had done nothing. [Wade] liked to drink and we had a woman name of Mrs. Abbie McGehee on the payroll. They got two quarts of pure corn and Savage[8] doped it a little. Wade did not have to be coaxed to drink it and after he got soused his brother Klansmen gently laid him in bed with Mrs. McGehee and took a nice flash-light picture. They presented this evidence to the firing board and they fired him. He kicked like a steer but to no avail. The Klan could not afford to keep a man who was caught in bed with a woman. Mr. Wade tried to explain, but they had the photos.[9]

---

[5] *New Orleans Times-Picayune*, 8 September 1922.

[6] *New York Times*, 26 June 1922.

[7] *New York Times*, 17 July 1922.

[8] Jett refers to Fred L. Savage, the Imperial Night-hawk and head the Department of Investigation.

[9] *Georgia Free Lance (Dublin, GA)*, 19 November 1925.

The effort was apparently successful. Both sides fired a few legal volleys at one another, but nothing of note came of the matter. Wade said he had been fired by Clarke for personal reasons, noting "Colonel Simmons was drinking so much liquor his mind is failing."[10] Once the immediate controversy had passed, little else was heard from Wade.

Clarke's choice to fill the open position of Imperial Kligrapp would change the future of the Klan, although no one could have realized it at the moment. In late 1921 or early 1922, he had recruited Hiram Wesley Evans, a rising star in the Texas Klan, to serve primarily as Simmons's assistant. A Dallas, Texas, dentist and at the time forty years of age, Evans was a short, pudgy man whose smile and affable manner easily won him friends and confidants. Like Simmons, he was a rousing orator, but with a streak of practicality that contrasted sharply with that of his new boss. Born in Alabama, Evans had grown up in the hill country of central Texas before attending Vanderbilt University in Nashville, Tennessee. After dropping out of college, he obtained a dental degree at age nineteen and opened a practice in Dallas. Evans was a fraternalist, rising high in the Masonic order and belonging to "many different lodges," a fact that impressed Simmons when he first interviewed him.[11] In replacing Wade as Imperial Kligrapp, Evans's duties included acting as liaison with Klan leadership across the Invisible Empire, a position that not only allowed him insight into the problems of the rapidly expanding organization, but also gave him a significant degree of political power on a grassroots level. Clarke was now firmly in charge. With Simmons on an extended vacation and those in power at the Imperial Palace owing their positions to the acting Imperial Wizard, there seemed little that could stand in the way of the Klan's spread.

Even as Clarke was consolidating power in Atlanta, the Klan nationwide was moving into politics. The transition to an active political role seems initially to have been less of a coordinated effort than the natural outgrowth of cadres of like-minded men gathered together in one organization. In mid-June, the *New York Times* featured a long article

---

[10] *Columbus (GA) Ledger*, 4 July 1922.
[11] Shepherd, "Ku Klux Koin," 39.

OFFICIAL DOCUMENT

--6--

firm on the firing line and will continue to stand there until
either we have won the victory or I have been shot down at my post
of duty.

      Duly signed and sealed at the Imperial Palace this
this the third day of July, Nineteen Hundred and Twenty Two.

IMPERIAL WIZARD PRO TEM.

ATTESTED:

IMPERIAL KLIGRAPP.

In the Spring of 1922, Hiram W. Evans, a former Dallas, Texas dentist who had become
an assistant to Imperial Wizard Simmons, was elevated to the office of Imperial Kligrapp
(Secretary). When Simmons elected to take a six-month sabbatical beginning in June 1922, E.
Y. Clarke became Imperial Wizard *pro tempore*, leaving the Klan in effective control of Clarke
and Evans. The signatures of both men appear on this final page of a missive sent to Klan
officers in July 1922. (Private Collection.)

In a carefully planned power coup, Hiram W. Evans (shown here in 1925) was elected Imperial Wizard in November 1922, in the process effectively stripping W. J. Simmons of control of the Klan. (Library of Congress.)

under the headline "Political Night Riders Invade State Campaigns."[12] Opening with the sentence, "The Ku Klux Klan is in politics," the report went on to detail the Klan's political success in electing friendly candidates across the nation. In Oregon, Texas, and Oklahoma particularly, Klan influence weighed heavily on electoral races, or appeared likely to do so in the coming fall elections. Klan-related political activity had been reported in "Illinois, Georgia, the Carolinas, Arkansas, Alabama, Indiana, California, Connecticut, and a dozen other states." A contemporary issue of *The Literary Digest* carried a similar article, noting with concern the Klan's growing political influence. The July issue of the *Atlantic Monthly* featured an editorial by former Mississippi Senator Leroy Percy condemning the actions of the Klan in the strongest terms: "[T]hey seek to overcome the powers of evil by donning a clown's garb, swearing to conceal their identity, and marching behind an Imperial Wizard whom they are sworn to obey. They fail to realize that our Government has been established by free American people, who will handle it without interference by, or dictation from, church or clan; that it is to be governed by neither priest nor wizard, knights or klansmen."[13]

At about the same time, *The Literary Digest* sent out a survey of over a hundred letters to newspaper editors "in various sections of the country where [the Klan] has been more active" seeking their opinion and recent news stories.[14] Not a single reply was favorable to the Klan. In responding, the *Macon Telegraph*, located in a city whose Klansmen wielded strong political influence, published a two-column editorial and a somewhat lukewarm chiding of the Klan:

> In the beginning, The Telegraph was inclined to view the modern Ku Klux Klan as no more than any other secret order holding forth for the protection of womanhood, the sanctity of the home and other such noble sentiment that have been instinctive in the human race from time immemorial....But as weeks and months have passed, it has become

---

[12] *New York Times*, 18 June 1922.
[13] Percy, "The Modern Ku Klux Klan," 128.
[14] *Literary Digest*, "Quaint Customs and methods of the Ku Klux Klan," 44-53.

plainly evident that the Ku Klux Klan was not simply a fraternity, but a financial scheme in the guise of a historical movement...Those who have gone into this organization with good faith and who are only trying to render a service to their country, are to be commended for their attitude, unfortunate though their method may be. But these well-intentioned men have not thoroughly looked behind the scenes of their organization; they have not given full consideration to the principles that the hood and mask represent. The conditions of the Sixties do not now exist; and present disorders call for altogether different methods. It is for the good of every Georgian, the Klan members themselves as well, that no secret organization that goes forth masked be allowed to exist. Many Klansmen have already come to this conclusion. All should eventually. However, American civilization cannot wait on a matter that holds such danger. The present session of the Legislature should take action.[15]

While well-meaning, the paper's editorial had little practical influence. The Klan's reign of terror in Macon had scarcely begun.

The potential and growing influence of the Klan vote was not lost on the state's politicians, however. In local, regional and state-wide races, candidates were often forced to take a stand as either for or against the Invisible Empire. A few days after the *Telegraph's* editorial, Governor Thomas Hardwick, engaged in what was predicted to be a close race in his bid for re-election, announced he planned to submit a bill to the General Assembly to make the wearing of masks in public a criminal offense. In strong words directed at the Klan, he said, "We have no room for invisible government in this State. So long as I am Governor and can prevent it we shall not have it, either in the Klan palace or the United States Capitol at Washington."[16] In a surprise move, Imperial Wizard *pro tem* Clarke wrote the governor stating that all members of the Klan in Georgia had been instructed to refrain from wearing the hood and mask "except in their lodge rooms."[17] His letter to the governor also noted that "lecturers will be sent throughout Georgia for sixty days, conducting an educational campaign, that Klan investigators will be busy in every part of the State, [and] that if a Klansman has broken the law he will have no

---

[15] *Macon Telegraph*, 5 July 1922.
[16] *New York Times*, 11 July 1922.
[17] *New York Times*, 23 July 1922.

protection from the order." Clarke assured Hardwick "the order stands for law and righteousness." The Governor, seemingly pleased with his victory and anxious to cater to the Klan vote, "reiterated that the principles of the organization are of the highest and denied that he had ever assailed any of those principles."

It is unclear if Governor Hardwick and his political advisors recognized the true purpose of Clarke's apparent concession. If they did not, the significance was certainly not lost on Julian Harris and the editorial staff of the *Enquirer-Sun*. Clarke's letter to the Governor said he planned to "gather a formidable body of Klan speakers and see to it that within the next sixty days public meetings are held in every county in the state of Georgia, setting forth the Klan's attitude to law enforcement and thus reaching the public as well as Klansmen with the right kind of message... I am determined that from the mountains to the seacoast in Georgia where the enemies of the cause are seeking to discredit same, that the good name of the Ku Klux Klan shall be protected and preserved." Sixty days was the approximate time before the Democratic Primary, which—in the de facto one-party atmosphere of 1920s Georgia—would determine the next governor. Clarke's true motive was to "put as many Ku Klux speakers in the field against Hardwick as he can possibly press into service."[18]

As the Georgia gubernatorial campaign moved into August, the rhetoric intensified with the late summer heat. Clifford Walker, the candidate backed by the Klan, the followers of Tom Watson, and similar groups, gained political momentum. Judge G. H. Howard, who had formerly directed three of Hardwick's campaigns, defected to the Walker camp. The Reverend Caleb Ridley, the Klan's Imperial Kludd, called Hardwick "a drunkard and lacking in morals."[19] In a seeming repudiation of the olive branch offered to the governor weeks earlier, the Ku Klux Klan drum and bugle corps, "dressed in full regalia and wearing masks," was the "outstanding feature" of Atlanta's Labor Day parade on

---

[18] *Columbus (GA) Enquirer-Sun*, 25 July 1922.

[19] *Columbus (GA) Enquirer-Sun*, 27 August 1922. This would seem to be a classic case of the pot calling the kettle black. Hardwick in response referred to Ridley as a "charlatan and blatherskite." (*Macon Telegraph*, 22 September 1922.)

September 4, less than ten days before the Primary. "They were the most conspicuous part of the parade through the principal streets of Atlanta, headed by a squad of mounted police offices, the line of march guarded by foot policeman, and the affair was developed into a huge advertisement of the fact that the Klan is bigger than Clarke's order."[20] Hardwick responded by saying he had "never seen a man wear a mask who was not bandit, a train robber, or some kind of criminal."[21]

The September 13 primary was a rout. Notwithstanding optimistic last-minute reports from the Hardwick camp, the Klan's candidate Clifford Walker was elected by an overwhelming majority. The *New York Time's* brief summary of the election was succinct and to the point: "It looks like the most tremendous landside in Georgia's political history."[22]

The Klan was on a roll, not only in the South, but nationwide and perhaps beyond. In July, Jesse O. Wood, Atlanta City Councilman, Klansman, and editor of *The Searchlight*, the Klan's semi-official organ, announced he was sailing for England on behalf of Edward Young Clarke to confer "with the leaders of the Second Hundred Thousand, an English organization whose purposes are somewhat like those of the Klan."[23] The trip was being undertaken in "hopes of effecting the formation of a world alliance of Caucasian Protestants." Closer to home, in mid-August some 4,650 candidates were initiated into the Klan in "a huge field just outside of Chicago." It was estimated that some 25,000 persons witnessed the ceremonies.[24]

Even with such high profile news and its repeatedly avowed respect for the rule of law, Klan-related intimidation and violence continued unabated. It is reasonable to say that many, perhaps most, such acts went unreported—or if brought to the attention of authorities, unpunished. Most often, the alleged deeds for which victims were warned or punished were not illegal *per se*, but rather perceived moral infractions such as marital infidelity, drunkenness, or consorting with members of another race. A few high-profile incidents made the press: Dr. E. C. Lindeman,

---

[20] *Columbus (GA) Enquirer–Sun*, 5 September 1922.
[21] *Columbus (GA) Enquirer–Sun*, 6 September 1922.
[22] *New York Times*, 14 September 1922.
[23] *New York Times*, 10 July 1922.
[24] *New York Times*, 21 August 1922.

the distinguished chairman of Social and Political Economy at the North Carolina College for Women in Greensboro, resigned his position and left the city after initially ignoring the Klan's warning "to discontinue certain alleged acts." It was reported that the Lindeman's cook "had entertained a number of her negro friends at the Lindeman home shortly after Christmas." [25] In another case, Hubert Kenneth Clay, a Harvard sophomore and descendant of the famed politician Henry Clay, had briefly been a member of the Klan in Colorado before moving East and renouncing the order's "un-American ideals" and its policy of "striking in the dark." After a series of increasingly threatening warnings for being "too indiscreet" with the secrets of the Klan, he "received a telegram, the contents of which he refused to divulge to his roommates. Immediately after opening and reading it he announced he was going to Florida," leaving that same evening on a southbound train.[26]

While such acts of mere intimidation were common, members of the Klan often resorted to violence. The Imperial Palace's repeated denials of responsibility were in part truthful. It would have been foolish for the organization to actively or openly encourage such activity. On a practical basis, however, the Klan hierarchy promoted the order's status as a regulatory force in a changing America, tacitly condoning not only action by intimidation, but also flogging, tar-and-feathering, and more. Episodes of violence that made the news were most often blamed on impostors seeking to discredit the Klan. When clear evidence of the Klan's involvement could not be plausibly denied, the responsibility would be laid on "renegade" Klansmen. For most of its existence the order's attempts to separate itself from violent acts was considered little more than a charade. One of the most egregious examples of Klan violence—and of the difficulty of bringing those responsible to justice— was the murder of two young men at Mer Rouge, Louisiana, in August 1922.[27]

---

[25] *Charlotte Observer*, 9 May 1922.

[26] *New York Times*, 4 December 1922.

[27] The events at Mer Rouge were covered widely in the contemporary press. The account given here is drawn in large part from summary articles by Robert L. Duffus, "How the Ku Klux Klan Sells Hate," in *The World's Work*, 1923, Vol. 46, No. 2, 174-183, and the *New York Times*, 26 December 1922.

In the early 1920s, Morehouse Parish encompassed a rural farming area in north Louisiana, adjacent to the Arkansas state line. Its two principal towns were the small villages of Bastrop and Mer Rouge, separated by some eight miles of dirt road. The exact date of the arrival of the Klan is not known with certainty, but thought to be in late 1920 as part of the rapid expansion under Clarke and Tyler. As revealed in later testimony, "the order first confined itself to lecturing and warning obnoxious persons," but grew more aggressive with the passing months. A former Klansmen would later testify that he resigned when "he was ordered to whip several men within an inch of their lives, take them to the Arkansas line, and order them not to return." The Klan, and for practical purposes the entire parish, was effectively ruled by J. K. Skipwith, known locally as "Old Skip," "the power-drunk Exalted Cyclops" of the local Klavern. According to a contemporary account of the events of August 1922, "The Klan went steadily from bad to worse for a long time prior to the fatal night…; decent men dropped out; the fanatical, violent, and vindictive got control; and Old Skip, tasting authority for the first time, grew more and more arrogant, more and more impatient of opposition or criticism."[28]

In mid-August, two young men, Watt Daniel, the son of a well-known planter, and Tom Richards, a garage mechanic, were kidnapped by masked men in broad daylight in the presence of witnesses. They were taken to the woods, questioned regarding their activities and general conduct, then released unharmed. The exact nature of their alleged offenses was never known. The rumor was the boys "knew too much." A week later, on the afternoon of August 24, Daniel, Richards, and a number of others from Mer Rouge attended a barbecue and baseball game in Bastrop. It was a pleasant day, with no hint of what was to come. Around dusk, a convoy of some fifty or sixty cars carrying the Mer Rouge delegation set off toward home. About two miles out of town, they found the road blocked by a stalled vehicle. Without warning, a group of armed masked men appeared, going down the line from car to car shining a flashlight into to each, searching. Five men, including

---

[28] Duffus, "How the Ku Klux Klan Sells Hate," 177.

Richards and Daniel were taken at gunpoint, thrown on a truck and driven away.

Of the five men kidnapped, one was released unharmed. Two others, including Watt Daniel's father, were brutally beaten before being pushed out of a car on the roadside in the village of Collinston. Richards and the younger Daniel were never seen alive again. Within days, Louisiana's Governor John M. Parker intervened. As he explained a few months later:

> On the 28th of August last, my phone rang late at night and a pitiful female voice appealed to me to try to help find the petitioner's husband. The lady stated that her name was Mrs. Richards; that she was from Mer Rouge, Louisiana; that her husband had been…torn away from her little three year-old child, and that an earnest effort had failed to produce any information in regard to him…. She said she was an orphan when she married Richards, that she had two little girl babies, that Richards was a kind, good husband, had never been in any kind of trouble, and as he was only a garage employee had left her absolutely destitute.[29]

Initial investigation of Richards's and Daniel's disappearance produced nothing. The Department of Justice's Bureau of Investigation sent agents to assist state and local authorities in seeking witnesses and gathering evidence. Unwilling to trust local law enforcement, Governor Parker dispatched state troops to help maintain order. On December 22, almost four months after the two men's kidnapping, the remains of their mutilated bodies were found floating in Lake La Fourche, a dozen or so miles from where they had been seized.

Evidence of the Klan's involvement was abundant and persuasive. Testimony revealed that the two men were likely killed because they recognized their kidnappers. When word reached members of the Klan that agents of the Department of Justice were investigating the case, they began secretly following them. The chief agent was observed to be carrying a large portfolio "which, the Klansmen believed, contained evidence against those implicated in the kidnapping and murder."[30] A plot was hatched to kidnap and kill the Federal agents, seizing the

---

[29] Duffus, "How the Ku Klux Klan Sells Hate," 176.
[30] *New York Times*, 26 December 1922.

portfolio in the process. Masked Klansmen planned to take them from a train as they traveled to the city of Monroe, but were thwarted when the scheme was revealed to the agents by undercover operatives who had infiltrated the local Klaverns. The mob assembled ready to act, but the agents had taken another route, thus foiling the plot.

Several arrests were made after the dead men's bodies were found. A "mysterious man" rumored to be "a high national official" of the Klan paid a brief visit to one of those arrested, but officially the Imperial Palace kept its distance.[31] Two grand juries, "at least two thirds of whose members were Klansmen," were assembled to hear the evidence.[32] Both failed to issue murder indictments. Despite reasonable public knowledge of their involvement, those responsible for the kidnappings and murders went unpunished.

While the authorities in Morehouse Parish were still searching for the missing men, Edward Young Clarke was in Muncie, Indiana, speaking on the subject of "Law Enforcement." His presence in the state reflected the Klan's phenomenal growth there, due in large part to the dynamic personality of a man named David Curtiss Stephenson. Stephenson, known best by his preferred nickname of "Steve," was a rising star in the Indiana Klan; he would be cited a few years hence as one of the chief individuals most responsible for the order's decline. But in these exuberant early days when the Klan seemed unstoppable, Stephenson was the prime mover in converting the state of Indiana into a near-fiefdom of the Imperial Palace. Clarke, the continuing subject of a number of lawsuits filed by disgruntled Klansmen, suffered another blow when he was charged by a federal judge with the possession and transportation of illegal liquor. Depending on whose story one believed, while in Muncie a bag containing a quart bottle of liquor and $500 in cash either *fell from*, or was *stolen out of* Clarke's automobile. In either case it came to the attention of the authorities, leading to the intervention of Prohibition officers. Clarke promptly surrendered to the

---

[31] Ibid. According to J. Q. Jett (*Georgia Freelance (Dublin GA)*, 26 November 1925) three of the Klansmen "who were in on this killing" were later murdered by other Klansmen for "talking too much."

[32] Duffus, "How the Ku Klux Klan Sells Hate," 176.

Federal Commissioner in Indianapolis and was released after posting a $2,000 appearance bond. Clarke issued a statement to the press avowing that he had no liquor in his bag when it was stolen, and that he "does not use liquor in any form."[33]

Despite whatever early stumbles the Klan may have had in its Indiana recruitment drive, the state was to become one of the foci of the order's power in the mid-1920s. In the words of one historian:

> Between 1922 and 1925, Indiana was the epicenter of the national Klan movement, the state that produced the Klan's largest, most enthusiastic membership, its greatest political victories, and its most powerful, well-known leaders outside of Atlanta. By any standard, Klan membership in Indiana was enormous. Between one-quarter and one-third of all native-born white men in the state paid ten dollars to become Klansmen during the 1920s; in some communities the figure was as high as 40 or 50 percent.... Hardly a fringe group, the Klan became the largest organization of any kind in the state. It was many times larger, for instance, than any of the veterans' organizations that flourished in Indiana at the same time and even larger than the Methodist church, the state's leading Protestant denomination.[34]

At first blush, Indiana would not have appeared to be a likely spot for the Klan to take root. The population was overwhelmingly white, native-born, and Protestant, displaying a noticeable absence of the usual targets of the Klan's vitriol. Blacks constituted less than three percent of the population, the foreign-born about five percent, and those of the Jewish faith about two percent. Catholics were more numerous, making up about a fifth of all church-goers in the mid-1920s.[35] Lacking its customary bogeymen, the Klan's recruiters relied more on the order's support of patriotism, the Christian religion, moral values, and Prohibition.

Much of the Klan's phenomenal growth in Indiana can be attributed to Steve Stephenson. A man of uncertain and varied background, he was born in Texas and raised in Oklahoma. The details of his early life are

---

[33] *New York Times*, 9 September 1922.
[34] Moore, L. J., 6-7.
[35] Ibid., 10.

murky, but he was said to have had a number of jobs, and was reputed to have married and abandoned two wives before ending up in Evansville, Indiana, working in a sales capacity for a retail coal company. During the Great War he served briefly in the military, completing officers' training. In joining the Klan at age thirty, Stephenson seemed to find his niche in life as a Kleagle and organizational promoter. "Part of his success can be explained by his shameless pretension and guile, his shrewd understanding of the Klan's potential, his forceful personality, and his fascination with military hierarchy and organization, which he put to good use in marshaling the recruitment campaign."[36] As a rising star in the Indiana Klan, Stephenson met and apparently worked closely with Hiram Evans, who at the time was serving as William Simmons's assistant and liaison to newly formed Klaverns across the rapidly growing Invisible Empire. His relationship with Evans would be vital in the events to come later in the year.

Indiana was but one of many states where the Klan's power, especially in the political arena, was obvious in the fall of 1922. Georgia, home of the Imperial Palace, was no exception. At the state Democratic Convention held in Macon in early October, the Klan was represented by the Rev. Caleb Ridley, the order's Imperial Kludd, and Walter Sims, Klansman and mayor-elect of Atlanta. The *Macon Telegraph* commented with some bitterness, "It was interesting during the night to watch the several candidates for the senatorship buttonholing Dr. Ridley. It has been a sickening play they have made for the Ku Klux support."[37]

Regardless of the growth in its political power, Klan leaders remained under legal siege by disgruntled Klansmen, a lingering residual from the *New York World's* revelations more than a year earlier. As Georgia Democrats vied for Klan support in Macon, a major announcement was made in Atlanta, less than a hundred miles to the north. On the morning of October 4th, Edward Young Clarke unexpectedly announced his forthcoming resignation as Imperial Wizard *pro tem*. Stating that "he had completed the organization of the machine," he intended to turn control back to Col. Simmons, now

---

[36] Ibid., 15.
[37] *Macon Telegraph*, 4 October 1922.

"completely restored to health" during his sabbatical. His job over, Clarke said he intended to become an ordinary Klansmen in order to have more time to devote to his personal business. Simmons was to resume his office of Imperial Wizard on November 10, several weeks before the scheduled Klonvocation celebrating the seventh anniversary of the Klan's founding.

Other factors were likely important in Clarke's decision. Elizabeth Tyler, his long-time business partner and management-savvy co-worker must have been sorely missed.[38] Clarke mentioned—somewhat in passing—that the ongoing lawsuits (of which he was one of the prime targets) were a distraction to the business of the order. His position of leadership had become an issue that he hoped to solve with his resignation. At the time no mention was made of rumors that a federal grand jury was at that very moment hearing charges accusing Clarke of mail fraud. The following afternoon, the jury issued an indictment alleging Clarke had designed a "rake-off" scheme to divert cash to his own use by charging local Klan officials inflated amounts for their required surety bonds. Once again, he dismissed the charges as "another effort on the part of the enemies of the Klan to hurt the Klan by discrediting me."[39] Simmons and the Klan's Kloncilium issued similar statements. For the second time in a month, Clarke paid his bond to a federal magistrate and was released pending trial.

With the impending return of Klan control to William Simmons, attention focused on the forthcoming First Annual Klonvocation of the Knights of the Ku Klux Klan to be held in Atlanta the last week of November. The gathering was Simmons's idea, an event to celebrate the seventh anniversary of the founding of the Klan, an event to showcase its growing membership and power. Some months earlier Simmons and Clarke had purchased for the Klan the Peachtree Creek Battlefield, the

---

[38] At 8AM on Saturday morning August 19, 1922, Elizabeth Tyler married Stephen W. Grow, "a well-known moving picture producer." The ceremony took place at her home on Atlanta's Howell Mill Road, with the Rev. Caleb Ridley officiating. (*Atlanta Constitution*, 20 August 1922) "Clarke offered strenuous objection to the match, doing all in his power to prevent it." (*Baltimore Sun*, 5 October 1922.)

[39] *Fort Worth Star-Telegram*, 6 October 1922.

scene of a major encounter between Confederate and Union forces during Sherman's Atlanta Campaign in the summer of 1864. It was to eventually become the site of the Klan's proposed University of America, an institution of higher learning serving to instill the tenets of One Hundred Percent Americanism in coming generations. In preparation for the meeting, Simmons had fenced in the battlefield for security, and constructed a "huge frame auditorium straddling the creek." An "Imperial Cottage" had been erected for the Klan hierarchy on a knoll some distance from the convention hall.[40] Fred Savage, as head of security, had trained guards and ushers to protect the secrecy of the proceedings.

As the Klonvocation date drew near, Atlanta anticipated a flood of Klansmen. "Entire floors were reserved in Atlanta hotels for the incoming Klan delegates. Pullman cars deposited loads of Klansmen in the railroad yards, whence they marched, in their costumes, under flags and banners, behind blaring bands to their assigned hotels. D. C. Stephenson, who by this time had gathered a quarter of a million new members of the Klan in Ohio and Indiana…came to the scene in a private Pullman car."[41] There were clues of exciting things to come. The Rev. Ridley hinted that the "rapidly increasing membership" of the Klan would lead to a four-degree order, with the higher grades of membership open only to the most faithful and active Klansmen. Simmons was said to be working on the ritual which was to be finalized at the convention.[42]

In many ways, the Klonvocation was to be a new beginning of sorts for the Klan, a transition to a more formalized structure to carry the organization into the years ahead. One major purpose of the gathering was to adopt bylaws and a permanent constitution for the order. Despite its growth and success, the Klan was still wholly owned by William J. Simmons, and still operating under a provisional charter granting him the offices of both Emperor and Imperial Wizard. It was assumed that he would continue in these roles, his titles and offices formalized with the new constitution. The previous year had been difficult following the

---

[40] Shepherd, "The Fiery Double-Cross," 8-9.
[41] Ibid.
[42] *Dallas Morning News*, 28 October 1922.

World's exposé and the Congressional hearings. Disgruntled current and former Klansmen were continuing their legal efforts against the Klan's leadership. But *within* the walls of the Imperial Palace it appeared that dissent had been quelled. It had not.

In the months prior to the November convention, it had become evident to a number of insiders that the management and direction of the rapidly expanding Klan left much to be desired. Simmons was both a dreamer and a drunk, a man with lofty ideas and a golden tongue for oratory, but lacking the practical skills to manage what was now a million-man organization with a steady stream of cash revenue. Clarke was certainly a marketing genius, but operating on the edge of both morality and legality. Under legal assault for his alleged financial mismanagement and federal indictment for mail fraud and possession of illegal liquor, he had indicated his plans to resign from the Klan's leadership. Elizabeth Tyler, the pragmatist and Clarke's one-time co-manager, had quit months earlier. Those who considered the situation could clearly see a pending leadership void as the Klan entered the eighth year of its existence.

The known conspirators were Hiram Evans, at the time Imperial Kligrapp, Fred Savage, the Imperial Night-hawk and head of Klan security, and Steve Stephenson, the rising star of the Indiana Klan. Edward Clarke's role—if any—in the events that followed, is unclear. It appears likely, however, that Clarke was aware of what was to happen and, if not an active participant, was at least passively complicit in the events that would remove William J. Simmons from his position of leadership in the Klan.

The Klonvocation began as scheduled on Monday, November 27, 1922.[43] The thousand-odd delegates gathered on the old Peachtree Creek Battlefield site, effectively shielded from outsiders by fences and

---

[43] The single definitive account of the events of the Klonvocation of November 1922 is found in a series of interviews given to William G. Shepherd by William J. Simmons in 1928 and published in a series of three articles that year in *Collier's* magazine. The source of this section is the third of those articles, "The Fiery Double-Cross," published in the 28 July 1928 issue. Shepherd, as a journalist, wrote a number of articles on the Klan during the first years of its existence in the 1920s.

Savage's well-trained guards. The highlight of the opening day was to be an address given by Simmons, refreshed and invigorated after his months in seclusion. After a prayer during which the Klansmen knelt, and the singing of "Onward Christian Soldiers," Simmons delivered an emotional oration, praising the Anglo-Saxon civilization and "the everlasting principles of white supremacy."

That night, Evans, Stephenson, and Savage quietly sent a number of men to talk with the delegates at their hotels. The vote on a permanent constitution for the Klan was scheduled to take place the following day. "'Tomorrow morning,' they would say, 'comes the election of Imperial Wizard. Emperor Simmons has so much work to do that he has asked us to select a wizard as an assistant for him. Simmons holds two offices—Emperor and Imperial Wizard. We think it will be best to elect Hiram Wesley Evans to be Imperial Wizard, and leave the greater powers of Emperor to Col. Simmons. Will you promise to vote for Evans in the election tomorrow?'" Almost everyone agreed, thinking the request had come from Simmons himself.

At approximately 4AM of the same night, Fred Savage and Steve Stephenson drove to Klankrest, Simmons's home on Peachtree Road, where they awakened the Imperial Wizard from a sound sleep. At first the two men told Simmons they were too excited to sleep and were out for an early morning drive. After a bit of hesitation, they brought up the subject of the upcoming election. Simmons averred that he presumed he would be confirmed without opposition for both Emperor and Imperial Wizard, the two offices he already held. Simmons recounted the exchange that followed:

> Finally Savage said to me, "Well, Colonel, we both just dropped around to tell you that whatever happens on the convention floor tomorrow, there will be armed men stationed around on the floor to protect your honor."
>
> "Protect my honor!" I said. "What do you mean?"
>
> "Why," said one of them, "there is a certain crowd of men here who say that if you are nominated for the office of Imperial Wizard tomorrow they will get up on the floor and attack your character. And we've just come to tell you that the first man who insults your name will be killed

by a sharpshooter right on the spot as he speaks. There'll be enough of us with firearms to take care of the whole convention, if necessary."

Before they went away, however, they told me that we could avoid bloodshed if I would agree to have Hiram Wesley Evans elected Imperial Wizard. I didn't know what kind of men these two fellows were, or I wouldn't have believed them. I found out afterwards that all this talk was a fine "frame-up"—a lie to deceive me, told by men I trusted implicitly. Well, I didn't sleep any more that night. I saw visions of a bloody shambles among the 1,000 delegates the next day.

At nine o'clock on Tuesday morning, the Klan hierarchy met for a "prayer meeting" at the convention site's Imperial Cottage. Clarke, Evans, Savage, and Stephenson were present, no doubt awaiting Simmons's decision. Other notable Klansmen present included James Lowery, sheriff of Atlanta's Fulton County, and noted sculptor Gutzon Borglum, now in the final planning phase prior to beginning the Stone Mountain Confederate Monument. Simmons gave a brief talk prior to announcing, "Evans is to be the Imperial Wizard."

The voting went as planned. In what was likely a stage-managed scenario, Clarke, whose resignation of the prior month seemed to be forgotten, was briefly suggested as a candidate for Imperial Wizard, but declined in favor of Evans. For his past service, however, he was willing to accept the office of Imperial Giant, a new title created for Imperial Wizards *emeriti*. Hiram Wesley Evans was named Imperial Wizard, while William Joseph Simmons retained his title of Emperor of the Invisible Empire, elected for life. The Associated Press news wires dutifully announced the change in leadership. Evans was described as a "practicing dentist"—something he had abandoned some time earlier— and "an active church worker [who] frequently lectures before Sunday School classes." The remainder of the Klonvocation went smoothly, one major achievement being the consideration of the formation of women's auxiliary to the Knights of the Ku Klux Klan.[44] Its creation was urged by Clarke, the newly elected Imperial Giant, who was no doubt well aware of the potential untapped income stream.

---

[44] *Flint (MI) Journal*, 30 November 1922.

In the weeks that followed, the newly elected Klan officers seemed to settle into their designated roles. In early December, Imperial Wizard Evans spoke in Texas, condemning Catholics, Jews, and Negroes while affirming that "Every resource that will make stronger and perpetuate the principles of the Knights of the Ku Klux Klan will be employed in the administration of its affairs to combat the attacks which have been and are being made against the order."[45] Meanwhile, Emperor Simmons and Imperial Giant Clarke traveled to Miami to participate in an event celebrating the Florida Klan and featuring a motorcade of "200 cars or more" between Miami and Homestead.[46] Little seemed to have changed.

Back at the Imperial Palace, Evans took over Simmons's office. The new Imperial Wizard's stated promise of creating a "great white throne room" for the Emperor never materialized. After a while, Simmons noted "a coldness among all the office help." As he explained it later, "I didn't have any office to go to. I just sort of had to hang around the place even though my title was Emperor." Shortly thereafter, Simmons noted pile of small booklets from the Klan printers, copies of the newly ratified "Constitution of the Knights of the Ku Klux Klan." Continuing his story, Simmons said, "I opened it. I discovered that it had been changed in many places. I looked at the paragraph covering the powers and duties of the Emperor. I saw that every power had been taken away from me and given to the Imperial Wizard. Evans and the rest of them laughed at me when I went to The Palace to complain. Evans had gotten his hands on the original constitution. 'Let's get the money, Colonel'—that's exactly what Evans said to me when I protested."[47]

"When a dreamer clashes with 'practical' men, he usually comes off second best. Col. William Joseph Simmons, founder of the modern Ku Klux Klan, was no exception."[48]

[45] *New York Times*, 8 December 1922.
[46] *Miami (FL) Herald*, 13 December 1922.
[47] Shepherd, "The Fiery Double-Cross," 47.
[48] Ibid., 8.

Chapter 19

Blackmail, The Mann Act, and Murder

By 1923, the Ku Klux Klan had become a firm part of the American mainstream, at least in certain areas of the country. In its home state of Georgia, some saw it as an unofficial regulatory auxiliary readily available to enforce moral infractions. In January, a Mrs. John Booth of Lawrenceville contacted Atlanta Chief of Police James Beavers "asking that the Atlanta police department find and arrest her husband and turn him over to the Ku Klux Klan for punishment," alleging he had deserted her two weeks earlier.[1] Later in the year a theater presentation of the comedy, "Polly With a Past," by the Georgia Tech Marionettes was sponsored by the Coca-Cola Company ("Delicious and Refreshing") and the Knights of the Ku Klux Klan ("The 100 Per Cent American Organization").[2]

While the Klan may have been gaining some degree of social approval in the state, the lame-duck Hardwick administration could do little but wring its hands in its efforts to stop growing reports of night-riding, flogging, kidnapping, and intimidation. In rural Barrow County for example, located between Atlanta and Athens, attempts to indict

---

[1] *Macon Telegraph*, 25 January 1923. Beavers was a Klan opponent, a rarity in Atlanta politics of the day. Instead of honoring Mrs. Booth's wishes, he called one of the local news correspondents.

[2] The program for the play is in the archives of the University of Georgia's Hargrett Rare Book and Manuscript collection. Georgia Tech was an all-male school at the time, requiring some of the Marionettes to appear in female garb. M. L. Brittan, Georgia Tech President, apparently found it appropriate to write a somewhat apologetic introduction titled "College Dramatics" for the program explaining that while "every young man is advised to take part in athletics…it is natural that some of our young men should be interested in dramatic art." He went on to say that "for years" Massachusetts Tech [M.I.T.] had sponsored a similar program, as if such unmanly activity was the norm in technical colleges of the day.

Klansmen for multiple acts of violence against local blacks were met with threats against the foreman of the Grand Jury. The Imperial Palace dispatched its "chief detective" who offered to assist the jury in bringing the culprits to justice. As it turned out, his services "consisted of disorganizing witnesses and setting up alibis for the accused men." Hardwick was quoted as saying, "I am powerless. God save the State."[3]

If the state government was powerless against the Klan, there were others—private individuals—who were determined to see its failure. John A. Manget was such a man. His experience is illustrative of the Klan's power in crushing such external opposition and of the attitude of the many newspapers of the day. Variously described in the press as a "millionaire," a "capitalist" and a "philanthropist," Manget was a prominent citizen of Atlanta and an early opponent of the Klan. When Governor Hardwick initially voiced timid opposition to the hooded order during his reelection campaign in the summer of 1922, Manget praised his stance. In an open letter to the Governor, with copies sent to the several newspapers in the state, Manget described Hardwick's speech as "among the bravest, most opportune, most beneficial utterances ever made by a chief executive of any commonwealth." Condemning the Klan as a "damnable bunch of grafters hiding behind cowardly masks [who] have made Georgia a stench in the nostrils of this nation," he declared the organization to have been "born of the ramblings of a helpless dreamer, engendered by a wife-deserting, grafting reprobate, and suckled and fed by the brain of a near-prostitute."[4]

In a January 1923 speech titled "Lawlessness in Georgia" delivered before Atlanta's Civitan Club, Manget averred "that the Ku Klux Klan is responsible, directly or indirectly, for many of the awful crimes that are disgracing Georgia and other Southern states." He sent a copy of his address to the *Atlanta Georgian* and the *Columbus Enquirer-Sun*, the only papers in the state that carried the *New York World's* exposé. His cover letter to Julian Harris noted, "your paper is the only one that seems to

---

[3] *Macon Telegraph*, 16 December 1922.
[4] *Columbus (GA) Enquirer-Sun*, 4 July 1922. In the latter phrase, Manget is clearing referring to Simmons, Clarke, and Tyler, respectively.

have courage enough to publish anything about the Ku Klux Klan."[5] In an editorial accompanying the *Enquirer-Sun's* publication of Manget's address, Harris openly denounced the failure of the state's larger dailies to criticize the Klan, calling them "stupidly blind as to the things that are daily becoming as menacing as they are already disgraceful," suggesting the papers "feared to lose a few thousand subscribers or find their profits falling below normal." In response, the *Macon Telegraph's* editorialist replied his paper "would rather find virtue in the Ku Klux Klan as in anything else than not, and it finds it much more congenial to recognize virtue than the opposite....The Klan has the same right to be a secret organization as any other." It was not an open endorsement of the Invisible Empire, but rather a veiled admission that the *Telegraph* was at times willing to look the other way.

A few weeks later, "thousands of people" watched as the Klan paraded in downtown Atlanta following a meeting at the City Auditorium, the procession headed by four mounted city police officers. Again displaying his willingness to take an outspoken stand against the Klan, Manget sent a letter of protest to Atlanta's Klansman-mayor Walter Sims, noting the organization "has prospered on account of its appeal to the ignorant and vicious based on religious intolerance, race hatred and determination to gain control of all governments, city, county, state and national." The mayor replied that he did not oppose "peaceful parades of American citizens in this city."[6]

In a strange turn of events, approximately two weeks after stating his opposition to the city-endorsed Klan parade, a letter from Manget appeared in a small eighth-page news item in the *Atlanta Constitution*. In it, Manget said that he "had scores of friends of mine" reveal they were members of the Klan, describing them as "prominent men professionally and in business, men of high standing in the community whose lives are above reproach." He stated, weakly, "that if the mask and robe were abolished there would be a cessation of antagonism toward the Klan." The bizarre twist was that the letter did not come directly from Manget, but rather was delivered to the *Constitution* by H. J. Norton, Exalted

[5] *Columbus (GA) Enquirer-Sun*, 14 January 1923.
[6] *Atlanta Constitution*, 2 February 1923.

Cyclops of Atlanta's Nathan Bedford Forrest Klan No. 1. Norton stated that he had received the letter from Manget with the specific request that it be printed in the newspaper. It was the last public statement Manget would make on the Klan.

The apparent reason behind Manget's stunning change of heart was revealed several years later in the rambling confession of J. Q. Jett published in ex-governor Hardwick's *Georgia Free Lance*. The Klan "went out and hunted up a painted woman, gave her $50.00 to sign an affidavit that Mr. Manget had relations with her. Well, we never heard any more from this. Sure, they would have published this affidavit in the *Searchlight* and would have probably ruined him, as many people will believe this kind of stuff."[7]

Meanwhile on a national level, Imperial Wizard Hiram Evans made a pilgrimage to Washington, D.C. where he "conferred with friends at the capital (*sic*) and the Senate and House office buildings."[8] The Klan's growing political success was phenomenal. In the 1922 off-year elections, estimates held that at least seventy-five members of the newly elected Congressmen owed their success to Klan support, not to mention those who had been defeated because of their opposition to the Invisible Empire.[9] Observers referred to Evans's visit as "a sort of scouting trip to line up things for an aggressive [political] campaign" in the upcoming 1924 elections.[10] Perhaps the only thing not going well at the moment for the Klan's growing power was news from Europe that some felt the order would not be welcome there. The *Echo de Paris* declared, "It is an organization of such character as is not wanted on this side of the Atlantic."[11]

---

[7] *Georgia Free Lance, (Dublin GA)*, 19 November 1925. In Jett's printed narrative, most likely recorded by a stenographer for publication, Jett refers to "John A. Monshet," close to the phonetic pronunciation of "Manget." There is little doubt that he was referring to "John A. Manget." In early 1923, the *Searchlight* was an unofficial Klan-related newspaper.

[8] *Philadelphia Inquirer*, 21 December 1922.

[9] *New York Times*, 10 December 1922.

[10] *Philadelphia Inquirer*, 21 December 1922.

[11] *Denver Post*, 30 December 1922.

Having effectively gelded William Simmons by elevating him to the powerless office of Emperor for Life, Evans set out to take over the one other power center in the Imperial Palace that he did not control, that of Edward Y. Clarke and the Propagation Department. On February 23, Evans's Chief of Staff Fred L. Savage announced that Clarke had "formally turned over to imperial headquarters" all of his propagation work.[12] The announcement implied that this was part of a larger plan, but the truth of this allegation is somewhat doubtful. The income from the ten-dollar Klectoken "donations" from new members was the true power behind the Klan, and Evans wanted to control it. Clarke was clearly an ally of Simmons, but he could not protest; his original contract contained a clause that allowed either party to cancel the arrangement. Six days later a Federal Grand Jury in Houston, Texas, revealed the indictment of Clarke for violations of the Mann Act that allegedly occurred more than two years earlier.

According to the accusations from Texas, on February 11, 1921, Clarke had transported twenty-something year-old Louise Martin from Houston to New Orleans for "immoral purposes." Under the Mann Act (formally known as "The White-Slave Traffic Act of 1910"), Clarke was indicted on two counts: the transportation of Miss Martin and the act of purchasing her ticket.[13] Individuals convicted of such crimes were usually subject to significant stints in Federal prisons. The details and timing of the indictment were quite suspicious. The alleged acts had occurred some two years earlier. The charges against Clarke were brought in Texas, Evans's home state and ultimate power center where the Klan was well represented in both politics and government. Although clear evidence for Evans's involvement is lacking, having the Imperial Giant put away on a

---

[12] *New York Times*, 24 February 1923.

[13] Interestingly, Clarke was apparently not the only fraternal order officer to run into trouble under the Mann Act. On 30 December 1922, the *Denver Post* reported that John Talbot, Supreme President of the Order of the Owls, was attempting to cut a deal in which William J. Simmons and E. Y. Clarke would take over the Southern portion of the Owls organization. Talbot was about to begin a five-year sentence in Federal prison at Leavenworth, Kansas, for violation of the Mann Act. *See Chapter Notes for further comments on this Federal Law.*

morals charge would certainly remove Clarke as an obstacle to Imperial Wizard Evans's domination of the order.

Clarke, now facing his third active Federal indictment, called this new charge "simply another effort to attempt to discredit me and through discrediting me, damage the Knights of the Ku Klux Klan."[14] After discreetly waiting a few days, Evans "gave out a statement formally announcing Edward Young Clarke's severance of official connection with the Klan," saying only that this was being done "for the good of the order."[15] No mention was made of the Mann Act indictment. Not missing the obvious irony of Clarke's situation, the *Macon Telegraph* pointed out in an editorial that in all likelihood, he would rather face a fair trial by his peers than the summary punishment he would likely suffer if left to the members of his own order.[16]

When Clarke failed to appear in court in Houston the following week, the federal judge increased his bond and ordered his immediate arrest. His attorneys stated that since he had paid his initial bond of $1,000, he was "at perfect liberty to go where he pleased, and he left [Atlanta] for a much needed rest."[17] Assurance was given that he would appear for his scheduled trial in September, notwithstanding the bench warrant issued for his arrest.

With Clarke effectively out of the way, Emperor William Simmons stepped back into the fray. His attempts to regain power over the coming months would unleash a dizzying array of legal actions and lead to the murder of one of his close associates. On March 22, Simmons announced the formation of Kamelia, a woman's order separate from but "ready to function alongside of the Ku Klux Klan."[18] It was to be open to white women over the age of eighteen and focus on the American home, American citizenship, and the American creed as taught by the Protestant church. Simmons proclaimed himself "El Magus" of the organization, head of its Krown Kourt. While the formation of a woman's order had been discussed at the Klan's November Klonvocation,

---

[14] *Macon Telegraph*, 2 March 1923.
[15] *Macon Telegraph*, 7 March 1923.
[16] *Macon Telegraph*, 9 March 1923.
[17] *Macon Telegraph*, 17 March 1923.
[18] *Augusta Chronicle*, 23 March 1923.

the announcement seemed to catch the Imperial Palace by surprise. Fred Savage, acting in his role as chief of staff, said, "We know of no such order nor have officials of the Klan been in communication with Mr. Simmons for several days." Imperial Wizard Evans responded the next day by saying, "all I know of any so-called Kamelia is what I have read in the newspapers." The Klan has no official women's order, he continued, and anything that Simmons had done in that direction had no official standing.[19] Evans issued a proclamation forbidding any Klansman from identifying himself with any women's organization, including Kamelia. Simmons promptly issued his own proclamation countering Evans's, citing his role as "creator and founder" of both orders.[20]

The fight escalated a few days later when a Federal judge in Atlanta issued an injunction that placed Emperor Simmons "over the Knights of the Ku Klux Klan," freezing the Klan's funds and effectively countermanding Imperial Wizard Evans's edicts. Evans was in New York at the time, leaving the Imperial Palace relatively unguarded. At 2:30AM the following morning, the same judge signed another order directing Fulton County Sheriff (and Klansman) J. L. Lowery to take possession of the Palace on behalf of Simmons. Within a day, the Simmons faction had charged several officers of the Klan—Evans's allies—with the embezzlement of more than $100,000 in cash which they had managed to sprit away during the take-over by the Emperor's forces. Simmons's victory was short-lived, as within twenty-four hours of his taking possession of the palace, complete control of the premises was turned over to Sheriff Lowery pending a resolution of dispute.

Meanwhile, Klansmen "from all parts of the county" began to descend on Atlanta in support of one side or the other. One early estimate of the number of Simmons supporters in town ran as high as 6,000.[21] Notable among them was Captain J. L. Skipwith and his delegation of thirty-three Klansmen from Morehouse Parish, Louisiana. Simmons seemed to welcome their support despite abundant evidence of Skipwith's and the Morehouse Parish Klan's involvement in the Mer

---

[19] *Charlotte Observer*, 25 March 1923.
[20] *New Orleans Times-Picayune*, 1 April 1923.
[21] *Augusta Chronicle*, 4 April 1923.

Rouge murders less than eight months earlier. On the other side, 140,000 Texas Klansmen from 275 Klaverns were said to be "solidly behind Dr. Evans."[22] While the Sheriff was officially in charge, "two sets of armed men guarded The Palace, and practically camped under the trees in The Palace lawn. One was Simmons's; the other, Evans's." As one writer later described the scene, "Famous and aristocratic old Peachtree Street shuddered with terror."[23] While the various court proceedings were in progress, an estimated three to five thousand members of the Nathan Bedford Forest Klan No. 1, the order's original Klavern, assembled in their lodge rooms and vowed their allegiance to Simmons, going so far as to proclaim him—not Evans—Imperial Wizard.[24]

In a series of hearings over the following days, charges and accusations flew back and forth from each side. The attorney for the Imperial Wizard's faction was confident of Evans's legal and legitimate election at the Klonvocation the prior November, stating he had been "wizarding right along" without interference until Simmons filed for his injunction. Simmons's attorney claimed various forms of fraud, including—in addition to the missing $100,000-plus—the alleged diversion by Fred L. Savage of $68,000 to his personal account, and the accusation that Imperial Wizard Evans was personally pocketing three dollars from the Klectokens of each new member.

After more than a week of legal bickering, the Fulton County Superior Court judge ruled that for the time being, the Klan was to be administered by a commission of three: Emperor William J. Simmons, Imperial Wizard H. W. Evans, and Municipal Court Marshall J. M. George. Evans and Simmons were enjoined from interfering with each other, and the "missing" $100,000 was returned to the Klan treasury, effectively dismissing the charge of embezzlement. A final decision as to the merits of each side's case was to be rendered in the weeks to come. Almost immediately Evans lashed out at E. Y. Clarke and Elizabeth

<hr>

[22] *Charlotte Observer*, 10 April 1923.
[23] Shepherd, "The Fiery Double-Cross," 48.
[24] *Augusta Chronicle*, 6 April 1923.

Tyler,[25] alleging the entire episode was a plot hatched by them to recover the income from the Propagation Department. "Mr. Clarke conceived the idea of ousting me as Imperial Wizard and substituting Colonel Simmons, so that he again might take charge of the propagation department and reap enormous profits from his rake-off from members who joined the Klan."[26] Evans also mentioned that he was just in the process of forming a women's auxiliary to the Klan when Simmons announced his formation of the Kamelia order. Rev. Dr. Caleb Ridley, the Imperial Kludd, spoke in defense of Clarke, stating, "there is no darker page of perfidy in the record of human relations than the conspiracy of H. W. Evans to crush E. Y. Clarke and to drive him out of the Knights of the Ku Klux Klan and make him an exile and wanderer on the face of the earth."[27]

With the standoff temporarily in abeyance, William J. Simmons, acting in his role as El Magus, addressed the first national meeting of the women's Kamelia order, held in Tulsa in mid-April. In addition to his usual praise of American values, Protestantism, and white supremacy, he trashed New York City as "the most un-American center on the American continent." "Within a radius of nineteen miles," he said, "there are more than seven millions of people congested. Of this enormous centralized population there are only 1,100,000 native-born, white Protestant Americans...The foremost political and social economist of the world recently made a survey of New York City, and after listening to its babble of tongues, after feeling its hot breath of anarchy, after touching its seething restlessness, he calmly turned away and said that Petrograd, in its dust and desolation, was of picture of New York City of the future."[28]

By early May a compromise had been reached between non-Klan mediators employed by the Simmons and Evans factions. Under the agreement, Evans was to be recognized as Imperial Wizard, but his orders were subject to veto by a supermajority of the members of the

---

[25] At the time often referred to by her new married name, Mrs. Elizabeth Tyler Grow.

[26] *Columbus (GA) Enquirer-Sun*, 8 April 1923.

[27] *Augusta Chronicle*, 9 April 1923.

[28] *Omaha World Herald*, 20 April 1923.

Klan's ruling council, the Kloncilium. Simmons was recognized as Emperor for Life, to be paid $1,000 a month during his lifetime with the annuity passed on to his wife after his death. Certain officials of the Klan who had displeased Simmons were to be let go, and their replacements decided by both the Emperor and Imperial Wizard. The Klan would recognize the Kamelia order, rescinding the edict that forbade Klansmen from having any association with it.

With the controversy seemingly settled, Simmons turned his energies to promoting the newly recognized—if not formally affiliated—order of Kamelia. On May 20, national newspapers carried a staged press photo of Kamelia initiation ceremonies in Atlanta's Emma Sansom Kourt No. 1.[29] A group of women wearing costumes vaguely similar to those of the Klan were shown kneeling in front of an American flag. Plans to form additional kourts throughout the nation were said to be underway. In defiance of the agreement, however, Simmons's organizational efforts were met by resistance from local Klan officials in Arkansas. Statements that Simmons made in response criticizing Imperial Wizard Evans were carried by a number of newspapers across the nation, resulting in another flurry of lawsuits.

On May 24, Evans filed suit against Simmons, alleging slander and libel, and demanding $100,000 for damage to his personal and professional reputation.[30] A week later, a group of Klan members from several states filed a separate suit against the Klan leadership, naming individually Simmons and Evans, as well as the members of the ruling Kloncilium. The action alleged "gross mismanagement" of the Klan's income and resources, and charged both Simmons and Evans with turning the Klan into a "personal machine for the enrichment and

---

[29] Emma Sansom was a fifteen year-old farm girl who assisted Gen. Nathan Bedford Forrest in an engagement against Union forces near Gadsden, Alabama, in May 1863. In 1907 a monument was erected in Gadsden in recognition of her heroism. Forrest's biographer, Wyeth, dedicated his book to Sansom.

[30] In an interesting side note, later in the year Evans amended his suit to add a demand for an additional $50,000 in damages, alleging that Simmons's answer to the initial suit was in and of itself libelous. (*Columbus (GA) Enquirer-Sun*, 28 November 1923.)

personal aggrandizement of themselves."[31] Evans response was a laconic, "Doesn't amount to a hill of beans."[32] Sculptor Gutzon Borglum, perhaps the most public figure on the ruling council, denied that he was a member of the Kloncilium, going so far as to deny that he was not even a member of the Knights of the Ku Klux Klan. Simmons was silent. The Atlanta court granted an emergency injunction, again placing the Klan under the court's control. Expenditure of funds was specifically prohibited, and the parties were enjoined from moving Klan headquarters away from Atlanta, an option that had apparently been discussed by Evans and his supporters.

The reason behind Simmons's silence in response to the new suit was soon evident when it became clear that the individuals filing the action were in fact the Emperor's supporters. The attorney for the plaintiffs, W. J. Coburn of Atlanta, explained that while Simmons was a defendant in the suit, he was an "innocent party." The action was "intended to straighten out and correct the very things alleged by Col. Simmons in his recent suit against Imperial Wizard H. W. Evans."[33]

Meeting in Washington D.C on June 2, the Kloncilium announced plans to investigate the charges brought in the most recent suit, and get to the "very bottom" of them. It was a somewhat disingenuous statement given the fact that the investigating body would be investigating itself. The Kloncilium also announced the formation of "Women of the Ku Klux Klan," a Klan-related women's group that would take in (or affiliate with) the League of Protestant Women, the American Women, the Puritan Daughters of America, the Ladies of the Golden Mask, and the Ladies of the Invisible Empire. Notably absent from the list was Simmons's Kamelia order, an apparent rejection of the agreement signed less than a month earlier.[34]

Playing an apparent game of tit-for-tat, Simmons escalated the dispute even further. On June 6, the front page of the *Columbus Enquirer-Sun* carried a banner headline reading, "Simmons Launches

---

[31] *Macon Telegraph*, 1 June 1923.
[32] *Columbus (GA) Enquirer-Sun*, 1 June 1923.
[33] *Macon Telegraph*, 2 June 1923.
[34] *Miami (FL) Herald*, 3 June 1923.

New Klan." Citing his authority as Emperor, Simmons announced that he was forming a new order "separate and distinct" from the Knights of the Ku Klux Klan. It was to be called the Knights Kamelia. While bearing a similar name to the women's order he had recently established, it was to be independent of it. Referring indirectly to Evans, Simmons said the "purpose of the [Knights Kamelia] is to afford a refuge to Klansmen who are now exposed to authoritative tyranny." Disgruntled or frustrated members of the Knights of the Ku Klux Klan would be allowed to "transfer without cost."

Less than two weeks later the fifteen-member Kloncilium met in Atlanta to examine the charges brought against Evans (and themselves) in the recent suits. Eleven were reported to favor exoneration, leading Emperor Simmons, Imperial Kludd Caleb Ridley, and two others to resign from the ruling body. Within days, the Knights of the Ku Klux Klan, Inc. had obtained a court order blocking Simmons from organizing the Knights Kamelia and thus revealing the "secrets and rituals of the Klan."[35]

Simmons immediately announced his intention to ignore the injunction (which had been filed in a Georgia court), and proceed with organization of the Knights Kamelia on a national level. He retained attorney Walter A. Sims, the Klansman-mayor of Atlanta, to represent him in fighting the ban, and implied that Evans opposed it as he was ineligible for membership. Simmons stated, "It is in response to the clamor of Klansmen from every section of the Invisible Empire that I am founding the Order of the Knights of Kamelia and that hundreds of thousands of Klansmen in a state of revolt against the administration of H. W. Evans may be restrained in their movement towards secession and may be saved to the great organization as it was originally founded and promulgated."[36] The same day, a Simmons representative announced the formation of a Knights Kamelia "castle"—the name given to local chapters—in Miami, Florida.

Over the following weeks, both Imperial Wizard Evans and Emperor Simmons traveled widely over the realms of the Invisible

---

[35] *Miami (FL) Herald*, 22 June 1923.
[36] *Columbus (GA) Enquirer-Sun*, 24 June 1923.

Empire, each encouraging their supporters while seeking to win often-uncertain Klansmen to their side. In late June, both men spoke to some 5,000 Klansmen gathered in Beaumont, Texas. A few days later, Simmons spoke to another Klan group in San Antonio, this time announcing his plans to "extend the work of the Ku Klux Klan beyond the shores of the United States." Klan headquarters in Atlanta had already received petitions to organize Klaverns in South Africa, Australia, Scotland, and Northern Ireland, he said. The first overseas chapter was to be in England, known as the Knights of the Universal Kingdom, or K.U.K.[37] On July 4, Evans was the featured guest at the tri-state Klonklave in Kokomo, Indiana, attended by more than 100,000 Klansmen and their families. It was here that Steve Stephenson was anointed as the Grand Dragon of Indiana, an office bestowed in no small part for his assistance in ousting Simmons and his support of the Evans faction of the Klan.[38] A few days later, Evans addressed a crowd of 40,000 or more at Buckeye Lake, Ohio.[39] In late July, Simmons spoke to a crowd of some 15,000 in Racine, Wisconsin, boasting—no doubt with exaggeration—that the Klan now had five million members.[40]

In mid-August, Simmons continued to feed the ongoing dispute by publically inviting Edward Clarke to return to the Klan, offering him

---

[37] *State Times Advocate (Baton Rouge LA)*, 2 July 1923. Based on contemporary news reports, it is possible that the Klan may have already gone "international." In January 1923, two masked men in Ku Klux Klan garb with fiery crosses on their breasts tried to blow up the a vault in the Hawaii Territorial Treasurer's office, hoping to steal $750,000 in cash and $7,000,000 in negotiable securities. They were thwarted by an "aged" and unarmed night watchman. (*New York Times*, 14 January 1923.). Near Mexico City, English-speaking hold-up men in Klan regalia were waylaying and robbing motorists. Though bandits, they were said to "be genial and courteous." (*Columbus (GA) Enquirer-Sun*, 4 February 1923.) Again in Mexico City, the director of the *Excelsior* newspaper was kidnapped following the publication of a series of articles denying the Klan's existence in the country. He was released when he promised to publish an article admitting to a Mexican Klan. (*New York Times*, 28 August 1923.)

[38] *Evansville (IN) Courier and Press*, 5 July 1923. See also Coughlan, "Konklave (*sic*) in Kokomo" in Leighton (1949), 105-129.

[39] *Cleveland Plain Dealer*, 13 July 1923.

[40] *New Orleans Times-Picayune*, 30 July 1923.

"full and complete executive administrative authority over all matters pertaining to the Klan and Kamelia."[41] Clarke would assume the new titles of Sir Knight Supreme of the Order of Knights Kamelia, and Herald Supreme of the Kamelia women's order. Clarke was in Indiana at the time, dealing with the Muncie liquor possession charge and trying to recover the $500 that had allegedly gone missing with the suitcase containing the illegal whisky. It was unclear how, if at all, Simmons proposed to get Evans's agreement for Clarke's return. The *Macon Telegraph* opined in a sarcastic editorial that "it is comforting to the public to know now that the one who was despised and ousted is the only source of hope for the perpetuity of the organization."[42]

By early fall, the nation as well as the citizens of the Invisible Empire seemed to be tiring of the constant bickering between their alleged leaders. The proliferation of parallel "klans" such as the Kamelia orders was both confusing and distracting. A long-planned regional Kloncilium in Dallas in October with Imperial Wizard Evans as the featured speaker drew only about 75,000 Klansmen, a third or fewer of the 200,000 to 250,000 publically predicted to attend.[43] In Atlanta, the very public squabbling among Klan leaders was beginning to turn opinion against the order. While the Klan remained strong in the South, in the words of one reporter, Georgia was "no longer a 100% state."[44] And if there were some in the state who were still uncertain, the events of the last two months of the year would do much to influence their opinion toward the negative.

After a number of delays, hearings on the suit for control of the Klan filed by the Simmons-backed faction in late May got under way on October 29. The plaintiffs presented a number of affidavits documenting alleged malfeasance and financial mismanagement on the part of the Evans administration. Among them was clear evidence of a plot to discredit Edward Y. Clarke. There was worry that "the [Mann Act] case against Clarke in Texas had apparently fallen through." An attempt was

---

[41] *Tampa Tribune*, 19 August 1923.
[42] *Macon Telegraph*, 21 August 1923.
[43] *New York Times*, 25 October 1923.
[44] *New York Times*, 18 November 1923.

KLANSMEN!
KAMELIA!

And to the Lovers of America

COL. WILLIAM JOSEPH SIMMONS

Founder and Emperor
Knights of the Ku Klux Klan

El Magus, Kamelia, the Woman's Klan

will relate the birth and history of the Ku Klux Klan, the principles of Klankraft, the elevation of Klansmen into Knights Kamelia, (second order of Klankraft) and the Creation of the Kamelia, (the woman's Klan) at

NIMISILA PARK

JULY 31st, 1923, 8:00 P. M

Auspices Canton Kastle, Knights Kamelia
and
Canton Kourt of the Kamelia

ADMISSION FREE

Klansmen, Their Families, Their Friends,
and the Public are Cordially Invited.

In case of inclement weather notices will be posted at Park as to meeting place.

T. O. TUTTLE, Imperial Kourier

Much of the year 1923 was consumed by a power struggle for control of the Klan between Imperial Wizard Hiram Evans and Emperor W. J. Simmons. Having been pushed to the side, Simmons started a women's branch of the Klan, naming himself El Magus as leader. (*Canton Ohio Depository*, 31 July 1923.)

made to ensnare him in further legal difficulties, this time by having a woman sue him for breach of promise, alleging that he had seduced and then abandoned her. The woman, Mrs. Helen K. Steele, had been coached and paid more than a thousand dollars by Tom Akers, an employee of the publicity department of the Klan. After taking the money, she contacted W. J. Coburn, lead attorney for the plaintiffs, eventually revealing the entire plot to Simmons's faction.[45] This, and similar evidence presented at the hearings, indicated that Coburn and others were gathering information on individuals directly employed in the offices of the Imperial Palace.

On Thursday, November 1, Fulton County Superior Court Judge J. H. Humphries lifted the temporary injunction, handing defeat to the Simmons side. In making his decision, the judge remarked, "It seemed to be an inside fight by about 300 members against 1,500,000 other members." The plaintiffs vowed to take the case to the Georgia Supreme Court.[46] The following Monday morning, Coburn, acting on behalf of Simmons, filed another action asking the same court to enjoin Imperial Wizard Evans from organizing the Women of the Ku Klux Klan, alleging they "were using secrets of the Klan." This was basically the same argument Evans had used against Simmons's formation of the Knights Kamelia. A hearing date was set for both sides to present their arguments. Late that same afternoon, Philip E. Fox, the director of Klan publicity, shot and killed W. J. Coburn in his law offices on the ninth floor of the Atlanta Trust Company Building.

According to multiple witnesses, Fox arrived at Coburn's office at about 4:30PM stating that he needed to talk with him. Coburn was speaking with another client at the time and sent word for Fox to wait until he was free. Instead, Fox barged into Coburn's office, stood in front of his desk and fired five times at the lawyer with an automatic pistol. Four of the bullets struck Coburn, three in the head and one in his stomach. He died within minutes. Fox then hurled the pistol at Coburn's body and fled down the building's stairs to the floor below where he was captured by bystanders and held until the police arrived. Fox was quoted

[45] *Macon Telegraph*, 30 October 1923.
[46] *Charlotte Observer*, 2 November 1923.

as saying, "I am sorry to have had to do it, but I am glad he is dead. He was planning to ruin me and I had just as soon be hung as hurt." [47] As subsequent investigation and evidence presented at Fox's trial would reveal, the situation was far more complex than it might have first appeared. Were it not for chance, Fox might have succeeded in his plans to kill William J. Simmons a day earlier.

On the preceding day, November 4, Atlanta's weather had been overcast with intermittent light rain and temperatures in the mid-fifties. Around eight o'clock that evening, Fox took a taxi to Klankrest, the Peachtree Road home of Emperor William Simmons. Unknown to Fox at the time, Simmons was in Birmingham visiting his elderly mother who had been hospitalized following a fall. Fred Johnson, Simmons's chief of staff, was staying at Klankrest in the Emperor's absence, and spoke with Fox. Johnson noted that Fox was wearing an unusually heavy overcoat for the mild weather, and thought it strange that kept his right hand in the coat pocket during the initial conversation. Fox demanded to see Simmons. He stated he had broken with Evans's faction of the Klan and needed to see the Emperor "for the purpose of revealing some information."[48] Johnson, suspicious of Fox's purposes, backed him into a corner. After some conversation, Fox showed Johnson the .45 automatic pistol that he had been holding in his pocket and revealed that he "had been sent there" to kill Simmons, Johnson, and Edward Y. Clarke, but Johnson "had talked him out of it." Fox indicated that he was going to return to his former home in Dallas, Texas, shortly. The significance of the visit did not become clear until after Coburn's murder.

Fortyish and overweight, Fox was an experienced newspaper man, having been most recently employed as the managing editor of the *Dallas Times-Herald*. He was quite well educated, being a graduate of Harvard who had later studied at Oxford in England. Lured away by an increase in salary and the opportunity to become the Klan's publicity chief and editor of official publication, *The Imperial Night-hawk*, he had moved to Atlanta with his wife and eight year-old son in March 1923. Fox

---

[47] *Tampa Tribune*, 6 December 1923.
[48] Ibid.

apparently had done his job quietly and well, and prior to the murder had never drawn undue attention to himself.

Immediately after Fox's arrest he was taken to police headquarters for questioning. As the word of Coburn's murder spread, two Klan detectives contacted Dr. Lincoln S. Smith, an alienist,[49] asking him to go with them straightaway to see Fox "for the purpose of above all things to make [him] keep his mouth shut."[50] Fox initially refused to see Dr. Smith, but when he was told that Mrs. Fox had sent him, relented and met with him. Smith later testified that he had in fact never spoken with either Fox or his wife prior to that time; the alleged request had come through the Klan detectives. Within days a grand jury had indicted Fox on a charge of capital murder, punishable by death in the case of a conviction.

The trial began in Fulton County Superior Court on December 12. Contemporary reports would describe it as "one of the most dramatic and bitterly fought murder trials in Georgia criminal history, and the defense one of the most unique ever offered in Fulton Superior Court."[51] The defense team seemed to initially lean toward a plea of insanity, but as the details of the crime emerged, it became clear that meeting the narrow legal criteria for such a plea would be nearly impossible. With former Governor Hugh Dorsey acting as lead defense counsel, Fox's lawyers asked the jury to find him innocent because he was insane *at the time of the murder*, promising that if the accused were freed, his family would take him back to Texas and be certain that he received appropriate treatment for his condition. Solicitor John A. Boykin, head prosecutor, scoffed at the idea, alleging instead that Fox killed Coburn because he knew the lawyer had embarrassing information about him that was likely to become public in further court proceedings. Both sides tried to avoid the elephant in the room, the fact that a member of the inner circle of

---

[49] The contemporary word for psychiatrist.
[50] *Macon Telegraph*, 18 December 1923.
[51] *Atlanta Constitution*, 22 December 1923.

one faction of the Klan had actively plotted to kill the principals of the other faction, succeeding in one of four planned assassinations.[52]

For the next nine days, attorneys for both sides fought tenaciously in a courtroom jammed with reporters, curious attorneys and members of the public. The fact that Fox had murdered Coburn was admitted; the question was why. The defense called a long list of witnesses, including many from Fox's former home of Dallas, to testify as to his intermittent mental instability. Three well-qualified alienists, including the superintendent of the Georgia insane asylum in Milledgeville, described the accused as a "paranoiac, the most dangerous type of a madman," who heard the voice of God instructing him to kill Coburn, whom he supposedly had never met.[53] The prosecution presented an equally impressive roster of witnesses who testified that Fox had been a high-functioning, successful worker with no evidence of insanity. To rebut the allegation that Fox did not know Coburn, one witness testified the two men met in Coburn's office about a week before the murder. Coburn had shown Fox some papers he had in his possession, the nature of which was unknown.

The defense described Fox as a devoted family man, going so far as to have his wife sit with him at the defense table during most of the trial, with his young son present in the courtroom several days. Boykin, speaking for the state, presented evidence that Fox was a womanizer and sometimes a heavy drinker. During his few short months in Atlanta, he had several brushes with the law. On one occasion, Fox had been arrested in an intoxicated state with a "scantily clad woman" in a hotel room and charged with drunkenness and disorderly conduct.[54] In another incident, he was discovered in a room with a woman during a police raid on a house of ill repute. Throughout the damning testimony, Mrs. Fox sat quietly at her husband's side, often patting him on the hand. According to observers, Fox himself seemed to take little interest in the proceedings, quietly staring at the table through horn-rimmed glasses,

---

[52] The obvious connection was not lost on the press. For example, one headline read, "Klan Leader is Slain by Member of Rival Faction." (*Cobb County (GA) Times*, 8 November 1923.)

[53] *Atlanta Constitution*, 16 December 1923.

[54] *Atlanta Constitution*, 19 December 1923.

displaying a twitching of the mouth and an incessant tapping of his feet. The prosecution alleged it was all an act to make him appear "crazy."

As the testimony unfolded, the name of a Mrs. Margaret Weaver was often repeated. It emerged that she was the woman in the hotel room with Fox, and the gun used to shoot Coburn belonged to her. She had skipped town immediately after the Coburn killing. Investigators for the prosecution finally tracked her down in Nashville. After the abortive attempt on Simmons's life the night before Coburn was murdered, she "admitted that she told Fox, 'Why you big fat baby. You haven't got the nerve to kill anyone.' To which Fox is said to have replied, 'I'll show you.'" The next afternoon she accompanied him to Coburn's office, but left when he did not emerge from the building after the shooting. A grand jury indicted Weaver as an accessory-before-the-fact, but by the time an arrest warrant was issued, she had disappeared once again.

While the defense alleged the murder was committed during a temporary bout of insanity, the prosecution presented evidence that the Simmons faction had been gathering evidence on Klan officials in their quest to oust Evans. Someone had been watching Fox. "Instead of being a quiet peaceful man of unquestioned sobriety, as witnesses described him, the Klan official in reality led a life of vice and drunkenness."[55] Fox, perhaps egged on by Weaver, knew Coburn had evidence of his iniquity and killed him in hopes of halting its release. On Friday, December 21st, the case was turned over to the jury. After deliberating for nine hours, they found Fox guilty, but with a recommendation of mercy. Judge G. H. Howard sentenced Fox to life in prison. William Simmons had attended several days of the trial; Hiram Evans was said to be out of town.

The next day the "mystery woman," Mrs. Margaret Weaver, was arrested in Birmingham, Alabama, and extradited to Atlanta where she was held without bail. She declined to discuss her case with newspaper reporters and spent Christmas day in the Fulton County jail "reading a mystery novel."[56] Shortly thereafter, Solicitor Boykin announced "that he

---

[55] *Atlanta Constitution*, 15 December 1923.
[56] *Atlanta Constitution*, 25 December 1923.

was not altogether satisfied with the case against her,"[57] and was uncertain as to whether she would be prosecuted. She was soon released; the matter never came to trial.

The question of the Evans faction's role—if any—in Coburn's murder was never settled. Many believed that Fox was goaded into killing the attorney. Whether or not Margaret Weaver had any connection to other Klan members was never established. In 1925, while Evans was still Imperial Wizard, J. Q. Jett opined that Coburn "had the goods on the present gang in power and they had to kill him or go to the [chain] gang. So they killed him in cold blood."[58] In 1928, Steve Stephenson gave a deposition in which he stated Hiram Evans had confided to him that "he was filling [Phil Fox] full of 'poisoned meat,' elaborating on this statement so that I was given to understand that he was telling Fox that he, Evans, could prove that Coburn was circulating stories derogatory to the character of Mrs. Fox. Finally [Fox] became so incensed that he said he was going to kill Coburn."[59] At the time, both Jett and Stephenson had become bitter enemies of Imperial Wizard Evans. Their stories, presented as alleged disclosures of embarrassing information, must be viewed in that light when considering their veracity.

---

[57] *Richmond Times-Dispatch*, 26 December 1925, *Atlanta Constitution*, 26 December 1923.

[58] *Georgia Free Lance (Dublin GA)*, 12 November 1925.

[59] *Augusta Chronicle*, 3 April 1928.

Part VI

New Directions?

There were many evidences here of the change which has taken place in the last two years—even in the last year. The delegates were mostly pious, sincere, rather simple men, of no great worldly success, but certainly without paranoiac tendencies. There were fewer of the politician type than at previous gatherings, but about every fourth man was a doctor of divinity. The convention lacked the prosperous smugness of a Republican assembly, but also the restlessness and incoherence of a Democratic one or the gayety of most fraternal conclaves. It was solemn, quiet, apparently sincere. There was constant reference to the "spiritual vison" or the "religious purpose" of the Klan. There has been improvement, too, in the caliber and seeming sincerity of the leaders. Many of the old ones are gone; those that are left appear to have changed and grown to meet the responsibilities that have come to them.

Stanley Frost, Writing of the Ku Klux Klan's Second Imperial
Klonvocation in Kansas City, Missouri in September 1924
"The Klan Restates Its Case"
The Outlook Vol. 138, No. 7,
October 15, 1924, p. 244

Chapter 20

Thirty Pieces of Silver and Political Aspirations

In many ways, the constant struggle for control of the Ku Klux Klan in 1923, culminating with the sensational murder of W. J. Coburn and the trial of Philip Fox, accomplished what the *New York World's* exposé and the Congressional hearings of 1921 could not. While the Klan was still growing in membership and power, these events served to reinforce the belief that, despite its high rhetoric, it was an organization of men with malleable morals. Many sought to crush the order, perceiving it as a threat to American democracy. Others, including current and former insiders, sought to salvage it through reformation. Edward Y. Clarke, now an outsider while still technically a Klan member, appeared to be one of these.

A few days after the Fox trial ended, Clarke sent an open letter to President Calvin Coolidge proclaiming "the Klan as now operated a real menace to law and order, individual rights and liberties and democratic political government." Continuing, he wrote, "I have received from widely scattered sections of the country direct and authoritative information that the Klan is rapidly developing nationally as a cheap political machine, a regulatory law and order league, and, in sections where it is strongest, brazenly and openly superseding the authority of the courts, and through character assassination, intimidation, and actual physical violence depriving American citizens of their constitutional rights without due process of law or a trial before a jury of their peers."[1]

Milton Elrod, spokesman for the Klan, replied dismissively that "Clarke had been trying to destroy the order for months," noting that membership had grown at the rate of 70,000 per week during the preceding month.[2] The clear implication was that the old order was dead,

---

[1] *New York Times*, 28 December 1923.
[2] Ibid.

and the new order ascendant—at least as measured by membership numbers. In response, Clarke called for a national meeting of the Klan to be held in Atlanta on February 26, 1924. It was to be a call for change: Either follow "the example of the founder of the original Ku Klux Klan" or disband altogether.[3] Unknown to Clarke at the moment, change was underway, but not in a direction that would have pleased him.

Only days later the Imperial Palace announced that both W. J. Simmons and E. Y. Clarke "had been expelled from the Klan for their opposition" to Imperial Wizard Hiram Evans.[4] Clarke's letter to President Coolidge in particular was cited as an act of "treason."[5] Clarke responded by calling the banishments a desperate attempt by Evans to hold on to power. Simmons called the action "unwarranted, illegal and beyond [Evans's] power," reverting to Biblical analogy by stating, "The fact is evident that while they are attempting to crucify me, it is for no other purpose than to procure opportunity under the fiery cross to cast lots for my garments and revel in the spoils."[6]

For much of the preceding year, Klansmen across the Invisible Empire had been divided in their loyalty. In Atlanta, the Nathan B. Forrest Klan No. 1 had become Simmons's most loyal supporter, going so far as to withhold payment of dues to the Evans-controlled Imperial Palace since July 1923. In addition to expelling the Emperor and Imperial Giant, a Klan spokesman announced that the Palace was revoking the No. 1's charter with plans to reorganize it under new leadership. Henry J. Norton, the Klavern's Exalted Cyclops, called on fellow members to support W. J. Simmons "as the only authorized legal officer…and not be deceived by a few employees of the present administration."

On February 12, announcements from both W. J. Simmons and H. W. Evans confirmed that in exchange for a payment of $145,500 in cash, Simmons had resigned as Emperor and as a Klansman, and in the process, deeded all of his copyrights, royalties, and other interests in the

---

[3] *Miami (FL) Herald*, 3 January 1924.
[4] *Greensboro (NC) Record*, 11 January 1924.
[5] *New York Times*, 12 January 1924.
[6] *Augusta Chronicle*, 15 January 1924. Simmons once again makes reference to the words of Jesus on the cross, paraphrasing Luke 23, Verse 34 (KJV).

Invisible Empire to the Knights of the Ku Klux Klan, Inc.[7] Simmons gave up his previously-granted $1,000 per month annuity, but was allowed to keep Klankrest, his home on Atlanta's Peachtree Street. As a condition of accepting the payment, Simmons "agreed to cease all opposition to the Ku Klux Klan and the regime of Dr. Hiram W. Evans and pledged himself not to participate in any movement or organization, the purpose of which is to disorganize, disrupt or in any way interfere with or cause dissatisfaction among members of the Klan."[8] In a bit of gloating, a Klan spokesman declared that Edward Y. Clarke had been left "high and dry, completely out of the organization."[9]

Two days after the signing of the agreement between Simmons and Evans, Simmons announced the formation of the Knights of the Flaming Sword, to be headquartered in Jacksonville, Florida. The order's initial membership was drawn from the ranks of dissatisfied Klansmen. Klan officials at the Imperial Palace were said to be "astounded."[10] Within weeks, the Klan's attorney, Paul Etheridge, announced that Simmons's formation of a new fraternal order was in violation of his buyout agreement and that he intended to enjoin Simmons use of Klankrest as home. Simmons replied that he "had taken up his residence in another portion of the city," effectively abandoning Klankrest.[11]

The reaction to Simmons's sellout was immediate and bitter. Henry J. Norton announced the secession of the Nathan B. Forrest Klan No. 1, stating that it would operate for the time being as the Mystic Castle, "an independent patriotic organization." In doing so, he denounced Simmons's withdrawal from "this great campaign," noting "the tragedy of

---

[7] The amount was determined by actuaries who calculated the monthly $1,000 benefit to be worth $96,000 and Simmons's ownership of rights for the Knights Kamelia to be worth $50,000 (*New York Times*, 13 February 1924). One presumes that the "missing" $500 payment was due to the agreement being signed at mid-month. Although news reports referred to the payment of $145,500 "in cash," Simmons apparently received only $90,000, all of which he used to start his new order, The Knights of the Flaming Sword. The details of this discrepancy are given in Chapter 24.

[8] *Columbus (GA) Enquirer-Sun*, 13 February 1924.
[9] *New Orleans Times-Picayune*, 13 February 1924.
[10] *Columbus (GA) Enquirer-Sun*, 13 February 1924.
[11] *Columbus (GA)Enquirer-Sun*, 26 March 1924.

it lies in the fact that he did it for money. No man in the nation now, who is both honest and informed, can follow him further. He will attempt to explain, but the whole story is told in these few words: He sold everything on earth he had, even his friends, for a small sum of money."[12] The Knights Kamelia expressed less sorrow; they simply "outlawed" Simmons and sued him for the sum of $25,000, alleging breach of contract.[13]

The conference of disgruntled and banished Klansmen called by Edward Y. Clarke met as scheduled in Atlanta on February 26. Roundly bashing both Simmons and Evans, the attendees voted on the first day to withdraw from any Ku Klux Klan affiliation and form a new order to be called the Knights of the Mystic Clan. The nucleus of the new organization would be formed by members of Atlanta's Klan No. 1 and the Knights Kamelia. Its principles would be basically the same as those of the Klan, but masks would be banned. Clarke spoke to the assembled group of the need for reformation and renewal, but refused to accept any position in the new order. Both the secession of the Nathan B. Forrest Klan No. 1 and the Knights of the Mystic Clan would be short-lived. Within months, the Klavern was reorganized under new leadership loyal to Hiram Evans, attracting back many of the former rebels.[14] The Mystic Clan, like many other secret fraternal orders of the day, rapidly faded into obscurity.[15]

The one ray of sunshine in this storm of troubles seemed for a brief moment to shine on Edward Y. Clarke. In early March, he surprised the Federal Court in Houston by pleading guilty to the outstanding charge of violating the Mann Act. His trial had been postponed twice, and it was assumed that he would carry out his pledge to fight the charges

---

[12] *Atlanta Constitution*, 18 February 1924.

[13] *Atlanta Constitution*, 22 February 1924, *New York Times*, 25 February 1924.

[14] Jackson, K. T., 40-41

[15] In an interesting side note, in May 1924, Wilmington, NC, police arrested Elder H. Johnson, a Mystic Clan recruiter, charging him with false pretense. H. F. Newwirk alleged that he paid Johnson a $10 initiation fee "under the impression that he was joining the original Ku Klux Klan and that he afterwards learned that the old Klan disowned the 'Mystics' and that they were not connected with the K.K.K." (*Greensboro (NC) Daily News*, 16 May 1924.)

against him. His attorney pled for leniency, "dwelling on Clarke's change of mind and his reformation." The judge, evidently both curious as well as suspicious, placed Clarke on the stand and questioned him under oath. In a lengthy and detailed examination, Clarke admitted that he and Imperial Wizard Simmons had visited "a house of ill repute" while attending a Confederate reunion in Houston. "At that time you were propagating ideals of purity, protection of virtue and so forth, weren't you?" the court asked. Clarke replied, "At that particular time I was not propagating any principles." After a stern lecture and the warning that he could imprison him for his admitted crimes, the judge freed Clarke with a $5,000 fine, which Clarke paid with funds borrowed against his two automobiles and his diamond ring. The government's "woman chief witness," presumably the "fallen woman" Louise Martin, was present in the court room during Clarke's testimony. A local reporter noted, "A smile was on her face throughout the proceedings."[6]

In early 1924, both as a result of the Klan's growing political aspirations and the negative publicity generated by the Coburn murder, Imperial Wizard Evans and his family quietly moved to Washington, DC, taking with them the Bureaus of Information, Education, and Publication, as well as the Department of Extension. Rumors of the move made headlines in the same accounts that announced the expulsion of Simmons and Clarke from the Klan. While the Klan hierarchy continued to insist that the order's headquarters remained firmly rooted in Atlanta, the empiric truth was that key management personnel and their staff now resided in the nation's capital. Evans justified these moves by alleging they were "forced by the exigencies of situations—there has never been a pre-arranged plan to take the Klan into politics."[17] Subsequent events would lead observers to doubt this statement. As W. J. Simmons would comment a few years later, "Within a few weeks [of the murder], Evans and his whole crowd cleaned out and moved to Washington."[18] Evans himself, speaking in the royal third person,

---

[16] *Dallas Morning News*, 11 March 1924. In April 1924, the Indiana charges of violation of federal Prohibition laws were dropped, solving for the moment most of Clarke's legal difficulties.

[17] Ibid.

[18] Shepherd, "The Fiery Double-Cross," 48.

phrased it a bit more subtly: "The situation made it necessary for the Wizard to spend much of his time in Washington, in order to be in close and first-hand touch with events."[19]

In the midst of the power struggle for control of the Klan that consumed much of 1923, Imperial Wizard Evans had been quietly restructuring the order. Many of his decisions, interpreted by Simmons, Clarke, and others as efforts to destroy the Klan's true purpose were in fact designed to create an efficient, national organization. There is little doubt that the criticism of Simmons as a hapless dreamer with poor management skills, or of Clarke as a money-driven marketing genius, were true. Under their control the order had been run in a seat-of-one's-pants management style, an uncontrolled push for expansion (and the income it generated) with few, if any, *practical* long-term goals. If the Klan was to see its avowed dream of a white-dominated, Protestant Christian-oriented America become a reality, it was necessary to move into the realm of politics. Issues such as the control of immigration, the suppression of the influence of the Catholic Church, the promotion of public (as opposed to parochial) schools, the enforcement of prohibition and similar divisive moral issues could most efficiently be achieved through legislative action on local, state, and national levels. Even as he consolidated his power, Evans was quick to point out, "The Klan is not in politics," while maintaining—paradoxically—"It is clear that the Klan programme must result in political action and can be carried out in no other way."[20] The movement of the Klan's major departments to Washington, DC, was in pursuit of this goal.

Both within and without the order, there were hopes and fears as to the eventual outcome. In one of a series of articles on the Klan published in early 1924, journalist Stanley Frost wrote,

> The upcoming National election, unless very carefully laid plans of the Ku Klux leaders miscarry, will make the Klan masters of Washington, with all that implies both in our Government and our National life. The hooded order expects to rule America, not only by controlling thousands

---

[19] Knights of the Ku Klux Klan, Inc., *Proceedings of the Second Imperial Klonvokation*, 65.

[20] Frost, "When the Klan Rules: The Plan to Capture Washington," 350.

of local governments, but from the very top down, by controlling the National Government. It expects, as a result of the coming election, to have in Congress a clear majority of members in both houses who are in sympathy with its aims or at least willing to vote for its programme, and in the White House a President, who will at the very least put no obstacle in the way of the Klan demands, and appoint to office no man the Klan disapproves, and who may actually be a member and a willing servant in the organization![21]

To Frost, and others, the Klan's agenda under Imperial Wizard Hiram Evans was clear.

With Simmons, Clarke, and their supporters no longer a major distraction, Evans was able to continue and focus on the reforms he had begun when he took control of the Klan. The order's basic mantra remained the same, but the message softened. Vigilante and extra-legal enforcement activity began to wane, replaced instead by "practical Klankraft," the implementation of the order's philosophy in the daily life of Klansmen: Rather than actively seek to harm or expel those whose religion or ethnicity differed, simply refuse to deal with them in business or politics. Do not attempt to impede the right of a Catholic to practice his or her religion, but make it clear that in matters of public life and policy, the tenants of that religion are basically anti-American. Assist lawmen in their enforcement of the law rather than administering extra-legal justice.

In some respects, changes in the Klan under Evans were less related to changes in philosophy than to the evolution of the order and its membership. In the early days, the Klan's growth was most prominent in the South and Southwest, a more rural region of mixed ethnicity bearing a historic association with lynching and vigilante action. As the Invisible Empire spread to the mid-West and North, the demographic of Klansmen changed. In states such as Ohio and Indiana, for example, the population was more homogenous, both ethnically and religiously. In Illinois and Michigan, the Klan recruited well in rural areas, but its strength in terms of numbers lay in the cities. To be sure, Klan continued

---

[21] Ibid.

to promote direct involvement, but in its new domains, this was often deemed best accomplished through the ballot box.

It is difficult to determine the overall political philosophy of those who were members of or supported the Ku Klux Klan in the early 1920s, though some did try. During the first third of 1924, *The Outlook*, a magazine of news and commentary, distributed ballots for its recurring survey, titled Platforms of the People. The idea was to determine where the average voter stood politically in view of the upcoming elections. In what would certainly be considered an unscientific poll by modern standards, *The Outlook* believed it could identify ballots mailed to individuals likely to be Klansmen (or their families). Some 10,000 were distributed to "a class of native-born, white, Gentile, Protestant Americans" in towns and small cities of New Jersey and Pennsylvania. The response was poor, only about 11%, but the results were most interesting. Surprisingly, the majority identified themselves as Independents, followed closely in numbers by Republicans. Fewer than 10% of respondents listed themselves as Democrats. Socially and economically, the respondents spanned the spectrum, but the majority came from "the less prosperous and less literate classes." Philosophically, their views varied widely on many political questions of the day, but were uniform in several specific areas. On average, more than 90% agreed on Federal support of education, a clear rejection of religiously-funded schools. Even greater numbers believed that foreign immigration should be further restricted, prospective immigrants screened at points of departure for the United States, and all alien immigrants registered on arrival. There was limited support for Prohibition, but many ignored the question, a direct conflict with stated Klan philosophy. "The Programme of the Klan" garnered strong support, nearly 100% from those listing themselves as Democrats or Independents, as well as more than four-fifths of self-identified Republicans. On numerous other issues, ranging from foreign relations to monetary policy to agriculture and taxation, responses varied widely, and in many cases were ignored on the ballot forms.

Despite its limitations, *The Outlook's* survey demonstrated that while many Klansmen or likely Klan supporters agreed on some key issues, on many others their opinions varied widely. This did not bode well for the

Klan's political future. Some races would be decided by votes based on issues central to the organization, but many would hinge on other concerns. This weakness in political calculation would become evident in the months that followed. While many Klansmen, their families, and others may have supported the order's agenda, votes were cast based on a variety of concerns, of which that may have been only one.

Perhaps the strongest political tool of the Klan was its secret nature. The Klan's presence in a given area was generally a known fact, but its membership numbers and rolls were guarded and unknown. As had been more than adequately demonstrated, Klan leaders were given to hyperbole and exaggeration when it came to the subject of membership. In contested elections, a matter of a few votes on one side or the other could spell a win or a loss for a candidate. Such a candidate approached by a trade unionist seeking support, for example, might be able to weigh the potential benefits or risks of endorsing a particular position based on the estimated voting strength of the persons the unionist represented. If the number of voters was small and the position risky, he could disavow it. With the Klan, on the other hand, no such calculus was possible. The mere name, "Invisible Empire," and the slogan, "We were here yesterday, we are here today, and we will be here tomorrow," was sufficient to raise uncertainty in terms of votes controlled or influenced by the order. In many cases, those aspiring to office deemed it better to be safe than sorry when it came to Klan-related issues. Either endorse the Klan (or at the least, its positions), or not oppose them with any degree of vigor.

As to political affiliation, the Klan was neither Republican nor Democrat. Ignoring the traditional Republican strength in the North and the Democratic strength in the South, the Klan eschewed party labels, preferring instead to give endorsement to candidates willing to support it regardless of political affiliation. In situations where the outcome of electoral contests was difficult to predict, the Klan would back candidates from both parties, or multiple candidates vying for nomination or election within a single party. While many Klan-backed candidates had done well in the 1922 elections, their success was more likely a reflection of local factors, not national strategy. In the two short years that had elapsed, the Ku Klux Klan had fully emerged as a force to be considered on the national scene. The need for a coherent and cohesive national political strategy would naturally follow.

One of the first major tests of the Klan's new political strategy came with the Indiana Republican primaries held in early May 1924. By that time, Steve Stephenson, to whom the Klan owed its strength in the state, had fallen out with Imperial Wizard Evans, resigning his office of Grand Dragon in the fall of 1923 but remaining influential in Klan affairs. In the spring of 1924, Evans brought in Walter Bossert, at the time head of the Klan's Propagation Department, to lead the Indiana Klan and guide its election strategy in the state. Bossert was a native Indianan, a lawyer by trade, and a "seasoned political strategist." Although there were Klan-backed candidates in the Democratic primaries, the order "elected to make its main drive for power though the Republican Party," considered at the time most likely to win in the November elections.[22] As one Klan insider confided to a journalist at the time, "[Indiana] is the best state in the union for trying out a new political idea. If we can get away with it here, we're all set to go."[23]

While the Klan may have initially sought to work behind the scenes, its early endorsement of several candidates in the Republican primary put those receiving its support squarely in the spotlight. The Klan's central theme was one of cleaning up government, the enforcement of existing laws, and the suppression of immorality. A card distributed to potential voters during the campaign read as follows:

REMEMBER

Every criminal, every gambler, every thug, every libertine, every girl ruiner, every home wrecker, every wife beater, every dope peddler, every moonshiner, every crooked politician, every pagan papal priest, every shyster lawyer, every K. of C., every white slaver, every brothel madam, every Rome-controlled newspaper, every black spider is fighting the Klan. Think it over. Which side are you on?[24]

---

[22] Frost, "The Klan Shows Its Hand in Indiana," 188.
[23] Ibid., 187
[24] Ibid.

Most of Indiana's Klan-backed candidates would go on to win in the fall election. In the end, the "Klan victory was as unexpected as it was complete." It was, in the words, of journalist Stanley Frost, "little less than a political miracle."[25] Frost described Bossert's campaign as "the most effective political organization the country has ever seen." At the same time he went on to observe "that the Klan is in danger of defeat whenever it comes into the open, and of disruption whenever it becomes tied to any party. Its power lies in its invisibility and its impartiality."[26]

With the stunning victory, Evans and his advisors set their sights on the next challenge, the November 1924 Presidential election. It was presumed that the incumbent president, Calvin Coolidge would be the Republican nominee to be pitted against an as yet-to-be-decided Democratic candidate. The opportunity lay with the Democratic Party which was strongest in the South, broadly overlapping the areas of the Ku Klux Klan's strength. Klan leaders themselves were for the most part Democrats. The Klan's aspirations were twofold: First, a party platform that endorsed the Klan by name, or barring this, a platform that mirrored the Klan's stated philosophy. Second, the nomination of a presidential candidate willing to openly accept the backing of the Klan with its social and political agenda.

The Republican National Convention was a brief and perfunctory affair, held from June 10th through 12th in Cleveland, Ohio. The platform committee struggled with a statement regarding the Klan, eventually deciding instead to call vaguely for "orderly government" and "improvement of naturalization laws." Failure to mention the Klan directly was considered the safest position for confronting an electorate with unknown allegiances. Coolidge was nominated as expected, reasonably confident of his reelection based on the then-booming economy.

The Democratic National Convention opened June 24, at Madison Square Garden in New York City. There was the usual hustle and bustle, including the concern that the local bootleggers would raise the price of

---

[25] Ibid., 187.
[26] Ibid., 190.

illegal liquor because of the strong demand created by the delegates.[27] In sharp contrast to the sedate Republican event, the convention would turn out to be a raucous and contentious affair, often described by reporters of the day in words usually reserved for descriptions of zoos, circus events, or street riots. It would set several records, including the dubious distinctions of being the longest continuously running political convention in American history, and as requiring the most ballots—103—to nominate a presidential candidate. Both of these were the direct result of the involvement of the Ku Klux Klan in the political process.

On the surface, it may have initially appeared that the Klan held a position of strength within the ranks of the 1,098 convention delegates. By some estimates, as many as a third of them were citizens of the Invisible Empire. The South, the traditional bastion of strength for both the Democratic Party and the Klan, might have been expected to give unswerving support to the Klan's agenda. But times and circumstances were changing. The Alabama delegation was led by Oscar Underwood, one of the state's United States Senators and long-time opponent of both the Klan and Prohibition. The strength of the party in the North had grown as well; at the start of the convention Alfred E. ("Al") Smith, New York's sitting governor, was considered to be the leading candidate for nomination.

The first major battle was over the wording of the Democratic platform. The party's fifty-four member Platform Committee had little trouble reaching consensus on the vast majority of issues. Only in two areas was there some dissention: the party's position on the League of Nations, and how to respond to the growing influence of the Ku Klux Klan. On the former issue, the differences were minor and easily resolved by a long-worded and equivocal statement of position on the League. The Klan was another matter. There was no major dispute among committee members in affirming the principles of American democracy, specifically freedom of speech, freedom of religion, the right to exercise one's political rights, and the notion that these rights extended to all, regardless of religion, race, or ethnicity. The problem arose in whether or

---

[27] They did not, reportedly in deference to the anti-Volstead "wets" among the party.

not the Ku Klux Klan, with its stated religious, racial, and ethnic biases, should be condemned by name. After much discussion, the Platform Committee submitted two versions of this platform plank under the heading of "Personal Freedom." The Majority Plank, written by Democratic grandee William Jennings Bryan, supported these rights but failed to condemn the Klan by name. The Minority Plank, endorsed by fourteen of the committee's members, specifically stated, "We pledge the Democratic Party to oppose any effort on the part of the Ku Klux Klan or any organization to interfere with the religious liberty or political freedom of any citizens, or to limit the civil rights of any citizen or body of citizens because of religion, birthplace, or racial origin."[28]

The debate and vote on the platform by the whole convention began on Saturday, June 28. It produced "some of the most disorderly scenes in convention history," so much so as to require "a heavy police guard," on the floor of the auditorium. Many of the delegates were armed, or so one man told Stanley Frost. To test this hypothesis, Frost wrote, "I tried the experiment of moving through the crowds in the lobbies and feeling for pistols, taking pains, of course, not to be misled by bottles. In one hotel lobby I found that one man in three was armed, in another it was three in five, and in the hotel where the faction of the friend who made the remark was staying, I found a weapon on every other man I got a chance to touch."[29]

The potential for violence was well recognized by the party leaders. For the three o'clock session that would address the Klan plank, "the hall was encircled by bluecoats standing shoulder-to-shoulder." The topic was opened by "a two-hour old-time convention debate" ending in a speech by William Jennings Bryan in support of the majority plank. The party, he said, was uniform in its thinking and should not be divided by "three little words," his euphemism for "Ku Klux Klan." His address and those that followed were frequently interrupted from both the convention floor and spectator galleries by exuberant applause, or loud boos and hisses, the nature of the expressions reflecting the wide division on the issue.

---

[28] *New Orleans Times-Picayune*, 29 June 1924.
[29] Frost, "The Klan's ½ of 1 per cent Victory," 385.

The presentation and defense of the Minority Plank followed, again eliciting an equally intense response.

After more than five hours of contentious debate, a roll-call vote was called shortly before two o'clock on Sunday morning. The count was almost equally divided: 542 and 3/20 votes against the plank naming the Klan, versus 541 and 3/20 votes in favor. It was a hollow victory for the Klan; a spokesman noted they "had won by a nose a victory of doubtful proportions."[30] Only the most politically naïve would fail to recognize the unspoken condemnation of the order. Several delegates went so far as to predict the imminent death of the Klan.[31] Humorist Will Rogers, who at the time was writing a nationally syndicated column, commented with a bit of irony, "They have been five days working on a plank on the Ku Klux Klan and finally brought in the same one the Republicans used."[32]

The next order of business was the nomination of a presidential candidate. Here the choice should have been easier. Al Smith, the nominal front-runner as the convention opened, stood for everything the Klan was against. He was Catholic, an opponent of Prohibition, and the governor of urban "Jew York," as some Klan members described his home state. Of Italian, German, and Irish descent, his power base lay in the support of "hyphenated"[33] Americans, another target of Klan disdain. The other leading contender was William Gibbs McAdoo, a sixty-one-year-old lawyer and former Secretary of the Treasury under President Woodrow Wilson.[34] Born in Georgia, McAdoo had been raised in Tennessee before entering the world of business and politics. He was rumored to be willing to work with the Klan, and in contrast to Smith, refused to condemn the order prior to the convention. There were more than a dozen other potential contenders for the candidacy, perhaps the

---

[30] *New York Times*, 30 June 1924.

[31] Ibid.

[32] *New York Times*, 29 June 1924.

[33] "Hyphenated Americans" was a favorite derogatory term used by Hiram W. Evans to describe recent immigrants, e.g., Italian-Americans, Irish-Americans, and the like.

[34] McAdoo was also President Wilson's son-in-law, having married the President's daughter in 1914 after the death of McAdoo's first wife. The couple divorced in 1935. Two months later the 71 year-old married Doris Isabel Cross, a 26 year-old nurse.

most prominent of whom was Alabama Senator Oscar Underwood, one of the leaders of the anti-Klan forces.

Balloting for the candidates began on June 30. The first few ballots placed McAdoo at the top, followed by Smith, but with the vote diluted by various "favorite son" candidates with no realistic chance of winning. By the fifteenth ballot, the trio of McAdoo, Smith, and John W. Davis emerged as frontrunners in that order. Davis, a relative unknown, was the former United States Solicitor General and later Ambassador to Great Britain. He was a conservative, but was rumored to side with the "wets" in his views on Prohibition. Day after day the balloting dragged on. The delegates squabbled amongst themselves in search of votes as no candidate seemed capable of achieving a majority. By the seventy-seventh ballot, the order of McAdoo, Smith, and Davis remained unchanged. By the eighty-seventh ballot, Smith had moved to the top, with McAdoo and Davis in second and third place, respectively. On the one-hundredth ballot, McAdoo slipped to third place, raising Davis to second. In frustration, both McAdoo and Smith released their delegates on July 9, giving the nomination to John W. Davis, a little known, dark-horse choice. In a post-convention analysis, Stanley Frost noted, "It is generally admitted privately, even by the Democratic leaders, that Davis is a poor candidate, no matter how good a President he would make."[35]

Within a matter of weeks, Democratic Candidate Davis had condemned the Klan from the campaign trail, stating, "If any organization, no matter what it chooses to be called, whether Ku Klux Klan or by any other name, raises the standard of racial and religious prejudice or attempts to make racial origins or religious beliefs the test of fitness for public office, it does violence to the spirit of American institutions and must be condemned by all those who believe, as I do, in American ideals."[36] The next day, the Republican Vice-presidential candidate, Charles Dawes, echoed Davis's sentiments, agreeing that the Ku Klux Klan "has no proper part in this or any other campaign."[37] In

---

[35] Frost, "Nomination by Exhaustion: Political Side-Lights on Democratic Strategy," 465.

[36] *The Outlook*, "The Klan as an Issue," 5.

[37] Ibid., 5-6.

the November elections, Davis would suffer an overwhelming defeat, polling only 28.8% of the popular vote and carrying only 12 of the 48 states.[38]

Although the Klan remained quite strong politically and did well otherwise in state and local elections in the fall of 1924, its image had been damaged by the divisiveness its supporters caused at the Democratic Convention. By early fall, some were beginning to predict the end of the Klan. An editorial in *The Outlook* opined, "The Klan…has not yet run its course, but one does not have to be the seventh son of a seventh son to find definite proof that the period of disintegration has set in and that its power both for evil and for good is slipping from its grasp."[39] Others, especially Imperial Wizard Hiram Evans, saw these perceived setbacks as mere bumps on the road to success, experiences from which to learn and grow. This outlook would be the dominant theme at another important 1924 convention, the Klan's Second Imperial Klonvocation held in Kansas City, Missouri.

---

[38] The winner, Coolidge, carried 35 of the 48 states while garnering 54.0% of the popular vote. The Progressive Party candidate, Robert M. LaFollette carried 1 state and received 16.6% of the popular vote.

[39] *The Outlook*, "The Rise and Fall of the Ku Klux Klan," 237.

Chapter 21

Apogee

The Second Imperial Klonvocation was held in Kansas City, Missouri, in September 1924, two and a half months after the disastrous Democratic National Convention. It was designed to be, as much as anything else, a display of the new public face of the Klan under Imperial Wizard Hiram Evans. As history would judge it, however, the event likely represented the high point in the existence of the Knights of the Ku Klux Klan, Inc.

There had been, of course, the First Imperial Klonvocation, held some twenty-two months earlier in Atlanta. It was brainchild of former Wizard and Emperor William Simmons, nominally timed to celebrate the seventh anniversary of the founding of the order, but more accurately to acknowledge the Klan's astounding success and growth in the face of determined foes. Those proceedings took on the air of a county fair *cum* tent revival, shielded by armed sentries from the prying eyes of the press and public, an emotional expression of self-defined American patriotism, evangelical Protestant Christianity, anti-foreign bias, and racial and religious bigotry. There were threatened killings, and a coup that toppled the old leadership and ushered in the new. In sharp contrast, its successor in Kansas City had all the verve and unpredictability one might expect from a national convention of actuaries.

With the Kansas City Klonvocation, the image the Klan sought to portray was one of respectability, that of a serious order with determined leaders and a legitimate American agenda. The mask was still part of the uniform, but the veil had been lifted. Klan officials registered under their own names in hotels and were accessible to reporters for interviews and commentary. There was a press bureau; reporters were even allowed on the floor of the convention hall during the last day of the proceedings as delegates were warned by their leaders that the "national press" was watching. The Klonvocation's program appeared equally divided between inspirational rhetoric and mind-numbing departmental and committee reports.

In no small part, one purpose of the well-ordered and businesslike program was to offset the impression left by the Klan's political antics at the Democratic National Convention earlier in the summer. There, the Klan became an obstructionist force, in the end costing the Democratic Party millions of dollars while weakening its chances for success in the upcoming November elections. In Kansas City, the Klan "presented a fairly definite and logical—although highly controversial—basis for its existence and purposes, claimed leadership in solving the present confusion and perplexities of thought, and made an open bid for the support of all people of 'American minds.'"[1]

The Klonvocation formally opened on Tuesday afternoon, September 23, with the singing of "America" followed by the formal entry of the Imperial Wizard and his Kloncilium. As the dignitaries made their way to the podium, throngs of Klansmen stood in silence, their left arms raised in the Klan salute.[2] The procession was followed by the singing of "Onward Christian Soldiers," then a prayer in which Imperial Wizard Evans's journey of leadership was compared to that of the two travelers on the Road to Emmaus.[3] This was followed by a lengthy "devotional" in which the speaker declared the Klan's Fiery Cross was in fact the cross of Jesus Christ. The mission of Christ, who was sent to save world, was similar to that of the Klan which had been ordained with the holy purpose of saving America. After yet another prayer, the Klonvocation moved to lighter fare, entertainment from several barbershop quartets and the group singing of a welcome to Imperial

---

[1] *The Outlook* , "The Klan Restates Its Case," 244.

[2] The Klan salute is best described as the left-handed equivalent of the so-called "Nazi salute." *See the Chapter Notes for further information and explanation of this gesture.*

[3] According to the Gospel of Luke, on the day of his Resurrection, Jesus appears to two of his disciples walking on the road to Emmaus. They do not at first recognize him but he later reveals himself, proving that he indeed lives. Later that day, Jesus appears to an assembled group of disciples, instructing them "that repentance and remission of sins should be preached in his name among all nations." The implication as to the Klan's propagation is obvious.

Wizard Evans: "How do you do?—Hello, Hiram—How do you do?" to the tune of the kindergarten ditty, "If You're Happy and You Know It, Clap Your Hands."

After a brief welcome to town by a prominent Klansman of Kansas City, the program moved on to the keynote address, titled "Americanism Applied." The Klonvocation at this time was still closed to reporters, but the Klan press office released excerpts from the speech, noting that it was delivered by the "governor of a great state." The failure to give the speaker's name might have seemed strange to some, but the Klan was known for its secrecy. The significance of this omission and its ramifications would become clear later.

The refined philosophy of the Klan under the leadership of Hiram W. Evans was detailed in a series of three addresses delivered to the delegates by the Imperial Wizard himself. Evans began, "I greet you, the Imperial Klonvocation, representing the millions of native-born, white, Gentile, Protestant citizens who have united under the banner of the Knights of the Ku Klux Klan for the protection of our nation and our race. You have assembled here at a time of great crisis. Events of overwhelming importance are waiting in the womb of history. The future of America, and of the white race, hangs in the balance."[4] The first discourse, "The Klan of Yesterday and of Today," outlined Evans's interpretation of the Klan's philosophy and the progress that had been made since he assumed power in late 1922. The second, "The Klan of Tomorrow," spoke of the challenges that faced the order in its drive for "true Americanism," especially the threat of non-Aryan "mongrel peoples," and "hyphenated" Americans. The third, "The Klan Spiritual," compared the Klan's quest to the ministry of Jesus.

Referring to the Klan as "the sole remaining hope," the Wizard outlined the struggles the Klan had endured, and how the purging of Simmons and Clarke had strengthened it. In what was perhaps an unconscious reprise of Simmons's testimony before Congress in October 1921, Evans stated "The Klan has not been alone in suffering under betrayal. American Independence had its Benedict Arnold, and even

---

[4] Knights of the Ku Klux Klan, Inc., *Proceedings of the Second Imperial Klonvokation*, 54.

Jesus Christ had His Judas."[5] Evans touted the progress his administration had made: the inauguration of a the K-Duo (a second, higher order of membership), the formation of the Women of the Ku Klux Klan, the establishment of the Junior Ku Klux Klan (open to boys between ages twelve and eighteen), and the establishment of the Empire Mutual Life Insurance Company, all of which represented new sources of income.[6] The all-important role of recruiting new members had been brought in-house. The Propagation Department ceased to exist after Clarke's firing, and a new Klan-controlled Extension Department was created, vastly increasing Klan income. New attention was given to the type of men chosen as Kleagles, deemphasizing the commission-based recruitment system. A National Lecture Bureau had been established to ensure uniformity of the Klan's message (and implicitly to avoid embarrassments like those caused by the former Imperial Kludd, the Reverend Caleb Ridley.

Clearly defining the Klan's new image under his rule, Evans stated: "The idea that the Klan is a social organization has been eliminated. There have been hundreds of so-called Klans organized for social purposes—dancing, cards, and what-not; they have either vanished or been reconstructed into real Klans. It is now well-established in the Klan mind the country over that the Klan is a militant, purposeful, patriotic organization—this, and nothing else."[7]

Between the prayers, inspirational speeches, and the occasional entertainment from various men's choral groups, the departmental and committee reports painted a vivid picture of the Klan of 1924.

---

[5] Ibid., 61.

[6] Like the Prudential Insurance Company whose symbol is the Rock of Gibraltar, Empire Mutual's symbol was Atlanta's Stone Mountain. Current ads of the day depicted a robed and hooded Klansman, backed by a fiery cross, handing a folder presumably containing cash to a young woman with two small children. The ad copy read in part, "The Empire Mutual Life Insurance Company is the only insurance organization that has dared to manifest its spirit of Americanism by reserving the benefits of its strong, solid policies for only White, Protestant Americans." Samuel H. Venable, whose family owned Stone Mountain, was the company's first president.

[7] Knights of the Ku Klux Klan, Inc., *Proceedings of the Second Imperial Klonvokation*, 77.

Ghey Shall Not Want!

Klansmen---and all white, protestant Americans---

What is in store for those most dear to you? Will they be able to "carry on" alone after the inevitable has overtaken you? Have you provided for the future of your loved ones in a manner that they deserve? You have not, unless they are protected, by a 100% *Protestant, American* policy no matter how much insurance you now carry! To find both the insurance of life and the continuance of Americanism in one policy is indeed as desirable as it is rare.

The symbolic cross marks the spot on Stone Mountain where the Knights of the Ku Klux Klan were organized, Thanksgiving night, 1915.

The Empire Mutual Life Insurance Company is the only insurance organization that has dared to manifest its spirit of Americanism by reserving the benefits of its strong, solid policies for *only* white, protestant Americans. Every cent of its financial assets is invested in 100% *American* securities and institutions, and will continue to be so invested. Can *YOU*, as a Klansman; can *YOU*, as a *white, protestant AMERICAN* neglect to give yourself or your family the incomparable protection of tried and true Americans and Americanism? Let us tell you more about the benefits you receive from the Empire Mutual Life Insurance Company. Write for particulars, stating date of your birth.

The Empire Mutual Life Insurance Co., 1700 Eye St., N. W., Washington, D. C.

    Gentlemen:
        Please send me more information about the Empire Mutual Life Insurance Co., without obligation. My age is____years. I am interested in the subject checked.

Agency ☐

A Policy ☐

Name_____ Address_____

As with other fraternal orders of the era, the Klan saw the sales of insurance to members as another source of income. The use of an image of Georgia's Stone Mountain in the advertisement may have been influenced by the Prudential Insurance Company's contemporary use of the Rock of Gibraltar as a symbol of stability.

Financially, the news was good. Net revenues had increased some 483% under the Evans administration as compared to a year earlier. A Klan-owned robe factory had been established, cutting the cost of production while increasing the Klan's profit margin. All publishing was now being done in a Klan-owned facility, allowing the creation of the order's new official periodical, *The Imperial Night-hawk*.

Most importantly, since the previous Imperial Klonvocation in 1922 the order's growth had been phenomenal. Although no membership numbers[8] were cited, the number of Klaverns was given as 2,982 nationwide as of September 1924, grouped into 22 Realms. Most striking was the shift in the location of the Klan's centers of gravity. In 1922, the combined South and Southwest accounted for 83% of the order's members. By June 1924, this had fallen to 40%. Klan members in the traditional South alone (Mississippi to Virginia, including Kentucky and West Virginia) now made up only 16.1% of the total. The Invisible Empire had become a true national organization.

The Klonvocation's business finished up with open-floor suggestions, motions and announcements, ranging from the idea that Kleagles be renamed "Field Representatives" in order to escape the bad name of those few who had left town without paying their bills,[9] to the information that there was now a Klan-associated tuberculosis sanitarium in Kerrville, Texas, with "Klan doctors, Klan nurses, and Klan help" for those in need.[10] Capt. J. K. Skipwith, the Exalted Cyclops of the Mer Rouge, Louisiana, Klavern, delivered in lively form his version of the Daniels and Richards murders, calling the suggestion that the Klan was somehow involved a plot hatched by local Catholics.[11] His testimony was answered with applause. The event ended on a positive note, with the presiding official mentioning in his farewell, "I was talking to the president of the hotel company this morning, and he advises us that this

---

[8] The numbers were apparently given verbally to the delegates, but were omitted from the final printed version of the proceedings. Delegates were specifically warned against taking notes.

[9] Knights of the Ku Klux Klan, Inc., *Proceedings of the Second Imperial Klonvokation*, 228.

[10] Ibid., 236.

[11] Ibid., 256.

is the best convention they have ever housed, that there was not found in any room occupied by any of you men a trace of liquor or moral degeneracy."[12]

Back in the Klan's home state of Georgia, Julian Harris was following the news of the Missouri Klonvocation with interest. Harris, never a fan of Governor Clifford Walker, noticed an Associated Press dispatch referring to "the governor of a great state," and that this unnamed governor had spoken of "building bridges across such chasms as ignorance, superstition, desolation, [and] disease." Walker, as Harris would note later, often waxed "pathetic and melodramatic in his speeches," usually referring allegorically to "chasms," etc. "But still further," Harris wrote in a subsequent editorial, "the *Enquirer-Sun* believes there is no other governor of any other great state as simple-minded and hypocritical in his view of the Klan as the governor of Georgia happens to be."[13]

On further investigation, Harris discovered that Walker had been out of town on September 23, the date of the "great governor's" address. Walker had let it be known that he would be in Philadelphia for "a much-needed rest." News reports also noted that Walker had been at a baseball game in Memphis, Tennessee, on September 25, accompanied by Tennessee's governor. On a hunch, Harris fired off a telegram on September 27, to the paper's Atlanta correspondent reading, "The *Enquirer-Sun* is informed that Governor Walker is the 'Governor of a Great State' who addressed the Klan at its secret meeting in Kansas City. Please see the governor and get a statement from him as to the accuracy or inaccuracy of our information." When asked, Walker "declined to make any statement on the subject one way or the other."[14]

Several days later, the *New York World* printed a story that it was in fact Governor Walker who had given the address on "Americanism Applied" in Kansas City. Citing excerpts from his speech promoting racial and religious discord, the *Macon Telegraph* again timidly chided the

---

[12] Ibid., 265.

[13] *Columbus (GA) Enquirer-Sun*, 28 September 1924.

[14] One cannot help but be reminded of the escapades of a more recent Southern governor, Mark Sanford, who was said to be off "hiking the Appalachian Trail" when in fact he was visiting his mistress in Argentina.

governor, saying "Governor Walker, as a private citizen, has just as much right to be any kind of Klansman as anybody else has; he does not have the right as Governor of Georgia to be a member of any secret organization whose purpose is not as large and whose methods are at least not as open and commendable as are those of the State he represents." The paper's editor hoped "the Governor will give the people of Georgia the truth in the matter."[15] The call for the truth was soon echoed in other of the state's papers. The *Greensboro (GA) Herald-Journal* called for the truth while further charging that Walker had been a Klan member for "over two years," and that there had even been "Klan initiations in the state capitol."[16]

On Monday, October 13, nearly three weeks after the opening day of the Klonvocation, Governor Clifford Walker admitted to a reporter for the *Atlanta Constitution* that he was indeed "the governor of a great state" who gave the address in Kansas City.[17] The mystery had become a national topic; there were rumors that a photograph existed showing Walker with Imperial Wizard Evans at the meeting, perhaps precipitating the governor's decision to come clean. He stated that he "had no apologies to make" for his actions. As to the racial and religious bigotry reported in excerpts of his speech, Walker implied that he had been misquoted. It did emerge in the conversation, however, that the governor had been a member of the Klan for four years. He was quick to qualify this, however, saying he was "also a member of the Odd Fellows, the Junior Order [of Mechanics], the Masons, the Farmers' Alliance, and the Missionary Baptist Church and I'm not ashamed of any of them." Under intense questioning, he acknowledged that he had been accompanied to Kansas City by two other state officials, both Klan members, J. J. Brown, the Commissioner of Agriculture, and Peter S. Twitty, the Game and Fish Commissioner. He admitted also that he had met with Nathan Bedford Forrest II, the Klan's Grand Dragon for Georgia, on the day of his inauguration, allegedly to discuss stamping out mob violence.

---

[15] *Macon Telegraph*, 4 October 1924.
[16] Quoted in the *Columbus (GA) Enquirer-Sun*, 12 October 1924.
[17] *Atlanta Constitution*, 14 October 1924.

Walker's revelations created a storm of criticism and controversy in the Georgia press. The *Macon Telegraph* issued a mild rebuke, while the *Athens Banner-Herald*, a former supporter of the governor, "parted political company" with him, stating, "No honest man can serve an invisible empire and the State of Georgia at the same time."[18] The *Greensboro Herald-Journal* was more scathing in its denunciation of Walker, saying that finally "Kautious Kliff" "had been smoked out of his hole." The editorialist, in noting that "Georgia office-holders are carrying the Fiery Cross—the symbol of the Klan—to distant states!" asked, "SHALL THE FIERY CROSS BE PLACED ON THE DOME OF THE CAPITOL?"[19] The *Americus (GA)Times-Recorder* was equally harsh in its denunciation of the governor, suggesting, "The decent thing for Walker to do now is resign."[20] The *Dalton (GA) Citizen* opined that "Georgia needs a governor, a representative of all the people, unbossed by any bloc or klan—just a plain 100 percent American."[21]

For more than a year, support for the Ku Klux Klan in Georgia had been waning. The killing of W. J. Coburn and the highly public trial that followed disgusted many. Now, the discovery that the state's chief executive was himself a prominent member of the secretive Invisible Empire convinced many others who may have been wavering in their opinions. In the weeks that followed, the rumor spread that Governor Walker was planning to pardon Philip Fox, currently serving a life sentence for Coburn's murder. The tale became so widespread that in December, the governor felt it necessary to issue a formal statement denying that any such plans existed. Given his recent deception, few knew what to believe.

There was no single event that definitively heralded the decline and eventual demise of the Knights of the Ku Klux Klan. In Georgia, it may have been Governor Walker's duplicity that marked the beginning of the end. More realistically, however, it was the subtle and gradual change in public perception of the order, often manifest in small and isolated ways.

---

[18] *Macon Telegraph*, 18 October 1924.
[19] Quoted in the *Columbus (GA) Enquirer-Sun*, 18 October 1924.
[20] Quoted in the *Columbus (GA) Enquirer-Sun*, 19 October 1924.
[21] Quoted in the *Columbus (GA) Enquirer-Sun*, 27 October 1924.

In Richmond, Virginia, in September 1924, a prominent local attorney engaged a Klan speaker in a fist fight at St. Paul's Episcopal Church over negative remarks on the Klan made by the church's rector.[22] In New Jersey, a *Jewish Chronicle* editorial averred:

> The Klan has reached the height of its development during the past year. The shadow of decline has already fallen on it. The candidate for President having denounced it; having been defeated in its alleged strongholds; having begun to provoke the disapproval of eminent Americans in all walks of life; having been revealed as a money-making machine for a group of higher ups; the American public are getting tired of keeping alive religious and racial hatred in order to make a holiday for some men interested in making quick money. In other words, the sound, common sense of the average American is asserting itself....[23]

In Worchester, Massachusetts, a group of young men attacked cars leaving a Klan rally at the New England Fair Grounds.[24] In New York, two wealthy men of the Jewish faith gave large sums of money toward the completion of two Protestant churches, one of whom said "he was investing...in the promotion of religion along the broader lines, as opposed to the narrowness of the Ku Klux Klan idea."[25]

All of these may have been events of local significance only, but taken together they pointed to a change in ordinary Americans' perception of the Klan. While the Klan remained yet strong, a small ad on page sixteen of the Marietta, Georgia *Journal* was in some ways most telling. It read:

> FOR RENT---Large hall vacated by the Ku Klux Klan Sept. 1st, at 112 Washington Ave. Apply 602 Church St., or phone 116.[26]

---

[22] *Macon Telegraph*, 22 September 1924.
[23] *Jewish Chronicle (Newark NJ)*, 3 October 1924.
[24] *Boston Herald*, 20 October 1924.
[25] *Macon Telegraph*, 30 November 1924.
[26] *Marietta (GA) Journal*, 16 October 1924.

Part VII

It All Falls Apart

The Ku Klux Klan is definitely on the wane. Everywhere it shows signs of dissolution; nowhere are there indications of gain....[I]nternal dissentions have contributed much to the defeat of this cause, undertaken with so great zeal by many thousands of people. Outside criticism and the wearing process of time have helped to bring about the decline, the novelty of the movement has lost its appeal and, most important, perhaps, of all, the Klan has not been able to achieve its advertised ends. It has failed of any outstanding accomplishment, even where its strength was greatest.

"The Klan's Invisible Empire Is Fading"
The *New York Times*, February 21, 1926

The Klan of the 1930s was primarily a social organization, stressing the fraternal side of its nature which had been its main appeal in countless communities during its better days. But even though there were Klansmen about and keeping busy, there was no disguising the hard times that had hit the Invisible Empire.

David M. Chalmers
Hooded Americanism: The History of the Ku Klux Klan,
Published 1965

Chapter 22

The Decline and Fall of the Invisible Empire

Every good tale deserves a moment that presages its end; an event, a *dénouement* or some great revelation that hints to the reader the game is soon to be over, justice will be served, or the final act played out. It was not to be that way with the Ku Klux Klan of the 1920s. Beginning in late 1924 or early 1925, the hooded order simply began to decline in both membership and political power. From a historical perspective, it would be beneficial to be able to point to some definitive break point, some happening or some person as being primarily responsible for the Klan's fall. Rather, the Invisible Empire's death took the form of the demise of an endangered species threatened by climate change and loss of natural habitat. For multiple reasons, some of which will be outlined below, the order's membership suffered a precipitous fall starting in the middle of the decade. By 1930, some estimates held that more than ninety-nine percent of Klansmen had abandoned the order, leaving as a total membership a tiny fraction of what it had been at the order's peak. And, like a species facing extinction, the Klan's range contracted, persisting most prominently in its traditional home of the South.

There were adverse events, to be sure. It is reasonable to speculate that at mid-decade in the 1920s the average man or woman could recount some outrage attributed to the Klan. Some—the Mer Rouge killings, for example—made national headlines. Others, however, were local. Perhaps it was the Catholic schoolteacher fired simply because of her religion by a local Klan-dominated board of education. Or the Greek-American restaurant owner whose once-popular business faltered and failed as a result of a Klan-promoted boycott. To others, their rejection of the Ku Klux Klan may have been its perceived perversion of the great American sport of politics, the heart of the democratic system. While never having enough numbers to become a true political party, the Klan had shown its willingness and ability to influence the balance of power through its secrecy, demanding in return support of what many saw as an anti-American philosophy. Whatever the cause, the public at large turned against it. Association with the order became toxic; membership in it spoke loudly of how one felt about American society. The end would eventually come, but it would be nearly two decades away in the midst of World War II.

This view of the Klan's demise is not to imply that it was obvious to all—or even a majority—of observers at the time. The failure of each of the nearly three thousand Klaverns that existed in the fall of 1924 was unique to that particular location and situation. Over the coming months and years some disbanded while others withdrew from the national organization, forming new and separate fraternal orders. Others continued while dwindling in membership and active participation until the point that it became obvious that continuation of the local group was useless.

The proximate causes of a Klavern's withdrawal or disbandment varied widely. Nationally, there was an overall growing public distaste for the Klan, the sense that its negatives far outweighed its positives in a pluralistic society. Many times there was an event, or series of events, that spelled the end. In other situations it may have been related to leadership, or lack thereof, a vital factor in any such social organization. In large sections of the country, especially the North and Midwest, there was the perception that the Ku Klux Klan as an organization had changed (or was not what it had been perceived to be), either because of the revelations and infighting of 1923 and 1924 or its direction under the leadership of Imperial Wizard Hiram Evans. And there were external factors. In some states, anti-mask laws were passed, as well as regulations requiring the membership rolls of fraternal organizations be made public. While often phrased generically, they were clearly aimed at the Klan. The boll weevil and crash of the cotton economy in the South in the early to mid-1920s added economic pressure, as did the Great Depression which began at the end of the decade. Money became scarce, and it was hard to spare even a few extra dollars for the local Klavern (or lodge). It was during this period of time that many of the nation's other fraternal orders failed, often to be replaced by mid-day businessmen's clubs.

Despite all, in some areas and especially in the South, there were pockets where the Klan remained a strong organization well into the 1930s and beyond, although operating on the margins of society. Klan-related floggings were common newspaper items in Georgia well into the 1940s. The difference was that now the victims were more likely to report them, lawmen more likely to pursue the culprits, and juries more likely to indict and convict the accused. In rural Wrightsville, Georgia, for example, the local Klavern continued as before for decades. In the 1930s a young local physician was said to have been castrated for repeated episodes of marital infidelity involving other men's wives. He left town and later committed suicide.[1]

Across the realms of the Klan, times were definitely changing. The 1925 New Year's Day edition of the *Charlotte Observer* reported that in Rocky Mount, North Carolina, a newly formed local Klavern sent a polite and "neatly typewritten" letter on official Klan stationary to the city's mayor bemoaning "deplorable conditions" that allowed local "mashers and other undesirables" to hurl "repeated insults" at "our mothers, daughters and sisters" in a certain area of one of the city's thoroughfares. The letter went on to call on city officials to "exterminate this blot on the face of the best city in the state of North Carolina." A year or two earlier, such a letter might have been unthinkable; the Klan would simply have taken action itself to "exterminate" the problem.

In cash-strapped St. Petersburg, Florida, the local police chief—unable to pay the salaries of additional officers—accepted the local Klan's offer to patrol the streets "without compensation," and in civilian clothes. The Klavern did kick off its campaign, however, with "a demonstration in full regalia in the negro quarters" of the city designed to search for "loafers or bootleggers."[2]

In Athens, Georgia, one of earliest sites of Klan organization, the order's efforts to "clean up" the city took a more complicated form.[3] In

---

[1] Private communication to the author. The informant wished to remain anonymous.
[2] *State Times Advocate (Baton Rouge LA)*, 11 February 1925.
[3] *Columbus (GA) Enquirer-Sun*, 9 January 1925, 18 January 1925, 25 January 1925; *Macon Telegraph*, 10 January 1925, 13 January 1925, 16 January 1925, 22 January 1925, 31 January 1925.

early January 1925, a grand jury announced the indictments of some forty local men including a member of the city council and the city recorder. The charges ranged from gambling, to vagrancy, to the possession of illegal whisky and the carrying of concealed weapons. The evidence for the alleged crimes stemmed from a newly opened nightspot, the "Jago House," set up and run for a number of months by a man named T. C. Husted. It was designed to be a trap, part of a "moral clean-up" of the city by the Klan. Husted was a spy of sorts, a Klan investigator known as "Operative H-1." Evidence gathered was turned over to the authorities, which resulted in the grand jury's action.

The indictment of a number of prominent citizens produced an immediate outcry, only made worse when it was revealed that the plan had been hatched with the approval of Klansman-Governor Clifford Walker. The fact that the local Athens newspaper had expressed its opposition to Walker for his deception with regard to his address to the Klonvocation in Kansas City may or may not have played a role. Unfortunately for the Klan, Husted was indicted with the others.

Walker initially denied involvement, then said that while he may have been present when the subject of the trap was discussed, he never expressly commented on it or approved it. His denial was vigorously repudiated by the Exalted Cyclops of the Athens Klan who was present at the meeting. Three weeks after the story broke, the Athens Klan, betrayed by higher-ups in Atlanta, voted to "sever all connection with the order known as the Knights of the Ku Klux Klan."

The decision of the Athens Klansmen to secede was a local story to be sure, but one repeated on multiple occasions for various reasons throughout the Invisible Empire. In July, sixteen local Colorado Klaverns resigned *en masse* from the Klan, citing differences with the national organization.[4] In November, it was announced that a large faction of the Arkansas Klan had seceded to form a new order named "The Grand Klan of America." The rebels claimed too much money was going to Klan officers' salaries, and not enough going to "causes of public welfare."[5] Anti-Klan pressure brought by states was taking its toll as well.

---

[4] *Atlanta Constitution*, 19 September 1925.
[5] *Charlotte Observer*, 7 November 1925.

In Vermont, the Klan's application to conduct business in the state was rejected.[6] In Louisiana, failure to comply with certain state laws caused the dissolution of several Klaverns.[7] The Supreme Court of Kansas confirmed the legality of regulations that effectively banned the Klan in the state.[8] On a national level, newly-reelected President Coolidge took part of his inaugural address in March "to speak out plainly against the principles of the Ku Klux Klan."[9]

Among the myriad of scandals that graced the pages of local and national newspapers during 1925, few were more salacious than that of D. C. ("Steve") Stephenson, the man whose name was inextricably linked to the Klan's power and political success in Indiana. In April, Stephenson was charged with the kidnapping, rape, and murder of "Madge" Oberholtzer, a young female employee of the State of Indiana. The widely reported accounts of Miss Oberholtzer's death, the details that emerged at the various hearings surrounding Stephenson's indictment, and the damning facts presented at the trial later in the year did much to destroy the reputation of the Ku Klux Klan, both locally and nationally. The fact that Stephenson was no longer a member of the Klan, having been banished nearly a year earlier, made the situation all the more ironic.

Steve Stephenson had been elevated to the office of Grand Dragon of the Realm of Indiana by Imperial Wizard Hiram Evans at the Klonklave in Kokomo in July 1923. Chaffing at what he considered Evans's dictatorial authority, it did not take long for the two leaders to arrive at loggerheads, leading to Stephenson's resignation from the high office less than three months later. Despite his relinquishment of the leadership post, Stephenson held on to significant political power, assisting Klan-backed candidates in the Indiana state elections of 1924. The long-simmering dispute burst into the open when in May of that year Stephenson called for the secession of the Klan in the northern Midwest, to continue as an independent body under his leadership.

---

[6] *St. Albans (VT) Messenger*, 1 January 1925.
[7] *State Times Advocate (Baton Rouge LA)*, 1 January 1925.
[8] *Macon Telegraph*, 21 January 1925.
[9] *Charlotte Observer*, 6 March 1925.

Walter Bossert, the Indiana Klan leader, expelled him from the order, while Stephenson in turn announced his resignation.

Even without formal status or membership, he retained significant influence in the Indiana Klan and perhaps more importantly, in state and local politics. Stephenson became a coal broker operating the Central States Coal Company, living comfortably in his mansion near Indianapolis and sailing his yacht, the Reomar II, on Lake Huron. In later testimony, Stephenson would estimate that he had taken in approximately $1,800,000 during his brief tenure with the Klan, not to mention what he raked in under-the-table in graft and bribes. The trial to come would bring forth tales of "alleged midnight revels" and parties featuring "rum and women."[10] At age thirty-four, Stephenson was living a life most men could only dream about. But with his rise to power had come enemies. Within days of his formal resignation from the Klan, his $95,000 yacht was destroyed by arsonists. Stephenson immediately blamed "unscrupulous leaders of the Klan."[11]

Even though the death of Madge Oberholtzer had nothing whatsoever to do with the Ku Klux Klan, Stephenson's fame and reputation was based on his initial rise to power as a Klan organizer and official. Nationwide newspaper accounts of the alleged kidnapping, rape, and eventual death of the victim and the reporting of the trial that followed almost invariably referred to Stephenson as "the former Klan Grand Dragon" or similar appellation. Fairly or unfairly, headlines connected the Klan to the proceedings: "Set Trial Date for Klan Case,"[12] "Klan Murder Trials Deferred Until Fall,"[13] "Klan Figuring in Murder Trial of Stephenson,"[14] etc. Such a connection, even if incorrect, should not have been unexpected. Going back as far as the *New York World's* exposé in 1921 and as reinforced by the accusations and name-calling of the preceding two years, it might seem quite possible that a leader of the Ku Klux Klan could find himself involved in such a situation. In the mind of many of the public, Stephenson was still a leader of the Klan,

---

[10] *Macon Telegraph*, 18 October 1925.
[11] *Evansville (IN) Courier and Press*, 28 June 1924.
[12] *Evansville (IN) Courier and Press*, 3 May 1925.
[13] *Boston Herald*, 7 July 1925.
[14] *Atlanta Constitution*, 14 October 1925.

and such men were seen as capable of this type of immorality and criminality.

On April 2, 1925, Steve Stephenson and two bodyguards were arrested on the basis of an indictment issued in Indianapolis charging them with five felony counts: kidnapping, assault and battery with intent to kill, assault and battery with intent to rape, malicious mayhem, and conspiracy to commit a felony. The charges were brought by George Oberholtzer, the father of Madge Augustine Oberholtzer, the alleged victim. "Madge," as she was known to her friends, was a twenty-eight year-old single woman, employed as a literacy consultant by the state. Oberholtzer had met Stephenson several months earlier at a dinner for the incoming Indiana governor whom Stephenson had helped put in office. She had been escorted by another date, but she and Stephenson danced, apparently displaying some attraction for each other. Subsequently, they had gone out on a couple of dates, and Madge had attended a party at Stephenson's home. He was an attractive and powerful man, she must have thought, someone whose attention was flattering. Over the coming weeks, the terrible details of events leading to her death would become public.

On Sunday evening, March 15, Madge returned home somewhat late after being out with friends. Stephenson had called on the phone for her earlier; her mother gave her the message and she returned the call, later going over to his house, supposedly to attend a party. Once there, she realized she was alone with Stephenson and his two bodyguards, and "was sure she was trapped."[15] Over her objections, she was pressured into drinking liquor, and was prevented from using the telephone to call home. Stephenson decided he wanted to go to Chicago, and Madge was too intoxicated to offer much resistance. By this time, the hour was quite late. The three men and Oberholtzer traveled to Union Station where they boarded a Pullman car in a train bound for the Windy City. There in the presence of one of his bodyguards, Stephenson—apparently intoxicated—ripped off Madge's clothes and proceeded to attack her. According to a physician who examined her later, her body was covered

---

[15] *Evansville (IN) Courier and Press*, 16 April 1925.

with bruises and bite marks on her breasts and elsewhere, all inflicted by Stephenson during the attack and rape.

Sobering up a bit and apparently realizing what he had done, Stephenson aborted the planned trip to Chicago. The four departed the train in Hammond, Indiana, just short of the Illinois state line. It was speculated that Stephenson did not want to be charged with violation of the Mann Act which would have been triggered if he proceeded into the next state. The group checked into a hotel under false names. Shortly after arriving, Madge was forced to send a telegram to her mother stating that she'd decided to go to Chicago and would be home later. She was also "forced to stay in the same room with Stephenson"[16] and was once again attacked by him. Afterwards, "as he lay on the bed sleeping she got up and took his pearl-handled revolver from his holster, intending to kill him. Then she thought of her family and decided the only thing to do was to kill herself. She said she walked in front of the mirror and held the weapon a moment to her temple. At that moment one of the other men entered the room," and jerked the gun away.[17]

Seeking a chance to escape, Oberholtzer told Stephenson she needed to buy a hat, having left home without one. He gave her fifteen dollars, but sent her out under the watchful eye of one of the bodyguards. She bought the hat, and then on the excuse of buying cosmetics, purchased a bottle of bichloride of mercury, a potent poison.[18] Back at the room, she secretly swallowed six tablets. Later in the afternoon, Madge confessed that she'd taken the poison. She was made to drink part of a bottle of milk, which she vomited up. The group soon departed back toward Indianapolis by car. Oberholtzer was acutely ill, vomiting blood and pleading to see a doctor. On return to Stephenson's mansion, she was "held a prisoner in a garage" until the next morning, March 18, when one of the bodyguards returned her to her home.[19] Her mother

---

[16] Ibid.

[17] Ibid.

[18] Bichloride of mercury (mercuric chloride) is a highly toxic chemical formerly used most commonly as a topical wound disinfectant. It was also used in the pre-antibiotic era to treat syphilis. Taken acutely, it can cause caustic burns to the gastrointestinal tract and renal failure, among other things.

[19] *Evansville (IN) Courier and Press* 16 April 1925.

recounted in a later interview, "A strange man...carried her upstairs, mumbled something about an accident in Muncie, and hurried away," apparently hoping to explain away Madge's battered condition.[20]

The family immediately called a physician to whom the now-dying girl gave the details of her ordeal. Within days, Oberholtzer slipped into a coma, dying of renal failure on April 14, almost a month after her kidnapping.[21] A grand jury issued an additional charge of first degree murder based on the failure to provide medical attention after Madge swallowed the poison, which was added to those already leveled at Stephenson and his bodyguards. Their bail was revoked; they were rearrested and held without bond pending a trial to take place later in the year. As the grand jury was considering the evidence, arsonists attacked Stephenson's mansion. In assessing the partially burned ruins, investigators found two cans of gasoline and one of kerosene and noted the gas jets had been turned on.

While the drama of the Oberholtzer rape and murder was playing out, Imperial Wizard Hiram Evans was forging ahead with his plans. The Klan issued a routine denunciation of Stephenson; they would not have been expected to do anything else. Whether or not Imperial Wizard Evans was truly concerned about fallout from the events in Indiana, or generally about the ongoing deterioration of the Klan is unclear. His focus, it seems, was on the Klan's strength as a player on the field of national politics. In stark contradiction of his pledge at the Klonvocation of September 1924, Evans made the decision to move the Klan's offices to Washington, DC. He himself had moved there with his family and the personnel of several key departments in early 1924. Over the following months, transfers of most of the remaining Imperial Palace employees had been "accomplished gradually and without public announcement." In early May 1925, it was disclosed that the Klan had "established elaborate offices for the Imperial Wizard and a large staff in one of the downtown office buildings [at 17th and I Streets] within a

---

[20] *San Diego Evening Tribune*, 8 April 1925.

[21] The details of Madge Oberholtzer's abduction and subsequent death were widely reported in newspapers nationwide. A somewhat more detailed account of the events and the legal and political fallout is available to the interested reader in Wade's *The Fiery Cross*, 239-247.

couple of blocks of the White House." The reason cited for not officially moving the Palace to Washington was the need to amend the order's constitution to do so. It was speculated that would take place at the next Klonvocation.[22] Evans was officially silent in his reasons for moving the Klan's center of power to Washington, but a caption under a large photograph of him in one newspaper read: "The Ku Klux Klan is attempting to set up in Washington a 'lobby' as powerful as that of the Anti-Saloon League, in the expectancy of influencing legislation in the direction of its 'ideals,' observers in the National capital believe."[23]

As spring became summer, the Stephenson scandal simmered quietly, garnering a few more headlines in June when the accused managed to secure a change of venue while delaying their trial to the fall session of court. In July, the great American orator and former presidential candidate William Jennings Bryan died unexpectedly. Within days, a rumor began to circulate that he had been a secret member of the Klan, having been "naturalized" into the order a few weeks after he referred to Klansmen as "misguided people" at the 1924 Democratic convention in New York. Bryan's family was quick to deny the allegation; most people considered it just another bit of Klan hyperbole.[24]

In order to celebrate the Klan's ascension as a national power player, the newly-moved Klan headquarters scheduled a massive parade to be held in Washington, DC on Saturday, August 8, 1925. Permits were properly requested and granted; in accordance with local regulations, masks were banned. The police, anticipating possible unrest, called every member of the force to active duty during the twenty-four hours that included the scheduled parade time. Local African-American groups were contacted and advised to keep a low profile. A white anti-Klan activist was briefly arrested and interrogated before being released. Philadelphia had turned down a contemporaneous request for a similar parade to be held there the following year, telling the Klan, "It would neither be good business nor good policy to authorize special days which

---

[22] *State Times Advocate (Baton Rouge LA)*, 12 May 1925.
[23] *Charlotte Observer*, 17 May 1925.
[24] *Macon Telegraph*, 7 August 1925.

might lead to misunderstanding or prejudice, and accordingly, although the necessity is regretted, your request cannot be allowed." [25] Washington, in contrast, was the nation's capital, its center of political power. Common sense and Constitutional freedoms would preclude any attempt to block a Klan parade there.

For days prior to the march, advance teams of Klan members poured into Washington. Preliminary estimates from insiders suggested that as many as 150,000 marchers from across the nation might participate. Three days before the parade, forty-three special trains bringing Klansmen, members of the Women's Klan and Junior Klan had been scheduled, with "more applications arriving daily."[26] Police detectives reported "many" automobiles had entered the city bearing tin plates affixed to their license tags "mystically marked KIGY." A news dispatch explained, "This is not a radio symbol, but denotes the Klan hail, 'Klansmen, I greet you,' as detectives decipher it."[27]

The day arrived hot and sunny. Promptly at three o'clock, the parade began at the capitol. For more than three hours, tens of thousands of white-robed Klansmen and Klanswomen formed a white river as they marched down Pennsylvania Avenue, skirted the White House grounds on Fifteenth Street and assembled at the base of the Washington Monument. Marines with fixed bayonets guarded the nearby Treasury Department building, unnecessarily as it turned out. Estimates of the number of marchers ranged widely. Klan members reported there were between fifty and a hundred thousand. One newspaper reporter who tried to keep tally estimated fifty thousand, of whom a quarter were women and children. Police estimates were more conservative, suggesting twenty-five to thirty thousand.

The spectacle went smoothly. As one reporter described it, "The show was as peaceful as a county fair or a small-town carnival, and had many of the aspects of those bucolic events."[28] The march was led by a lone white-clad Klansman, followed by Imperial Wizard Evans

---

[25] Ibid.
[26] *State Times Advocate (Baton Rouge LA)*, 5 August 1925.
[27] *New Orleans Times-Picayune*, 7 August 1925.
[28] *Greensboro (NC) Record*, 9 August 1925.

resplendent in his silk robes of purple and gold. There were American flags and bands playing popular airs, patriotic tunes, and Christian hymns. As the last of the robed throng arrived at the Mall and Washington Monument, the heavens opened with a heavy thundershower, abruptly cutting short the religious ceremony and planned speeches. Despite entreaties from the speakers' podium, the crowd quickly scattered, scurrying for shelter from the downpour. Another reporter, sensing that the parade was an effort to show the continuing pertinence of the Invisible Empire, commented, "Undoubtedly, the Klan has been losing members—in certain sections losing its grip on the situation, almost disintegrating. But the Klan is not dead and it convinced itself that it is alive by this display of vitality. A good many backbones beneath the bed-sheet robes have been strengthened, doubtless."[29] Some would say later that the 1925 Washington march was the high point of the Klan. It was, to be certain, a massive show of strength, but the decline was well underway and would accelerate in the months and years to come.

A few weeks later, Imperial Wizard Evans held a national meeting of Klan leaders at a resort at Buckeye Lake, Ohio. The gathering was held to chart the future of the order, to lay plans for the "capturing of the second offensive in the Klan program." Announcing that, "the Klan has grown up. It is no longer a child; it is an adult," Evans asserted, "The Klan has taken its place in American social life as a dignified influence for civic righteousness." There were calls for further strengthening of the women's branch and junior orders of the Klan, and the necessity for the order to take "a militant stand against modernism in the Protestant church."[30] There was little doubt that Evans's vision for the Klan was not that of his predecessors. The problem would be convincing the nation at large of that change.

Meanwhile, in the home state of the Klan, the atmosphere was becoming increasingly chilly. The *Dalton (GA) Citizen*, commenting

---

[29] Merrit, "The Klan on Parade," 554.
[30] *State Times Advocate (Baton Rouge LA)*, 25 August 1925; 26 August 1925.

The Klan's Washington, DC, march in August 1925 probably marked the high point of the order. As many as 150,000 Klansmen (and auxiliaries) marched down Pennsylvania Avenue in a show of strength. (From the collections of the Manuscript, Archives, and Rare Book Library, Emory University.)

In September 1926, for a second year in a row, Imperial Wizard Hiram Evans led a Washington, DC, march of Klansmen. (Library of Congress.)

The September 1926 Washington, DC, Klan parade was a much-diminished event compared to the preceding year. The march attracted only about 15,000 to 20,000, of whom as many as one-third were from women's auxiliaries. (Library of Congress.)

editorially on the Washington march and the Buckeye Lake meeting, opined:

> Wearing masks, practicing sacrilege in burning fiery crosses, appealing to race and religious hatreds is so thoroughly un-American and so contemptible that we are surprised that any intelligent person would engage in such perfidy for even one performance, even though possessed of an overwhelming curiosity to know something about nothing. The dollar and curiosity, spiced with hatred and bigotry, are the dragons that make "grand dragons" grandiose, superior to all surroundings, and "smart alecks" of the most advanced types.[31]

Even in Macon, where the Klan had held significant power, the city council voted against allowing the order to parade unless masks were removed.[32]

In Indiana, the second installment of the Stephenson scandal was unfolding. The trial of the former Grand Dragon and his two bodyguards began on October 11, and would drag on for more than a month. It was, in the words of one reporter, "one of the most sensational [trials] in Indiana court annals."[33] The revelations were the topic of daily headlines, the vast majority of which continued to associate the accused with the Klan, even though the connection had been severed nearly a year and a half earlier.

The proceedings opened with a long wrangle over whether or not to admit Madge Oberholtzer's dying declaration, prepared from her testimony by attorneys before she slipped into a coma. The judge allowed most of it to be read in open court over the objections of defense counsel. The words of the now-dead victim began, "I, Madge Oberholtzer, being in full possession of my mental faculties and conscious that I am about to die, make as my dying statement the following...." She spoke in a way that was both simple and damning as it described her ordeal, including the "unprintable details" of her rape by Stephenson.[34] Stephenson's legal team alleged that she was under the influence of sedatives when the

---

[31] Quoted in the *Columbus (GA) Enquirer-Sun*, 13 September 1925.
[32] *Macon Telegraph*, 30 September 1925.
[33] *Rockford (IL) Republic*, 14 November 1925.
[34] *Rockford (IL) Republic*, 31 October 1925.

statement was given. Subsequent witnesses for the prosecution attributed Oberholtzer's death to the combined effect of self-administered poison and infection from the wounds inflicted by her attacker. The defense presented a relatively brief case, attacking the character of the dead girl, implying that she had a drinking problem and was of questionable morals. Her death, in their view, was simply due to suicide. Stephenson's actions following the revelation that she had taken poison were appropriate.

Throughout the course of the trial, the Ku Klux Klan figured prominently. Examination and cross-examination of witnesses shed light on Stephenson's lifestyle, his political connections, and his influence in the legislative activities of the state. In their closing argument, the prosecution referred to Stephenson as a "man who holds himself above the law and a destroyer of the virtue of women." As to his bodyguards, one was described as a "gorilla," and the other an "iron man" and "slugger." The defense, in its closing arguments, said simply "regardless of what might have been done, Stephenson was not guilty of murder."[35]

It took the jury less than six hours of deliberation to convict Steve Stephenson of second degree murder while acquitting his two alleged accomplices. Stephenson, apparently expecting to be exonerated, was described as "stunned," and "angry." Two days later at his sentencing hearing he proclaimed his innocence, calmly predicting, "Time will unfold the cold white light of truth and show this honorable court and the world that D. C. Stephenson is not guilty of this or any charge brought against him."[36] Within days, he assumed his new identity as Prisoner No. 11,148 in the Indiana penal system, destined to be his home for the next three decades.

In early 1926, the *New York Times* featured a long article titled, "The Klan's Invisible Empire is Fading," based on a nation-wide survey of the order's current fortunes.[37] An accompanying editorial stated, "The evidence seems to be conclusive that [the Ku Klux Klan] is everywhere on the decline." Indiana was cited as a particular example. At its peak in

---

[35] *New York Times*, 13 November 1925.
[36] *Evansville (IN) Courier and Press*, 17 November 1925.
[37] *New York Times*, 21 February 1926.

the state three years earlier, the order numbered some 400,000 members. Based on "a sworn statement" by a local official, the numbers had fallen to "only about 50,000." Similar situations were reported in multiple other states. The cause of the decline was attributed to "internal quarrels, disputes over finances, and accumulated disappointments in the field of politics." The paper's editorialist confidently averred that, "All genuine and reflecting Americans will be glad to believe that this curse is about to be removed from our public life." Within weeks, Imperial Wizard Evans announced, "The policies of the Klan have changed and it is now completely out of politics. It is not interested in the candidacy of any man or woman."[38] While perhaps trying to appear proactive, the "change" was most likely something beyond the Klan's control.

In early May 1926, the Pulitzer Prize Committee announced that the gold medal for "the most disinterested and meritorious public service rendered by any American newspaper in 1925" was awarded to Julian Harris's paper, the *Columbus Enquirer-Sun*. Cited particularly were the paper's editorial stance against the Ku Klux Klan, its campaign for clean government, its defense of religious freedom, and its rejection of racial intolerance. In responding to the award, Harris said, "For more than five years, the *Enquirer-Sun* has fought the Klan, denouncing it as 100 percent un-American and as a cowardly masked gang which attempted to usurp the rights of constituted authority and foment racial prejudice and religious intolerance....The fight against the Ku Kluxers was continued until the local chapter disbanded and efforts to get any strength have failed. Its first and last entry into local politics resulted in a 4-to-1 defeat."[39] Harris was particularly proud of having exposed Governor Clifford Walker's attempted deception in his supposedly secret address to the Klan's 1924 Klonvocation.

The Klan's Third Klonvocation was scheduled to take place in Washington, DC in September 1926. Hoping for a repeat of the previous year's show of strength, the order once again planned what was scheduled to be a massive parade. If anything, however, the event became a graphic display of the Klan's decline. This time "the most liberal

---

[38] *Atlanta Constitution*, 13 March 1926.
[39] *Plaindealer* (Topeka, KS) 14 May 1926.

estimate of the number of marchers was 20,000;" a more realistic guess was closer to 15,000. Of that number, "probably a third…were women and girls."[40] The conclave that followed once again elected Imperial Wizard Evans for another four-year term; he would be reelected to similar terms in 1930, 1934, and 1938.

While plans for the Klonvocation and parade were being formulated, the Fort Cumberland Klan No. 24 in Cumberland, Maryland, slightly more than a hundred miles to the northwest, seceded from the order, "denouncing the national Klan as a fraudulent and dishonest organization, operated primarily for the purpose of gouging money from its organization."[41] In Georgia, Klansman-Governor Clifford Walker had apparently also seen the (political) light, stating "mobs with heads covered with flour sacks shall not rule in Georgia" in response to the abduction and flogging of an attorney near the community of Lyons. Walker declared that martial law might be imposed, "if the regular processes of the courts fail to curb these outrages."[42]

With the passing months, news reports of the Klan faded from the national press. If there was an item worthy of reporting, it was often negative. In mid-1927, Klan supported candidates were defeated five-to-one in Indiana.[43] In early 1928, another of the *New York Time's* surveys of the strength of the Klan reported that the order nationally "has lost the greater part of its membership and influence."[44] Near the same time, the Klan announced it would abolish two of its most sacred icons, the mask and the "secrecy in membership" of the order. A spokesman denied this change was in response to anti-mask laws pending in several states.[45] In Atlanta, the once-proud and elegant Imperial Palace had essentially been abandoned, allowing thieves to strip it of lighting fixtures, plumbing,

---

[40] *New York Times,* 14 September 1926.
[41] *Atlanta Constitution,* 6 September 1926.
[42] *New York Times,* 29 December 1926.
[43] *Atlanta Constitution,* 23 June 1927.
[44] *New York Times,* 5 February 1928.
[45] *Atlanta Constitution,* 26 January 1928.

The Klan remained strong in Georgia for a number of years, despite declines elsewhere in America in the late 1920s. Klan-related events such as this "Klan Day" at Atlanta's Southeastern Fair remained common. (Kenan Research Center at the Atlanta History Center.)

The *Columbus Enquirer-Sun*, under the editorship of Julian L. Harris, was awarded the 1926 Pulitzer Prize, based in part on the stand the paper had taken against the Ku Klux Klan. (From the collections of the Manuscript, Archives, and Rare Book Library, Emory University.)

"and practically every movable object."[46] It would soon be sold and turned into an apartment building by a local developer.[47]

In the spring of 1929, acknowledging the obvious, Imperial Wizard Evans announced that the Klan's offices would be returning to Atlanta, with the move expected to take place in early summer. A new location in Buckhead at the intersection of Roswell Road and Peachtree Road was to be the Klan's home. Concomitant with the announcement of the move, Nathan Bedford Forrest II, now the national Kligrapp (secretary) for the Klan, announced the order's agenda for 1929. This included "education, good roads, health, tax revision, law enforcement, and a new constitution for Georgia." "We have adopted a constructive program to work for in Georgia as a means of justifying the Klan's existence," Forrest explained.[48] The once-bold proclamations of One Hundred Percent Americanism, white supremacy, and promotion of Protestant Christian values appeared long forgotten.

By 1930, it was—for practical purposes—all over for the Ku Klux Klan as a national power. A widely circulated article in the *Washington Post* observed, "Today a crumbling shell of juggernaut skidding dizzily toward oblivion, the Klan makes a last desperate stand, casting a faltering shadow athwart the ballot box to exact tribute for a political power exposed as colossal myth, and ruling a vanishing domain, fantastically small even now."[49] Americans for the most part seemed to have figured it out. There were supporters, however. In Berlin, Germany, the leader of the increasingly powerful National Socialist German Workers Party expressed his admiration for the Fascists in Italy, the White Terror in Hungary, and the Ku Klux Klan in America. His name was Adolf Hitler.[50]

At the decade progressed, Klan organizations persisted in a few areas, generally keeping a low profile. The much-reduced Georgia Klan borrowed the Red Men's Wigwam to hold its 1934 Klorero (state convention), announcing "a program to combat and eliminate alien

---

[46] *Atlanta Constitution*, 16 June 1928.
[47] *Atlanta Constitution*, 3 February 1929.
[48] *Atlanta Constitution*, 5 May 1929.
[49] Quoted in the *Tampa Tribune*, 6 November 1930.
[50] *Prensa (San Antonio TX)*, 17 November 1930.

radicalism in industrial centers of Georgia."[51] In 1937, the order again made the news when President Roosevelt nominated ex-Klansman Hugo Black for a seat on the United States Supreme Court. Black had been a member of the Alabama Klan in the 1920s, hoping at the time that joining would help further his political career. Despite the controversy, he was overwhelmingly confirmed by the Senate.

In 1938, with the fear of rising German militarism and the threat of war in Europe, the Congressional House Committee on Un-American Activities heard testimony that in some sections of the United States the Klan and the German-American Bund were "working hand-in-hand." John Metcalfe, an investigator for the committee and a former Bund member testified, "The Bund believes the Klansmen will be among the host of 'kameraden' who will join it in a battle against its enemies when 'der tag' arrives."[52] While widely reported, there was little if any clear evidence of extensive cooperation between the Klan and pro-Nazi groups, despite both espousing anti-Semitism and racial prejudice. Subsequent events and America's entry into World War II did little to help the Klan's reputation among those who recalled the alleged collaboration.

By 1939, Imperial Wizard Evans was supplementing his salary from the Ku Klux Klan by operating a company that supplied asphalt emulsion to the Georgia State Highway Department. In what appeared to be a change of heart, he accepted an invitation from the Bishop of the Georgia Roman Catholic Church to attend the dedication of the new Cathedral of Christ the King, situated on the site of the Klan's former Imperial Palace. When questioned about this, Evans refused comment, but it was pointed out by reporters that a few months earlier he had announced "that the Klan had abandoned racial and religious issues, and that he planned to have its effort devoted to fighting communism and

---

[51] *Atlanta Constitution*, 21 July 1934. The Improved Order of Red Men was a secret fraternal order tracing its origins to the eighteenth century. Its meeting places were referred to as "Wigwams." Unlike many such organizations, it continues to exist in limited form in the early twenty-first century. The fact that by 1934 the Georgia Klan no longer had a fixed meeting site is significant as a measure of its decline.

[52] *San Francisco Chronicle*, 6 October 1938.

the C.I.O."[53] Several weeks later, Evans's name came up in testimony before a legislative investigative committee looking into possible corruption in the Highway Department. It may have been these issues that led him to announce his premature retirement as Imperial Wizard in June 1939. Others asserted that the Klan under Evans's leadership had become increasingly irrelevant, failing to change with the times.

Evans, the Klan's leader since 1922, was replaced by his chief aide, forty-two year-old James A. Colescott. Colescott, a native of Indiana and former veterinarian, had been a member of the Klan since 1923, and had held a number of offices in the order, including a brief tenure working with D.C. Stephenson. The new Imperial Wizard immediately announced "the Klan nourishes no hates, loves everyone, bears no grudges [and] believes in letting the other fellow mind his own business." The Klan, he explained, "shall ever strive to promote the interest of the native-born white, Protestant, Gentile population of America. Doubtless, the well-organized minority groups will take care of their interests. It is at least their problem."[54]

Interest in the Klan and its activities was soon overshadowed by the conflict in Europe and America's subsequent involvement in the war. Little was heard of the order until June 1944 when it was discovered by a local Atlanta newspaper that the Klan's national headquarters were vacant and that Imperial Wizard Colescott had sold his home on Collier Road and left the city.[55] Reached by telephone, Colescott told the newspaper that in April 1944, the remaining members of the Klan had held a secret Klonvocation and "voted to suspend the Constitutional laws of the Knights of the Ku Klux Klan, Inc., to revoke all charter Klans, and to order disbandment of all provisional Klans." He went on the say, "This does not mean the Klan is dead," but that local chapters were freed from any national organization or obligation, and thus able to function as they saw fit. The fact that the Internal Revenue Service would later file a

---

[53] *New York Times*, 17 January 1939. The C.I.O. (Congress of Industrial Organizations) was a consortium of labor unions formed by John L. Lewis in 1928. A number of its leaders were said to be socialists or communists. In 1955 it merged with the American Federation of Labor to form the AFL-CIO.

[54] *Atlanta Constitution*, 11 June 1939.

[55] *New York Times*, 5 June 1944.

lien for $685,305 against the Knights of the Ku Klux Klan, Inc. for unpaid taxes dating back to the 1920s was likely to have influenced the Klan's decision to disband.

Part VIII

In The End

In the final analysis, the Klan was not alien to society or un-American. If it were, the problem would have been much simpler. Rather the Klan was typically American. It prospered and grew to national power by capitalizing on forces already existent in American society: our readiness to ascribe all good or all evil to those religions, races, or economic philosophies with which we agree or disagree, and our tendency to profess the highest ideals while actually exhibiting the basest of prejudices. To examine the Ku Klux Klan is to examine ourselves.

Kenneth T. Jackson, from the Preface to
The Ku Klux Klan in the City 1915-1930,
published 1967

The ultimate weakness of the Invisible Empire, however, was its lack of a positive program and a corresponding reliance upon emotion rather than reason. The distinctive white garb, super-secret ritual, and guarded open-air meeting were calculated to appeal to man's weakness for the mysterious. But emotion proved to be a two-edged sword. Having aroused eager patriots to the imminent dangers facing Americanism, the Klan could not pacify them by repeating an eight-page ritual four times a month and passively awaiting election day. Inevitably, the unusual became the commonplace, and emotional fervor waned. Without a meaningful raison d'être *the Invisible Empire was exposed as a ludicrous sham, for neither its infantile mumbo jumbo nor its exaggerated claims could bear objective scrutiny, even among those it counted as Knights. The genuine sense of American decency finally asserted itself and consigned the once mighty Klan to obscurity.*

Kenneth T. Jackson, from the Epilogue to
The Ku Klux Klan in the City 1915-1930,
published 1967

Chapter 23

What Was the Klan?

The simple question that forms the title of this chapter is one that has challenged historians for nearly a century. In 1930, an editorialist writing for the *Norfolk Virginian-Pilot* noted, "The Klan phenomenon is for future historians to dissect. They will dig out the facts, study the underlying causes and publish fascinating accounts of this manifestation of mass psychology."[1] The supposed occult nature of the organization, its secrecy, its willingness to use violence while espousing Protestant Christian values, its political aspirations, and its corruption have all provided fodder for endless speculation ranging from casual magazine articles to scholarly treatises and academic dissertations. There is no single answer. In many ways, the Ku Klux Klan of the 1920s was a historical accident, an organization whose creation, persistence, and success required a series of fortunate twists and turns of fate, each building upon the other: If the Lost Cause movement had not glorified the Klan of the Reconstruction era, if the American fraternalism movement had not popularized secret fraternal orders, if *The Birth of a Nation* had not raised the name of the Klan in the American consciousness, if Edward Young Clarke and Elizabeth Tyler had not been willing to take over the Klan's propagation, and so on, the order would have dwindled, perhaps becoming an obscure footnote in history. As it were, the stars aligned in such a fashion as to allow the existence and exploits of the Knights of the Ku Klux Klan to occupy a firm place in the American story.

Attempts to explain, classify, and categorize the phenomenon of the Klan of the 1920s date from its earliest recognition as a potentially potent social and political force in American life. Over the years, academics and historians alike have compared it to other movements that

---

[1] Quoted in the *Macon Telegraph*, 20 November 1930.

preceded or followed it, their interpretations often bathed in the light of the social theory *du jour*. In 1924, Mecklin attempted to describe the Klan in Freudian terms, explaining it as a refuge for rural and unsophisticated small-town minds. Political scientists often compare the Invisible Empire to the Know-Nothing movement of the mid-nineteenth century, citing comparisons between the two for their secretive nature, and anti-immigrant, anti-Catholic bias.[2] Others have focused on the more mainstream populist nature of the Klan, especially when interpreted in terms of its widespread geographic range.[3] The fact is, the Klan was what it was, at once both similar and unique in each of many footholds across the great expanse of the American nation. To attempt to summarize the exact character of the organization in a few brief paragraphs is both disingenuous and misleading.

In terms of general commonalities, the Ku Klux Klan in practice might be best described as an organization manifesting a uniquely American version of fascism, similar in a number of ways to contemporary fascist movements of the day, most prominently the National Socialists (Nazis) in Germany and Mussolini's black-shirted National Fascist Party in Italy. All espoused ultra-nationalism, a distrust of things perceived to be foreign, an anti-labor, anti-communist bias, anti-Semitism, distinctive uniforms, and an emphasis on direct action.[4] It is notable that after the Ku Klux Klan's decline in the late 1920s, a number of prominent ex-Klansmen joined the Fascisti movement in Georgia, including Walter A. Sims, former Atlanta mayor, J.O. Woods, former editor of the Klan-related *Searchlight* newspaper, and Rev. Caleb A. Ridley, former Imperial Kludd. There were populist elements as well, an opportunity to oppose or strike back against those segments of society, both high and low, which deviated from the Klan's perception of what American society should be. Hence, for example, the suspiciousness regarding the Catholic hierarchy, the vigilante role in support of unwritten moral codes, etc.

---

[2] *See Chapter Notes for a brief explanation of the Know-Nothing movement.*

[3] See, for example, Lay, "Hooded Populism: New Assessments of the Ku Klux Klan of the 1920s."

[4] Think of the brown shirts in Germany, the black shirts in Italy, and the white sheets in America.

Descriptive categories aside, the Ku Klux Klan might also be compared to the mythic deity Proteus, Homer's Old Man of the Sea, a shape-shifter capable of assuming multiple physical manifestations when pressured to tell the truth. In this regard, descriptions of an individual Klavern of the Ku Klux Klan of Minnesota might differ from that of the description of one in Georgia, which would differ yet again from one in California, and so on. The large number of published works and academic treatises that focus on local, state, or regional Klans, each somewhat different, reflect this fact.

Perhaps then, when considering the Ku Klux Klan during its glory period of the 1920s, it is appropriate to address the nature of the order in a series of individual statements rather than a single unifying description:

The "philosophy" of the Knights of the Ku Klux Klan was less of a unitary value system than it was a hodge-podge of generic statements designed to appeal to a significant segment of American society. The details and implementation of this philosophy changed over time and in response to ambient social and political conditions.

The Klan, in its original conception by William J. Simmons, was to be a beneficial, fraternal order created primarily as a business enterprise. Its appeal of One Hundred Percent Americanism and old-time Protestant Christian values were congruent with the thinking of a significant segment of the American population of the day. Its racism, while abhorrent to many, was not too far removed from the mainstream of American thought in the early twentieth century era of *Plessy v. Ferguson*.[5] The same might be said of both the Klan's anti-papist and anti-Semitic philosophy. Right or wrong, the Klan's message had broad appeal as witnessed by the multiple millions of members who called themselves Klansmen at the order's peak. At various times during its three decades of existence, both the positive and negative focus of the Knights of the Ku Klux Klan changed with changing times. During the

---

[5] *Plessy v. Ferguson*, 163 U.S. 537 (1896), refers to a United States Supreme Court decision upholding the constitutionality of state laws requiring racial segregation in public facilities under the doctrine of "separate but equal."

World War I era, the enemies were slackers, labor organizers, and German sympathizers. In the post-war Prohibition years, Bolsheviks and bootleggers were its targets. Later, the Klan focused more on social issues and political power. Eventually, it lost pertinence as circumstances changed more rapidly than its philosophy and actions.

The creation, propagation, success and failure of the Ku Klux Klan during its existence between 1915 and 1944 were far more dependent on the actions of individuals than any other single factor.

Unlike a number of other contemporary social and religious movements of the day, the Klan had no messiah, no single figure on whom its existence depended. W. J. Simmons founded the order and was inextricably associated with it, yet the order prospered and spread primarily due to the marketing skills of E. Y. Clarke. Even then, it reached its peak of power and membership under Hiram W. Evans, the man who deposed Simmons and Clarke in an ugly public coup. It could be argued that it was also Evans's efforts to redirect the focus of the order that contributed to its demise and eventual dissolution. There was clearly a divide between higher level leaders of the Klan and the common Klansman. In large measure, the former saw it as an enterprise that bestowed wealth and power, while the latter perceived it as offering an opportunity to do beneficial works for his community and nation.

The wildly successful growth of the Ku Klux Klan in the early 1920s was due to a set of social, political, and economic conditions combined with aggressive marketing unique to that era. Had the Klan been formed at another time or under other conditions, it is unlikely that it would have prospered.

The period of the Klan's most rapid growth was one of social and economic transformation in the United States. There was a sense among many that the country was headed in the wrong direction, that threats to the very ideals that made America great were lurking in the shadows, ready to strike. In these uncertain times, the Klan offered sharp rhetoric combined with the willingness to take direct action. Similar periods in history have produced similar movements, perhaps the best comparison being the right-wing fascist movements in Europe of the same era. Although the Klan's message changed somewhat with time it failed to adjust many of its core values. By the 1930s it had become a small and relatively insignificant group in American society.

It is a mistake to lump together the "Klans" of the Reconstruction era, the 1920s, and the post-World War II era. While sharing the same name, their genesis, raison d'être, *and actions were and are fundamentally different on many levels.*

While many historians and several published histories of the Ku Klux Klan trace the order from the 1860s to the present day, this is—in the author's opinion—a mistake. The single thing the Klans of the three periods share is the name, and fundamentally little else. The Ku Klux Klan of the Reconstruction era was a product of the conditions of the day, an attempt on the part of local citizens to regain political power and social dominance. The "Klan" was but one of many local regulatory groups that arose spontaneously across the conquered Confederacy. The collective movement represented by these groups assumed the name of the Ku Klux Klan most prominently because that individual group was better organized than most, its nominal leader former Confederate General Nathan B. Forrest was well-known, and the Congressional hearings held in 1871 popularized the name by generically referring to "the Ku-Klux conspiracy."

The Klan of the 1915-1944 era was created as a beneficial, fraternal order whose ultimate purpose (no matter what its members might have thought) was to make money for its founder. Its costume and prime symbol, the burning cross, had nothing to do with the Klan of the 1860s, having been drawn directly from the movie, *The Birth of a Nation*. In addition to being a money-making scheme, it later became a source of political power. Although many, perhaps most, members joined with good intentions, the order was basically corrupt on a leadership level. It failed because of this innate corruption, internecine fighting, social violence, and failed political aspirations as well as its apparent inability to adapt to changing times.

The various organizations that arose after World War II and identify themselves as units of the Ku Klux Klan are generally fringe groups whose prime agenda is the promotion of racial hatred and white supremacy. They were able to adopt the regalia and symbolism of the 1920s Klan as it fell into the public domain with the failure of the Knights of the Ku Klux Klan, Inc. in 1944. They are often described as "hate groups," an appropriate appellation.

In summary, while the Ku Klux Klan of the 1915-1944 era was formally organized and generally managed under a common leadership, any description of its philosophy, goals, and deeds must be examined in the context of both time, place, and situation. In many respects, there was no single Klan, but rather a unique chimera of an organization that defies description unless carefully placed in context. The many disparate and differing accounts of the Ku Klux Klan are at once both correct and incomplete. The order and its significance will provide ample research material for historians and social scientists for generations to come.

Chapter 24

There Are No Second Acts[1]

The genesis, success, and failure of the Ku Klux Klan of the 1920s were driven as much by individuals as it was by circumstances and events. From the perspective of time, the order's history over the unsettled years of the decade might be considered as a great national drama in which characters, many of them larger than life, wandered on and off the stage, playing their assigned roles before disappearing into obscurity. But the lives of the men and women who achieved such notoriety through their association with the Klan rarely sank into anonymity once their association with it ended. It is interesting and perhaps instructive to review for a moment the subsequent life courses of some of the major figures in this tale of American history. The paragraphs that follow are not meant to be a definitive biography of these individuals, but rather a brief look at their lives after the Klan.

William Joseph Simmons

The name most frequently associated with the Ku Klux Klan of the 1920s is that of William Joseph Simmons, the founder, original Imperial Wizard, and Emperor of the Invisible Empire. Numerous accounts describe Simmons as a dreamer, a man with grand ideas but little skill in converting them to reality. He was known to be a poor manager of money; the Klan was essentially bankrupt when he contracted with Clarke and Tyler to recruit new members. Behind the carefully crafted public image of the Imperial Wizard, there appears to be little doubt that Simmons saw the Knights of the Ku Klux Klan as a business, a way to

---

[1] The title of this chapter is derived from the phrase, "There are no second acts in American lives," from notes for *The Last Tycoon*, an unfinished novel by F. Scott Fitzgerald, the subject of his current work at the time of his sudden death on December 21, 1940

car skidded over an embankment on the way to the Colonel's Nacoochee Valley farm. M. A. Moore, the Flaming Sword's Supreme Recording Knight died instantly of a broken neck. Simmons suffered a fracture of his collar bone, four broken ribs, and a punctured lung. A third occupant of the car was unharmed.[7] Simmons's recovery was slow. The Knights of the Flaming Sword went into receivership in April 1925, its assets distributed to its creditors.

Not to be kept down, in 1930 Simmons was once again in the news as head of "The White Band," a secret organization chartered in 1927 with its "international headquarters" in Atlanta. Simmons was quoted as saying, "the purpose of the international organization is to preserve the ethnic integrity and sovereign supremacy of the white races of mankind. It is non-partisan, non-sectarian, and non-radical. It has no quarrel with the Klan. It is an original and unique organization, independent of any other organization." He went on to assert the "Band" had "several thousand" members.[8] By 1931, Simmons was railing against "the hellish scheme of the rapidly rising tide of color and communism" and the "senseless seethings of shallow sentimentalists." The White Band specifically disclaimed racial prejudice, "saying it merely wants to keep the negro a negro and in his place."[9] This order, too, like the ones before it, would fail.

William J. Simmons, ex-Imperial Wizard, ex-Emperor for Life, ex-Grand Magus, ex-Supreme Monarch, etc., died "in virtual obscurity" at the Atlanta Veterans hospital on May 18, 1945 after being in failing health for four years. The *New York Times* ran a rather longish notice of his death, together with his photo.[10] The *Atlanta Constitution*, Simmons's home newspaper, granted him a brief and neutral obituary of only a few paragraphs, noting his association with the Klan as well as a couple of other fraternal orders.[11] A few days later, Ralph McGill, at the time the *Constitution's* editor-in-chief, devoted an entire column to

---

[7] *Columbus (GA) Enquirer-Sun*, 22 February 1925.
[8] (Boise) *Idaho Statesman*, 22 July 1930.
[9] *Milwaukee Journal*, 23 December 1931.
[10] *New York Times*, 22 May 1945.
[11] *Atlanta Constitution*, 21 May 1945.

Simmons's passing.[12] His assessment of Simmons's life was not a kind one.

Edward Young Clarke, Jr.

If any one person should receive credit for the success of the Ku Klux Klan in the 1920s, it would be Edward Young Clarke. Without his marketing genius, assisted by the most able Elizabeth Tyler, the order would have failed. The Knights of the Ku Klux Klan, Inc. would have been long forgotten, having joined the ranks of other fraternal orders who disappeared in the early twentieth century. Rightfully, Clarke was characterized as a huckster and con-man during his tenure with the Klan. In late 1923 and 1924, he seemed to have had a change of heart, calling for the Klan to eschew its violence and attempts to subvert the rule of law and return to its true roots as a patriotic, Christian-based organization. His open letter to President Coolidge in late 1923 and his meeting with disillusioned Klansmen in February 1924 were indicative of this change. Or were they? Was Clarke nothing more than a highly intelligent disciple of P. T. Barnum as some alleged, or had he reformed?

Leopards rarely change their spots. By July 1924, Clarke was again making headlines as "Supreme Scout," or Organizing Director, of the Mystic Kingdom, "an organization devoted to religious tolerance and benevolence and declared to be created to weld together the Protestant white people of the world into a universal movement for the furtherance of the Protestant faith and the preservation of racial integrity." [13] If membership numbers could be believed—by this time no rational person would do so—the Mystic Kingdom already boasted more than 4,500 members in diverse cities ranging from Milwaukee in the North, to Philadelphia in the East, and Jackson, Mississippi in the South. According to a press release, the order planned to spend $1,000,000 on a maternity hospital in Atlanta, $2,000,000 on a narcotic sanitarium in Chicago, and was considering a music conservatory. There were plans to raise a million-dollar educational fund to be loaned to students for their

---

[12] *Atlanta Constitution*, 24 May 1945.
[13] *New York Times*, 16 July 1924; *Charlotte Observer*, 20 August 1924.

college education. How these plans coincided with the "movement's" stated mission is unclear.

For nearly a year and a half, Clarke's name disappeared from the public eye, appearing again in January 1926 with the announcement that "a new movement designed to bring back the honesty and simplicity of the religion of our fathers" was being formed in Atlanta. One of the main purposes of the as-yet-unnamed organization would be "to secure the dismissal of school teachers who teach evolution and profess atheism in the schools and colleges of the United States." There were plans to set up local chapters "in every town and city in the country."[14] The *Macon Telegraph*—no fan of Clarke—commented editorially that "there are suckers who will bite upon such a proposition—suckers enough to send a flood of gold in to the depleting Clarke exchequer."[15]

Within weeks, the new order had been given a name, the Supreme Kingdom, and shortly thereafter suffered its first defeat when the Atlanta Board of Education refused to set up a committee to determine if any teachers in the city's schools were teaching evolution.[16] The order continued to progress, however, soon hiring as the Supreme Kingdom's director, Fred W. Rapp, former executive organizer and business manager for the evangelist Billy Sunday. It was also announced that new members would have the opportunity of purchasing bonds issued by the order in amounts ranging from $20 to $500.

The Supreme Kingdom continued to grow quietly until January 1927 when the *Macon Telegraph* began a full-fledged campaign to expose the true nature of Clarke's latest fraternal order. Having obtained an extensive collection of Supreme Kingdom documents and contracts from disillusioned insiders, the paper published a series of articles detailing the methods and finances of the organization.[17] In order to create concern about the threat of atheism in the minds of potential recruits, the newspaper revealed that the Supreme Kingdom was secretly reprinting "literature issued originally by the American Association for the

---

[14] *Springfield (IL) Republican*, 18 January 1926.
[15] *Macon Telegraph*, 23 January 1926.
[16] *Macon Telegraph*, 13 May 1926.
[17] *Macon Telegraph*, 7 January 1927.

Advancement of Atheism" and distributing it as if it came from the atheistic society. As with the Knights of the Ku Klux Klan, Clarke had set himself up to receive the lion's share of any "donations" made by new members. There were multiple levels of membership, each with a designated fee ranging from $12.50 for the lowest to $1,000 for the highest. Clarke's cut was 50 to 75 percent depending on the level. For those who were interested in helping finance the new and growing order, Clarke promised that each $1,000 invested would yield a return of $20,000 once the total membership reached one million. As an additional income source, the Supreme Kingdom was selling "at cost" life insurance policies "declared by the Comptroller General of [Georgia] to be not only of doubtful character but...not consistent with good insurance methods."[18]

The series of articles were published at the same time Dr. John R. Stratton of Calvary Baptist Church of New York City was scheduled to speak at the Macon Municipal Auditorium on behalf of the Supreme Kingdom. The *Telegraph* had obtained a copy of a contract calling for him to be paid $30,000 during the year to deliver a total of sixty lectures. News of Rev. Stratton's association with the Supreme Kingdom created a crisis in his home pastorate.[19] Backpedaling, he described his connection with the order as "temporary and tentative," and that he had only joined because of its stand against Bolshevism, atheism, and evolution. He denied the existence of the purported contract, saying the documents obtained by the *Telegraph* were fakes. Dr. Stratton was soon replaced by a familiar face, that of the Reverend Caleb A. Ridley, former Imperial Kludd of the Ku Klux Klan. [20]

By mid-1928, Clarke had created the Mystic Castle of the Supreme Kingdom, an order-within-an-order. Potential members were offered the chance to buy a life membership for $500. The membership certificate, promoted as a worthwhile investment, would entitle the holder to share in the profits of the sale of regalia, literature, books, etc. The payout for

---

[18] Ibid.
[19] *New York Times*, 20 January 1927.
[20] *Macon Telegraph*, 25 August 1927.

the membership certificates over a ten-year period was projected to be $25,000.[21]

Within a year, Edward Clarke had formed a new and completely separate order, The Esskaye, Inc., the name based on the initials of the Supreme Kingdom. It was to be the second in a grand plan that included seven interrelated orders. Despite his negative encounters with the local newspaper, he chose Macon, Georgia for The Esskaye's headquarters. Once again, the *Telegraph* was on the case, skeptical of Clarke's intentions. The purpose of order was to fight Tolerance, whatever that might mean. A pamphlet issued by the order read:

> An octopus whose branches are spreading even into little hamlets of America, growing and prospering under the title of "Tolerance," is slowly sapping the lifeblood, and lulling to sleep the conscience of a great and glorious people through the mistaken idea that "Tolerance" is a virtue. Patience and sympathy and kindness and recognition of the rights of others, are great virtues and are to be cherished. "Tolerance" is an insidious, ever growing and ever creeping serpentine octopus, spreading the poison that lulls to sleep, and would make us tolerant of and consort with sin, death, and eternal destruction....The "Tolerance" thought is being shot into the American mind by an organized force that is the greatest enemy to real Americanism, human liberty, and religious freedom this country has ever had to face, and the battle against this organized force has just started.[22]

It was a bizarre statement, to say the very least.[23] The Esskaye was being funded by the issuance of $250 certificates, each certificate entitling the bearer to twenty cents for each new member initiated over the next decade. By Clarke's stated estimate, with a million members the $250 investment would be worth $20,000.

---

[21] *Macon Telegraph*, 19 August 1928.

[22] *Macon Telegraph*, 2 July 1929.

[23] It is the author's opinion that Clarke was suffering from what would now be termed bipolar disorder, though not recognized in that era as a distinct diagnosis. Judging from Clarke's interviews and activity at the time, his grandiosity, increased self-esteem, flight of ideas, intense goal-oriented behavior, and foolhardy money-making schemes would seem to support this diagnosis, being indicative of a manic episode. Further events in Chicago would tend to bear this out.

It did not take long for the scheme to fall apart. On November 1, 1930, Atlanta police arrested Edward Clarke and his wife, Martha Anna Clarke, on charges of embezzlement filed in Jesup, Georgia. The couple were quickly released on bond, but Clarke was arrested again a few days later, charged with leaving the Georgian Terrace Hotel in Atlanta without paying a $50 bill. The matter of the embezzlement charge was eventually settled by the payment of a $1,000 fine.

A year-and-a-half later The Esskaye, Inc. popped up once again, this time in Chicago. News reports spoke of Clarke organizing this "new group," which already had 75,000 members in 38 states. Chicago was to be its headquarters. The Esskaye's stated purpose this time was to combat atheism, end the Depression, and restore prosperity. A "founder" membership was available for $300, but the "rank and file" could join for only $10.[24] The following month, Clarke was voluntarily admitted to the Cook County Psychopathic Hospital for observation prior to a scheduled hearing "to determine his sanity." The admission was apparently prompted by Clarke's friends, including the local attorney for The Esskaye.[25]

An initial evaluation by an alienist found "no evidence of psychosis or mental disease," but the examining physician wanted to have him seen by "several other alienists."[26] After ten days and the examination of four psychiatrists, Clarke was pronounced sane, but with a caveat. One physician, Dr. C. A. Newman, said, "I believe this man should be held in an institution but not this kind of an institution. He should be in jail."[27] That assessment would eventually come to pass. In December 1933, the Clarkes were indicted on mail fraud charges related to activities of The Esskaye in Jacksonville, Florida.[28] They were tried and convicted in July of the following year. Clarke was sentenced to five years in the Federal penitentiary in Atlanta, while his wife received a sentence of two years to be served in a West Virginia prison. Witnesses at the trial "told of buying

[24] *Register-Republic (Rockford IL)*, 2 May 1932.
[25] *Daily Illinois State Journal (Springfield, IL)*, 22 June 1932.
[26] *Morning Star (Rockford IL)*, 28 June 1932.
[27] *Daily Herald (Biloxi MS)*, 1 July 1932.
[28] *Augusta Chronicle*, 29 December 1933.

thousands of dollars' worth of 'Pioneer Certificates' in the organization on the promise of rich profits from membership fees."[29]

Clarke was eventually released from prison on parole, spending the last years of the 1930s in Chicago as "a dabbler in advertising, literature, and publishing."[30] In 1939, Monarch Publishing, Clarke's company, released Thomas Dixon's last novel, *The Flaming Sword*. In failing health, Dixon chose Clarke "because he was too ill to seek a good publisher."[31] Doubleday Page, the publisher of Dixon's best-known work, *The Clansman*, had rejected the manuscript for *The Flaming Sword*, likely because of its extremely negative portrayal of blacks. The dystopian novel takes place in the 1930s, ending with a communist takeover and the formation of the "Soviet Republic of the United States." Its plot line reflected what Dixon considered to be a vast conspiracy by blacks and Communists to destroy America.[32]

In July 1940, Clarke, now described as "white-haired and dignified," was arrested once again on a variety of charges, including failure to pay a $600 hotel bill, passing a worthless check for $76, fraudulently obtaining $9,600 in cash and services, and conning a woman out of $600 "by telling her he was soon to inherit a three million dollar legacy."[33] The outcome of these charges is unknown, but by 1943, Clarke was apparently free once more as he was arrested in Griffin, Georgia on charges of giving a bogus check for $22.64 to an Athens, Georgia hotel. He pled guilty and was sentenced to seven years in prison, to serve a minimum of two years before being eligible for parole.

March 24, 1949, marked the last date of any public record relating to Clarke. He apparently had been released on parole after three years in prison and had absconded to New York. He was subsequently arrested there as a parole violator. As reported by a number of newspapers: "Seventy-three year-old Edward Young Clarke, Imperial Wizard of the

---

[29] *Richmond (VA) Times Dispatch*, 20 July 1934.
[30] *Rockford (IL) Morning Star*, 12 July 1940.
[31] Cook, 129.
[32] See the Introduction by John D. Smith in the University of Kentucky's 2005 reprinted edition of Dixon's *The Flaming Sword*.
[33] *Rockford (IL) Morning Star*, 12 July 1940; *The Garfieldian (Chicago IL)*, 18 July 1940.

Ku Kluxers in the twenties, slipped away from Fred C. Kendrick, elderly parole supervisor of the Board of Pardons at Atlanta. The escape was made while Kendrick was buying tickets to take Clarke to Atlanta at the Pennsylvania Railroad's 30th Street station. Railroad police and Philadelphia officers immediately pressed the hunt—but Clarke was gone."[34]

Elizabeth Tyler (Grow)

Having resigned from her position with the Ku Klux Klan in early 1922, Edward Young Clarke's associate married an Atlanta movie producer, Stephen W. Grow, later that year, apparently over her former business partner's (and lover's) objection. In retrospect, her decision to distance herself from the Invisible Empire was a wise one. The following year, Tyler and her husband moved to Altadena, California, a suburb of Los Angeles, to pursue his movie career.

In September 1923, Tyler's grand house on Atlanta's Howell Mill Road was rented to a Mrs. Elfrieda Wagner. Three months later, Mrs. Wagner was arrested on charges of violating the Prohibition law based on the discovery of "what police classed as an elaborate distillery" in the basement of the house. Mrs. Wagner said the still was there when she rented the house.[35]

Elizabeth Tyler Grow died in California on September 10, 1924. The cause of death was said to be high blood pressure.

Hiram Wesley Evans

In the late 1930s, prior to his unscheduled resignation as Imperial Wizard, Hiram Evans had settled into a comfortable life, residing in "a palatial modernistic home" in Atlanta at the prestigious address of 300 Peachtree Battle Avenue, apparently possible by making very efficient use of his $1,000-a-month-plus-expenses stipend from the Klan.[36] His lifestyle, however, was certainly supported in large part by his other businesses, mainly having to do with supplying material to the Georgia

---

[34] *Augusta Chronicle*, 25 March 1949.
[35] *Cleveland Plain Dealer*, 30 November 1923.
[36] *Atlanta Constitution*, 31 May 1940.

State Highway Department. It was a strange but lucrative sideline for someone trained as a dentist who had spent much of his working life as head of a fraternal order. There had been hints of malfeasance in Evans's business dealings prior to his leaving the Klan leadership post, but it was a year later that the matter exploded into public view.

On May 30, 1940, a Federal grand jury indicted Evans and a State Highway Department purchasing agent (who also happened to be the Clerk of the Georgia House of Representatives) for mail fraud and conspiracy to violate the Sherman Anti-Trust Act. The activities in question dated back to the late 1920s, though the focus was on the years 1937 through 1938. In his testimony before the jury, Evans admitted that though his own company and acting as an agent for others, he held "a monopoly on the emulsified asphalt business in the state." As to the issue of price-fixing, he said his type of business did not involve "collusive bidding," but rather "co-operative selling." [37] The distinction seemed lost on prosecutors; Evans pled no contest to the charges and agreed to pay a $15,000 fine plus court costs.

Evans's legal troubles were not over. In January 1942, a Fulton County (Atlanta) grand jury indicted Evans along with former Georgia governor and Klansman E. D. Rivers and nineteen others on a variety of charges generally described as a "conspiracy to defraud the State."[38] The grand jury's investigation continued, with Evans, under indictment, refusing to answer further questions. His wife admitted working with Evans's secretary to remove from his office potentially incriminating documents sought by the investigative body, but refused to say more, citing her Fifth Amendment rights. Their actions earned the Evanses fines for contempt of court.

Among the multiple defendants, the state chose to try Hiram Evans first, perhaps thinking that their case against him was strongest. For six weeks between April and June 1942, the jury heard witness after witness describe a far-reaching web of governmental corruption. There were well-substantiated tales of bid-rigging, kickbacks, bribery, and retaliation against state employees who refused to go along with the schemes. Evans

---

[37] Ibid.
[38] *New York Times*, 4 January 1942.

had even kept a "secret" house in the middle of a lake in south Fulton County described as "a heavily-barred sound-proof place where Evans, former Governor E.D. Rivers, and others were wont to meet in secrecy" to discuss their plans. Evans described it in turn as merely "a quiet, rustic retreat where [he] and his friends could catch a breath of cool air on a summer day." [39] After three days of deliberation, the jury declared themselves hopelessly deadlocked, with six voting for acquittal and six voting for conviction. The judge declared a mistrial; the prosecutor stated he planned to bring the case back to trial in the next term of court. In the meantime, ex-Governor Rivers was brought to trial, primarily on the charge of embezzlement of state funds while in office. His case resulted in a mistrial as well.

In April 1943, Solicitor John A. Boykin announced that the State had decided not to pursue further prosecution again Evans, Rivers, and the others indicted the previous year. Citing the mistrials as well as the fact that many necessary witnesses were unavailable because of involvement in the war effort, "he felt it would not be proper to put the State or the county to the additional expense" of the trials.[40] Based on newspaper reports, the evidence against the accused seemed overwhelming. How much, if any, the lingering influence of the Klan had to do with the mistrials and the decision to forgo further prosecution cannot be determined.

Evans did not escape totally unscathed. He had paid approximately $8,105.56 in Federal income taxes for the years 1937 through 1941.[41] The various court proceedings had placed his business dealings, both legitimate and otherwise, under a microscope. After several years of squabbling with the Internal Revenue Service, in 1947 the United States government filed tax liens against Evans totaling $339,665.[42] For the last two decades of his life, Hiram Evans kept a low profile, almost completely disappearing from the public eye. He died in Atlanta at age eighty-four on September 14, 1966.

---

[39] *Macon Telegraph*, 8 May 1942.
[40] *Evening Star (Washington DC)*, 9 April 1943.
[41] *Kansas City (MO) Star*, 21 June 1946.
[42] *Marietta (GA) Journal*, 10 January 1947.

David Curtiss ("Steve") Stephenson

Steve Stephenson, the man who was famously quoted as having said, "I am the law in Indiana," began serving his life sentence for the murder of Madge Oberholtzer in November 1925. There seems little doubt that Stephenson thought his tenure in prison would be a short one. After all, it was through his efforts and support that Indiana Governor Ed Jackson was elected, not to mention numerous other Indiana office holders on state and local levels. While not officially associated with the Ku Klux Klan, he still retained significant influence among its members. Or so he thought. In truth, the brutal circumstances of Oberholtzer's death and the revelations brought forth at Stephenson's trial had been so controversial that even his closest allies abandoned him. Stephenson sat quietly in jail, waiting for the pardon that would never come.

Based in large part on the testimony and relationships brought out at the trial, an Indianapolis grand jury began a probe into allegations of corruption in the state and local governments, and their relationship to the Klan. After weeks of testimony, the jury failed to deliver any indictments to frustrated prosecutors. Stephenson himself testified, but revealed little of use. By early January 1927, local news reports were calling the probe a "failure." Suspicion was cast on two jury members who adamantly refused to vote for indictments, raising the specter of outside influence.[43]

Six months passed with no sign that Stephenson would be pardoned or paroled. In late June 1927, he announced, "I've been double-crossed for the last time," stating "You can tell Prosecutor Remy of Marion County that I have numerous things that I am prepared to talk about freely and they are matters which I believe will start a much needed cleanup in Indiana politics."[44] A new grand jury was impaneled and began hearing testimony. Stephenson, it seems, had kept documentary evidence of widespread corruption in the state, referring to it as his "black boxes." Within weeks, local newspapers began printing copies of incriminating documents from Stephenson's trove as rumors of

---

[43] *Evansville (IN) Courier and Press*, 2 January 1927.
[44] *Evansville (IN) Courier and Press*, 29 June 1927.

indictments swirled. Governor Jackson tried to explain the $2,500 check he received from Stephenson in 1923 as "payment for a valuable saddle horse."[45] Few believed him. In early September, the grand jury issued indictments charging Governor Jackson with bribery, John L. Duvall, the mayor of Indianapolis, with violation of the corrupt practices act, as well as other charges against the chief counsel for the Klan in Indiana and the chairman of the local Republican Party. The governor managed to elude prosecution by successfully pleading that his alleged crime fell outside of the statute of limitations. Others, including Duvall, went to prison. A local judge was impeached.

For the next twenty-three years, Stephenson remained a prisoner. Finally, on his forty-seventh appeal to the State Parole Board, he was granted freedom, the conditions being that he remain under the supervision of a parole officer and that he leave the state of Indiana. The now balding and pudgy prisoner was set free on March 22, 1950. Six months later, he disappeared from a Carbondale, Illinois rooming house while his parole officer and sponsor were on vacation. After being free for two months, Stephenson was rearrested in Minneapolis, Minnesota where he had taken a job working in a newspaper print shop under the name Frank Carl Wright. His fellow employees turned him in after seeing his photo in a news story in a local paper.

For more than a year, Stephenson remained in a Minnesota jail while he fought extradition to Indiana where he was destined to resume serving his life sentence. He eventually lost and was returned in November 1951. A ten-year penalty was tacked on to his punishment. Despite this, a "last-time" parole was granted to Stephenson in December 1954. He was not freed until December 1956 because of difficulties in arranging an employment sponsor, and the prisoner's refusal to take a mental status exam. The only condition of his parole this time was that he leave Indiana. In the next few years, Stephenson was married twice, appearing in news reports only once in 1961 for alleged sexual assault against a sixteen year-old girl in Missouri. The charges were reduced to "common assault." Stephenson was fined $300 and

---

[45] *Greensboro (NC) Daily News*, 15 July 1927.

sentenced to four months in jail.[46] He died in 1966 at age seventy-four and was buried in a veterans' cemetery in Johnson City, Tennessee.

Julian LaRose Harris

An acclaimed writer and newspaperman, Julian Harris is often best remembered for the fearless stand he took against the Ku Klux Klan in Georgia in the early 1920s. The award of the Pulitzer Prize to his newspaper, the *Columbus Enquirer-Sun*, in 1926 was a validation of his courage, honesty, and willingness to pursue what he believed to be the right course, often ignoring the personal consequences. Unfortunately, these same attributes contributed heavily to Harris's failure as businessman-owner of a newspaper. Harris's and the *Enquirer-Sun's* stands in favor of the teaching of the then-controversial theory of evolution, the calls for justice and equal rights for blacks, the recognition of the inevitable failure of Prohibition, and the often-unpopular positions on politicians and political issues did little to help the paper's bottom line. Each contrarian position cut into subscriptions and advertising revenue. In the end, the *Enquirer-Sun* under Harris simply lost money. While the Pulitzer Prize brought accolades and national recognition, it did nothing to stem the financial losses. Coupled with this was the implosion of Georgia's cotton-based economy in the 1920s, the failure of many agriculture-related businesses, and the demise of nearly half the state's banks. By 1929, the paper was bankrupt, went into foreclosure and was sold to a newspaper chain. Julian Harris and his wife Julia remained as employees of the paper in non-administrative positions. When Julia was let go in December 1929, Julian also resigned. He was soon back with his old newspaper, the *Atlanta Constitution*.

In May 1930, the *Enquirer-Sun* was sold to the parent corporation of its local rival, the *Columbus Ledger*. On the same day that the sale was announced, the *Enquirer-Sun's* long-time bookkeeper, Francis E. LaCoste disappeared. He hanged himself less than a month later in a Cincinnati, Ohio hotel room. An audit of the paper's books revealed that

---

[46] *Greensboro (NC) Record*, 17 November 1961.

LaCoste had embezzled some $60,000 during his tenure, most of it while the paper was owned by the Harrises.[47]

Harris remained on the *Constitution's* staff until 1935, when he became the editor of the *Chattanooga Times*. In 1942, Harris moved back to Atlanta as a correspondent for the *New York Times*, finally beginning his retirement at age seventy in 1945. For years he worked on his autobiography but never completed it, dying in 1963 at age eighty-eight.[48]

Philip E. Fox

Of all the men associated with the Ku Klux Klan of the 1920s, Phil Fox's career was one of the more curious. A well-educated, successful newspaperman prior to his employment with the Klan, his murder of Simmons's attorney W. J. Coburn might have seemed totally out of character for a man of his situation. D. C. Stephenson, J. Q. Jett, and William J. Simmons all alleged that the killing was part of a plot formulated by Imperial Wizard Hiram Evans to suppress his rivals. These allegations were vigorously denied by Fox from his prison cell and were never pursued by the legal system.

Fox began serving his prison sentence in late 1923. In the early 1930s, after serving more than seven years, there were attempts to obtain his release on parole. During his incarceration, Fox had been a model prisoner. B. H. Dunaway, superintendent of the state prison at Milledgeville, sent a letter of endorsement stating, "He is not a criminal type, but a man of principle, education and refinement," continuing, "Fox has as good a record as any prisoner who was ever confined in the Georgia penitentiary system."[49]

Efforts to obtain Fox's release finally paid off in May 1934 when he was paroled by Governor Eugene Talmadge into the custody of none other than Imperial Wizard Hiram W. Evans. Evans said Fox was to be his personal employee earning $75 per month. Notices of his release gushed with praise for his accomplishments in prison: He had become

---

[47] Lisby and Mugleston, 219-224.
[48] *See the Chapter Notes for additional reading on Julian and Julia Harris.*
[49] *Macon Telegraph*, 6 June 1931.

known as "Doctor Fox" because of his service in the prison pharmacy. He had created a beautiful flower garden in front of the main prison dormitory, giving "many of the old and crippled prisoners jobs and enabl[ing] them to get out in the sunshine."[50]

It is unclear how long Fox stayed in Georgia after his release. His name surfaced again in 1938 in a news article stating that after his parole he "returned to his home in Dallas to hit the comeback trail." That year, country singer W. Lee O'Daniel was elected governor of the state of Texas in a surprise upset victory. According to one account, "Virtually unknown a few months ago, [O'Daniel] gained the public's eye (and its votes) by barnstorming the state with a group of hillbilly musicians, the candidate himself helping to render many of the mountain songs which he composed.[51] With the hillbilly music as a side attraction, O'Daniel had an eleven-point program—'the Ten Commandments' and an antipathy for 'those professional politicians.'" O'Daniel's campaign manager was Philip E. Fox. "The shrewdness of the former Atlanta slayer and Klan leader was in a great measure responsible for the 'hillbilly' candidate's amazing triumph."[52]

The Reverend Caleb Alford Ridley

Caleb Alford Ridley was born under trying circumstances in North Carolina, earning money to pay for his first schooling by hoeing tobacco in the fields. He later went on to attend Wake Forest, Mercer University, and the Moody Bible institute in Chicago. He became, as one report described him, "one of the most widely known platform speakers of the South."[53] Despite his Horatio Alger upbringing and his good works as a

---

[50] *Macon Telegraph*, 4 May 1933.

[51] O'Daniel later went on to be elected as US Senator from Texas, in the process becoming the only man to defeat Lyndon B. Johnson for elective office. O'Daniel was a prolific songwriter; some of his works included "The Yellow Rose of Texas," "Teenage Boogie," "Pussy, Pussy, Pussy," "Cripple Creek," "It's No Sin to Rock," and "Don't Lie to an Innocent Maiden." Audio recordings of many are available on *www.youtube.com*.

[52] *Augusta Chronicle*, 27 July 1938.

[53] *Atlanta Constitution*, 22 August 1926.

minister, he is most often remembered for his role as the Imperial Kludd in the early days of the Ku Klux Klan.

Ridley, a supporter of W. J. Simmons, split with the Klan at the same time as the Emperor. By 1926, he was holding a pastorate in Sour Lake, Texas, but took time off that summer to become the field director for the gubernatorial campaign of J. O. Wood, former Klansman and publisher of *The Searchlight* during the days of the Simmons regime. The following year he became involved with Edward Y. Clarke's Supreme Kingdom, paid $6,000 per year as "spiritual advisor" and sometimes lecturer.[54]

After a hiatus of several years during which time he moved to North Dakota, Ridley was back in Georgia in 1930 helping organize a local division of the American Fascisti, a black-shirted organization of fascists inspired by Mussolini in Italy.[55] At the time, the Great Depression well underway and jobs were increasingly scarce. The organization's plan was to "serve notice on business firms in Georgia to get rid of negro employees and give the jobs to white men."[56] After a change of name of the organization to the Knights of America, Ridley settled in Waycross, Georgia as editor of the group's official organ, *The Black Shirt*.[57]

Shortly after the publication's initial issue, Ridley was arrested in Waynesville, North Carolina, charged with violation of the Prohibition law and driving an automobile while intoxicated. His court date was postponed; newspaper reports said he was "suffering from a complete nervous breakdown."[58] A month later Ridley's case was *nolle prossed*; he was said to be "seriously ill in Atlanta."[59] He died there on January 20, 1932, at the age of fifty-eight. Multiple obituaries did not give a cause of death. In an editorial titled, "His Talents Wasted," the *Macon Telegraph* said, "Dr. Ridley might have been a really useful member of society if he

---

[54] *Macon Telegraph*, 8 January 1927.
[55] *Macon Telegraph*, 18 July 1930.
[56] From the *New Republic*, reproduced in the *New Yorker Volkszeitung*, 12 October 1930.
[57] *Macon Telegraph*, 16 June 1931.
[58] *Charlotte Observer*, 1 September 1931; *Macon Telegraph*, 3 November 1931.
[59] *Augusta Chronicle*, 2 December 1931.

had turned his talents and his tremendous energies in the direction of something which was of real service to the American people."

John Gutzon de la Mothe Borglum

Gutzon Borglum is best known as the sculptor of South Dakota's Mount Rushmore. Few are aware that Borglum was an early member of the Ku Klux Klan and sat on the Klan's Kloncilium, the order's ruling council during the Imperial Wizardship of William J. Simmons. Though his role in the Klan saga is a relatively minor one, were it not for his membership, it is quite conceivable that the massive granite heads of Mount Rushmore would have never been carved.

Borglum was recruited by Helen Plane in 1915 to design and build an appropriate memorial to the Confederacy on the sheer face of Georgia's Stone Mountain. Borglum was at the time, and remains in the annals of history, one of America's most talented and prolific sculptors. On his first visit to Georgia to assess the proposed task, Borglum met Sam Venable. Venable's family owned Stone Mountain and had given permission to build the monument. The project, which was to have started in the late 'teens, was deferred due to World War I. By the time of its resumption in 1920, the Klan had been formed and was about to begin its rapid period of growth under the guidance of Edward Young Clarke and Elizabeth Tyler.

Borglum was apparently introduced to the Klan by Venable, one of the order's charter members. Despite being a member of the Catholic faith, Borglum joined it because he agreed with its ideals for America. In short order he became a friend and supporter of William Simmons, and soon thereafter, of D. C. Stephenson in Indiana. Another significant reason for Borglum's membership in the order was the possibility of the Klan's monetary support for the expensive Stone Mountain memorial project. Edward Clarke promised to assist in fund-raising, but his rapid fall from power in 1923 after the coup that toppled Simmons as Imperial Wizard destroyed that possibility. During the internal struggles for power in 1923, Borglum was a supporter of both Simmons and Stephenson, both of whom lost out in the end. The taint of these ill-fated political alliances extended to the Board of the Stone Mountain Confederate Monumental Association and likely had some bearing on the Association's decision to cancel Borglum's contract in February 1925. The sculptor moved on to his next major project, the Mount Rushmore Memorial. Had the contract been continued, it is quite conceivable that the massive heads of Washington, Jefferson, Lincoln, and Roosevelt, a twelve-year project, would not have been created out of the stone of South Dakota's Black Hills.[60]

Thomas Dixon

Thomas Dixon, author of the novel *The Clansman* which was later adapted for the silver screen in the form of *The Birth of a Nation*, was an early and frequent critic of William J. Simmons's Knights of the Ku Klux Klan. Speaking before a meeting of the American Unity League in 1923, Dixon said,

> The original Klan was founded as a weapon against a corrupt and intolerable tyranny by the bravest and noblest men of the South, but the proscription of the negro by the modern Klan is inhuman. The Klan's assault upon the foreigner is the acme of stupidity and inhumanity. We are all foreigners, except the few Indians we haven't killed. Our fathers blazed the way through the wilderness and for the trembling feet of liberty they built a beacon on these shores, flashing its rays of hope to all the oppressed of the earth. Shall we, their sons, meet the humble immigrant of today with a mask and dagger and push him back into hell? If this is 100 percent Americanism, I, for one, spit on it.[61]

---

[60] *See Chapter Notes for additional information on Borglum and Stone Mountain.*

[61] *Evening Post (Charleston, SC),* 23 January 1923

Epilogue...

In October 1945, a huge cross burned once again on Stone Mountain, said to be visible from as far as sixty miles away. A few days later an article in the *New York Times* featured an interview with Dr. Samuel Green, Atlanta obstetrician and Grand Dragon of the revived Georgia Ku Klux Klan.[1] Green, whose photo accompanying the article bore an uncanny resemblance to the recently-deceased Adolph Hitler, said, "The Klan has as much right to exist as the Masons, Rotarians or any other organization." The organization was "voluntary," and its main purpose, beyond those of the recently disbanded Knights of the Ku Klux Klan, Inc., was to fight communism. Some eight months later agents of the Georgia Bureau of Investigation filed court documents accusing the Klan "of a conspiracy to seize key governmental agencies and of employing secret propaganda to enforce its doctrines upon the State by violence, terrorism, and hate."[2] At the same time, agents of the Federal Bureau of Investigation advised Georgia Governor Ellis Arnold of an assassination plot on his life hatched in Atlanta's Oakland City Klavern. Dr. Green stated he had "thoroughly investigated" the reports and found them to be "wholly false."[3]

And so it continued....

---

[1] *New York Times*, 21 October 1945.
[2] *New York Times*, 21 June 1946.
[3] *New York Times*, 23 June 1946.

Appendix

A Glossary of Ku Klux Klan Terms

Contemporary Newspaper Coverage of the
Ku Klux Klan 1910-1940

A Glossary of Ku Klux Klan Terms

Like many fraternal orders of the era, the Knights of the Ku Klux Klan, Inc. had their own terminology to describe various offices, positions, and functions within the organization. For the most part, these sprang from the mind of the Klan's founder, William J. Simmons, who appreciated the semi-mystical and dramatic nature of such in the order's ritual and reputation. As a matter of convenience the terms listed below are given in alphabetical order. Many, though not all, begin with the "kl" alliteration. Some titles are taken from those used by the Ku Klux Klan of the 1860s.

The names of offices or officers were modified by the addition of various adjectives signifying level in the organization. For example, the order's national chaplain would be referred to as the *Imperial* Kludd, whereas the chaplain of a local Klavern (chapter) would simply be the Kludd.

Term	Meaning
Aliens	All persons who are not Klansmen
Exalted Cyclops	The highest officer of a Klavern
Furies	Collectively, the sub-offices of a Province
Genii	Collectively, the sub-officers of the Klan on a national level
Grand Dragon	The highest officer of a Realm
Great Titan	The highest officer of a Province
Hydra	Collectively, the sub-officers of the Klan in a Realm
Imperial Wizard	The Supreme Chief Executive of the Klan
Invisible Empire	The geographic distribution of the Klan, i.e., "the whole world"

Klabee	Treasurer
Kladd	Conductor
Klaliff	A second-in-command, equivalent to a vice president
Klanishness/Klancraft	The practical implementation of the philosophy of the Klan
Klansman	A member of the Klan in good standing
Klanton	The division of the Klan below the Province level
Klarogo	Inner Guard
Klavern	Local Klan Chapter
Klazik	A third-in-command, equivalent to a second vice president
Kleagle	Recruiter and membership officer
Klectoken	A *donation* given as an initiation fee for membership in the Klan
Klepeer	Delegate to the Imperial Klonvocation
Klexter	Outer Guard
Kligrapp	Secretary
Klokann	A board of auditors, investigators and/or advisors when assembled to judge on a matter
Klokard	Lecturer
Kloncilium	Collectively, the officers of the Klan—equivalent to a Board of Directors
Klonklave	A secret meeting of the Klan
Klonsel	Attorney
Klonverse	Convention of a Province of the Klan
Klonvocation	Convention of the Imperial Empire
Kloran	The book containing the Klan's constitution and rituals
Klorero	Convention of a Realm

Kludd	Chaplin
Naturalization	The ritual and process by when a candidate is admitted to membership in the Invisible Empire
Night-hawk	Courier of the Klan, in charge of candidates for naturalization on a Klavern level
Terrors	Collectively, the sub-officers of a Klavern

Contemporary Newspaper Coverage of Ku Klux Klan 1910-1940

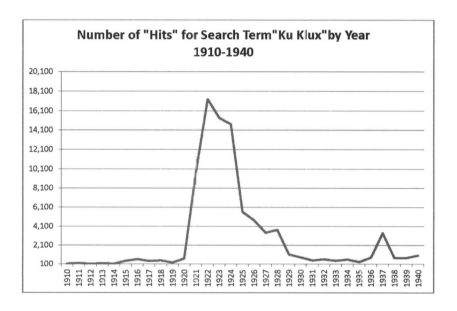

The membership of the Ku Klux Klan of the 1920s roughly mimicked its press coverage. This graph details the number of "hits" for the search term "Ku Klux" entered into a single American newspaper internet archive search engine. Even though the Knights of the Ku Klux Klan, Inc. was founded in 1915, it was only in 1920 with the employment of Edward Y. Clarke that the Klan became a national news story. The order's membership (and power) peaked in 1924-25 and fell into a sharp decline thereafter. The peak in 1937 represents news coverage surrounding President Roosevelt's nomination of ex-Klansman Hugo Black to the United States Supreme Court. (Chart based on data derived from *www.genealogybank.com*. Accessed 1 November 2014).

Chapter Notes

Chapter 1

The Founding of the Ku Klux Klan: The building where the members of the Klan allegedly first met in 1865 was, at the time, the law office of Judge Thomas Jones. It still exists on a side street within view of the Pulaski courthouse. In 1917, it was adorned with a bronze plaque erected by the United Daughters of the Confederacy commemorating the site of the founding of the Ku Klux Klan. As of 1924, the building had been purchased by the then-newly revived Klan to be "kept as a shrine." The plaque itself was stolen in 1972, but returned four months later after a $50 reward was offered. The current owner of the building, understandably uncomfortable with publicity generated by the plaque, has left it in place, but reversed, such that only the blank back side is visible.

As to the Klan's name, an alternative and seemingly highly speculative explanation for its origin is given by the authors of a 1924 pamphlet (Romine) published in Pulaski by the local newspaper. It was pointed out that a number of men from the Pulaski area were veterans of the Mexican-American War (1846-48), and consequently might have heard of Cukulcan, described as "the god of light" in "Mexican mythology." Based on the theory that some of the Klan's founders might have "learned the story of Cukulcan" from their fathers or uncles, the writers suggest this as a possible alternative source of the name. They point out that Klan members sometimes referred to themselves as "sons of light" as the primary justification for this possibility. The name "Cukulcan" does not correspond to any recognizable Aztec deity.

Chapter 3

Gen. Nathan B. Forrest and the Ku Klux Klan: Some historians note that there is little hard evidence to prove that Forrest was the first Grand Wizard, or even that he was a member the Ku Klux Klan. Most, however, agree that he was, with the lack of documentation to be expected given the secret nature of the organization. The Klan of the 1860s remained controversial well into the twentieth century prior to its revival in 1915, and it is quite conceivable that subsequent admirers of Forrest did not wish to stain his name by promoting any association with the order. His leading biographer, John Allen Wyeth, first published *The Life of General Nathan Bedford Forrest* in 1899, with the book remaining in press for a number of years. Despite Forrest's well-publicized link to the Klan, Wyeth devotes a dismissive two paragraphs to the subject in the 600-plus page text. (See Wyeth, *That Devil Forrest: Life of General Nathan Bedford Forrest*) Stanley Horn addresses this issue in some detail in his *Invisible Empire: The Story of the Ku Klux Klan 1866-1871.*

Chapter 4

Albion Tourgée: Tourgée later went on to achieve success both as a writer and in politics. His commitment to civil rights led him to become lead attorney for Homer Plessy, the losing plaintiff in what would become the landmark 1896 Supreme Court case of *Plessy v. Ferguson* which established the "separate but equal" doctrine that upheld legalized segregation for decades. Tourgée later served as United States consul to France, appointed by President McKinley. Tourgée's book, *A Fool's Errand*, was in some ways a *roman à clef* based on his experience in Reconstruction North Carolina. His description of a carpetbagger, being himself one, is telling:

> "Carpet-bagger," which was in some sense the lineal descendant of "abolitionist," was, as was very proper for a second edition, a considerable improvement on its immediate predecessor. It was undefined and undefinable. To the Southern mind it meant a scion of the North, a son of an "abolitionist," a creature of the conqueror, a witness to their defeat, a mark of their degradation: to them he was hateful because he recalled all the evil or shame which they had ever known. They hissed the name through lips hot with hate, because his presence was hateful to that dear, dead Confederacy which they held in tender memory, and mourned for in widow's weeds, and as was but natural that they should do so. They hated the Northern man, who came among them as the representative and embodiment of that selfish, malign, and envious North, which had sent forth the "abolitionist" in ante bellum days, had crushed the fair South in her heroic struggle to establish a slave-sustained republic, and now had sent spies and harpies to prey upon, to mock and taunt and jeer

them in their downfall and misfortune. To their minds, the word expressed all that collective and accumulated hate which generations of antagonism had engendered, intensified, and sublimated by the white-heat of a war of passionate intensity and undoubted righteousness to the hearts of its promoters. (Anonymous (Tourgée), p.160)

Chapter 5

The End of Fraternalism: The decline of fraternal societies in the United States began in the late 1920s for a number of reasons. Perhaps most prominent was the changing tastes of the American population—folks simply got tired of them. With the automobile in common use, Americans became more mobile and found other interests. Radio and movies opened new worlds to be explored. Wives tired of their husbands spending one or more nights a week away from home "at the Lodge." Many societies promoted insurance and other financial benefits for their members, often without adequate underwriting standards. This aspect, especially with the onset of the Great Depression, caused the collapse of many. Others, e.g., the Woodmen of the World (founded in 1890), transitioned over the years to a role of primarily offering commercial financial products, including life insurance. Additionally , the very closed nature of many secret organizations became less attractive when compared to the open lunchtime meeting format of a new wave of civic, business, and service clubs, including Rotary, founded in 1910, Kiwanis, founded in 1915, Lions, founded in 1917 and Optimists, founded in 1919.

Chapter 6

More on William J. Simmons and the Woodmen of the World: Simmons's oratory abilities were well displayed in his address in a memorial service honoring Joseph C. Root, founder of the Woodmen of the World. "All humanity was his friend: for in his heart of hearts, his soul of souls, there was no Gentile or Jew, no bonded or free. He walked in the darkness of morality's night giving hope and cheer and died with a prayer on his lips for the work he began. He did not allow himself to become saturated with small things and driven by every wind, nor to be at the mercy of small minds. He lived to make secure the bulwarks of the people." (*Atlanta Constitution* 2 February 1914) He remained active in the Woodmen of the World even while planning for the Knights of the Ku Klux Klan. In July 1915, three months before the initial Klan organizational meeting, he was given credit for helping Atlanta win the venue for the 1916 WOW convention. (*Atlanta Constitution* 7-20-15)

Chapter 8

The Flaming Cross: In the days prior to the Internet, many households with school-age children possessed a copy of *The World Book Encyclopedia,* the quintessential home reference source for much of the twentieth century. A student of the 1960s researching "Ku Klux Klan" would have found a large photo of a group of white-robed hooded men standing in a circle around a flaming Christian Cross. Although the location of the photo was not given, it was taken in Wrightsville, Georgia in the late 1940s. More so than any other symbol, the burning cross has become inextricably associated with the Klan. But what are its origins?

The so-called "Fiery Cross" had no association with the original Klux Ku Klan of the 1860s. This symbol, like much of the iconography of the 1920s and subsequent Klans, was directly adopted from D. W. Griffith's movie, *The Birth of a Nation.* In the film, hooded Klansmen arrive to save the day, carrying the symbol of flaming crosses. Griffith's movie was adapted from Thomas Dixon's 1905 romantic novel *The Clansman,* wherein "the old Scottish rite of the Fiery Cross" is invoked to call the Klan to action after the summary execution of a black man who had attacked a white woman. Dixon, in turn, had adopted the symbol from Scottish lore of the *Crann Tara* (Gaelic for "Fiery Cross"), when a small burning cross was used to summon the clans in time of war. Sir Walter Scott recounts its use in his 1810 narrative poem, "The Lady of the Lake."

Stanley F. Horn, author of *Invisible Empire: The Story of the Ku Klux Klan 1866-1871,* expressed some annoyance that Simmons's revived Klan had adopted the flaming cross as a symbol. In an epilogue to 1969 edition of his history, he wrote, "When I had concluded my rather extensive research into the origin and practice of the original Ku Klux

Klan, it suddenly dawned on me that there had not been any mention of any use of a 'fiery cross' in any of the recorded public appearances of the Ku Klux of the 1860s, either in newspaper accounts of parades or demonstrations or in the testimony of any of the cloud of witnesses who testified in the Congressional Inquiry in 1872. (*sic*) This seemed strange so I wrote to Dixon and asked him what authority, if any, he had for introducing this feature in his novel." Dixon gave a vague reply, and when Horn pressed for further details on the subject, Dixon refused to answer his letters. Horn then concluded, "Griffith, probably not knowing (and not caring) about the attenuated basis for associating the fiery cross with the actual activities of the actual Ku Klux Klan, certainly recognized the dramatic possibilities of this gimmick and made it an outstanding and impressive feature of his motion picture. Thus, the fiery cross become erroneously but indelibly fixed in the public mind as an essential feature of the official ceremonies of the original Ku Klux Klan...." (Horn, p. 438)

The outrages committed by the Klan have transformed a burning cross into a powerful symbol of hate and bigotry, equal to that of the Nazi swastika. States and municipalities across the nation have passed laws and ordinances banning its display, resulting in a number of legal actions, some of which have reached the United States Supreme Court. Perhaps the most well-known of these is *Virginia v. Black* et al., decided by the court in 2003. The State of Virginia had passed a statue declaring that the "burning of a cross shall be *prima facie* evidence of an attempt to intimidate a person or a group of persons." As such, the mere act would fall into the category of intimidating "hate speech," certain types of which have been found to be illegal despite the free speech guarantees of the First Amendment. The majority of the court held that while the burning of a cross "with the attempt to intimidate" could be proscribed, use of the symbol itself was protected as free expression under the Constitution.

Simmons undoubtedly adopted the flaming cross symbol from Griffith's movie. There is one suggestion, however, that it had been used previously in the same general time frame. In his dramatized account of the Leo Frank case (*A Little Girl is Dead*, The World Publishing Company, New York, 1965) author Harry Golden states, "Two months to the day after they had lynched Frank, the Knights [of Mary Phagan] climbed to the bald top of Stone Mountain outside of Atlanta and burned a huge cross, visible throughout the city." This statement is unreferenced, and no confirmation could be found from other sources. Perhaps the most detailed and objective account of the Frank case is that of Steve Oney in *And the Dead Shall Rise* (Pantheon Books, New York, 2003). Contacted via email for his opinion on this possible event, Oney related that he, too, had never seen any other documentation of the alleged event. This bit of unsubstantiated information is presented for the reader's interest, but in the opinion of the author, it is considered unlikely to be factual.

Chapter 16

Politicians in the Klan: In a series of articles on the Ku Klux Klan in *The World's Work* in mid-1923, journalist Robert L. Duffus proposed that men who joined the order fell into six broad categories: "(1) organizers and promoters; (2) businessmen, who joined to get or keep trade; (3) politicians; (4) preachers, honest fanatics, and people who have been misled as to the Klan's real inwardness; (5) the 'horse play' crowd, 'joiners,' men looking for excitement; (6) bootleggers, joining for protection." (*The World's Work*, Vol. 46, No. 2, June 1923, p. 183) Between 1922 and 1926 or so, the third of these classes, politicians, thrived because of support of the Klan, and in turn, many were eventually turned out of office for the same reason. Klan-backed candidates on local, regional, state, and national levels were elected to office in many areas of the United States. As politics is often a game of polarity, for similar reasons many others were elected based on their opposition to the Klan.

In Georgia, more so than any other state, the Klan gained an early political foothold. In the early to mid-years of the 1920s, Klan-supported elected and appointed officials—in many cases Klansmen themselves—held sway in Atlanta, Macon, and Columbus. Clifford Walker, a Klansman, was elected as the State's governor in 1922. Tom Watson, a Klan supporter if not a member, was Georgia's United States Senator at the time. United States Supreme Court Associate Justice Hugo Black joined the Klan briefly as a young man. A number of other prominent politicians on a regional or national level did so as well, or were rumored to have done so. Generally, these issues arose later in their political career when a history of association with the Ku Klux Klan would have been a political liability.

Perhaps the most prominent national political figure alleged to have been a Klan member was President Warren Harding. His induction as a citizen of the Invisible Empire is presented as fact by at least one prominent historian, Wyn Craig Wade, in his book *The Fiery Cross*. (Wade, 165) The exact timing of Harding's alleged joining is not given, but is presumed to be sometime in 1921 or 1922 after the Congressional Hearings. Harding died suddenly while in office in August 1923. According to Wade, whose account is based on the evidence of others, Harding was "naturalized" in the Green Room of the White House by a five-man "induction" team led by Imperial Wizard William J. Simmons. The brief account contains enough details to give it an aura of verisimilitude, but most historians and others who have examined the allegation doubt its truth.

Numerous references regarding politicians who supported or who were or were alleged to be members of the Klan are available via routine internet search. More specific information is available from the many written books focusing on various regional activities of the Knights of the Ku Klux Klan across the United States and Canada. For a review of the Klan's political activities in its home state of Georgia, the interested reader is directed to C. C. Moseley's article, "The Political Influence of the Ku Klux Klan in Georgia, 1915-1925." (*The Georgia Historical Quarterly*, Vol. 57, No. 2, 235-255.)

Chapter 19

The Mann Act: The White-Slave Traffic Act of 1910 was named after Congressman James R. Mann of Illinois, one of its prime sponsors. The law made it a felony to cross state lines or international borders transporting "any woman or girl for the purpose of prostitution or debauchery, or for any other immoral purpose." While the Act still forms the basis of Federal law it has been modified extensively by congressional amendments and court interpretations. The deliberately vague original wording, citing "immoral purpose" and "debauchery" could be, and in the past has been, construed to represent consensual sexual relations between unmarried persons. Under current amendments, the Act has been made gender neutral and broadened to include such activities as child pornography.

Prosecutions of alleged offenses under this Act have often been selective, frequently targeting high-profile individuals who might have otherwise offended law enforcement officials. Over the years, the list of persons investigated, charged, or tried under provisions of the Mann Act is quite interesting, including such notables as Frank Lloyd Wright, Charlie Chaplin, Chuck Berry, Charles Manson, Tony Alamo, Warren Jeffs, associates of New York Governor Eliot Spitzer, and Anwar al-Awlaki. The outcome of their cases varied—some were convicted, others found innocent, and in some instances the charges were dropped or never formally brought to trial. The case of al-Awlaki was an exception; he was killed in a CIA-led drone strike in Yemen in 2011.

Chapter 21

"The Nazi Salute": Americans rarely salute. Historically, we are not a militaristic society, reserving overt displays of patriotism for times of national crisis and war. In our daily lives we tend to limit our salutes to the playing of the national anthem or during the Pledge of Allegiance to the flag. Most Americans of the current day would be astonished to discover that up until the late 1930s, the standard and accepted way of saluting the American flag was what we now refer to as the "Nazi Salute," the right arm extended upward and outward.

The Pledge of Allegiance was written by Francis Bellamy in 1892. It was originally published that year in a children's magazine, *The Youth's Companion*, accompanied by instructions that the right arm be extended, palm upward, toward the flag during the recitation of the pledge. The gesture soon became known as the "Bellamy salute," and became the standard way of addressing the flag over the following decades. It was incorporated in The National Flag Code in 1923, which in turn was voted into Federal law in June 1942 during the early days of World War II.

The Klan adopted the Bellamy Salute, but altered it by changing it to a left-handed gesture. Perhaps the framers of the Klan's signs and rituals simply wanted to be different; one explanation offered is that the left hand is nearer the heart

During the same era in Europe, Italian Fascists had adopted the so-called "Roman salute," exactly equivalent to Bellamy's. In the early 1920s, German National Socialists—the Nazis—embraced it, making its use in certain situations a compulsory part of daily life after they came to power in 1933. During the turbulent years of the 1930s, the Bellamy salute remained in common use in the United States while becoming increasingly associated with the militarism and oppression of Hitler's Germany.

In December 1942, some six months after making the Bellamy—and now Nazi—salute a part of the law, Congress modified its language to make the hand-over-the-heart gesture the prescribed form of addressing the flag during the Pledge of Allegiance. So it remains today. In Germany and other parts of the former Third Reich, the raised hand salute has been declared illegal and its use can result in imprisonment.

Chapter 23

The Know-Nothing Movement: The "Know-Nothing" movement was a uniquely American social movement that briefly wielded some political power in the 1850s. It is generally described as "nativist" in that it grew out of resentment of the growing waves of European immigrants that arrived in the United States in the 1830s and 1840s. Major issues were competition for jobs and other social resources, but a more prominent focus revolved around anti-Catholicism and papal conspiracy theories as many of the newcomers were of the Catholic faith. Adherents often formed local secret or semi-secret societies whose purpose was to oppose immigration and the granting of citizenship and other rights to new immigrants. Members of these organizations were advised to reply, "I know nothing," if asked about affiliation with such a group or the group's activities. Know-Nothing support helped elect a number of political candidates in the early 1850s. The short-lived American Party was an outgrowth of the movement. Regional differences and attitude to the issue of slavery did much to dissolve the cohesiveness of the movement, which was essentially defunct as a uniform political force by the start of the Civil War.

Chapter 24

Julian Harris: Despite his fame as a newspaperman and recipient of the Pulitzer Prize, relatively little has been written about Julian Harris. Indeed, his wife Julia, a most talented writer and historian, may be better known. The couple's life and careers are detailed in Julian Harris's biography, *Someone Had to Be Hated*, published by Lisby and Mugleston in 2002.

Gutzon Borglum: Gutzon Borglum's brief membership in the Ku Klux Klan was apparently a source of embarrassment to his family. There are two major biographies of his life, *Give the Man Room* by Robert J. Casey and Mary Borglum, published in 1952, and *Six Wars at a Time* by Howard and Audrey Shaff, published in 1985. Both address the major points in Borglum's life and career, but differ markedly in one fundamental way. While the latter work goes into some detail regarding the sculptor's Klan membership and the associated politics thereof, the former—of which his wife was a co-author—fails to mention the Klan at all. Likewise, Borglum's papers in the Library of Congress contain a number of items of correspondence relating to the Klan. Those in Emory University's Manuscript and Rare Book Library, however, a gift of family members, appear to have been sanitized to remove correspondence and other documents relating to the Ku Klux Klan.

An additional work that refers to Borglum and the Klan is David Freeman's *Carved in Stone: The History of Stone Mountain* (Mercer University Press, 1997).

Author's Note and Acknowledgments

Writing is a voyage of discovery; the process of creating this book was no exception. As noted in the Author's Preface, much of my interest in the Ku Klux Klan of the 1920s sprang from the research I did for my previous book, *A Killing on Ring Jaw Bluff*. That morphed into an article published in the Winter 2012 issue of *Georgia Backroads* magazine which, in vastly expanded form, became this current work. Perhaps the biggest discovery for me during the process of research and writing was the large amount of information on the Klan that had not been included (or only mentioned in passing) in previous works on the subject. Over the last decade or so, a vast treasure trove of historical newspapers, magazines, out-of-copyright books, pamphlets, and other ephemera has become available via the internet. This collective resource is a rich store of fresh data on then-current events of the past, often opening new doors, or providing new and expanded perspectives.

Like most historians, I tried whenever possible to draw my story from primary sources, the most valuable of which turned out to be these newspapers. There are a number of internet sites offering historical newspapers dating from recent times back to the eighteenth century. All are quite incomplete in their coverage of the American press, but between their various offerings, and often relying on proprietary sites run by existing major dailies, one can obtain a fairly comprehensive record of events of the day as well as public and private opinion based on editorials and letters to the editor. Through careful reading and term-specific searches, it is often possible to piece together a story that a few years ago would have been quite difficult to decipher.

As an interesting observation, newspaper coverage of the Ku Klux Klan, at least as measured by internet search result "hits," closely tracks the Klan's rise and fall in the 1920s. A chart of search results for the term "Ku Klux" derived from one historical newspaper site for the years 1910-1940 reveals very few mentions prior to 1920 when Clarke and Tyler took over recruitment and publicity. (See Figure, page 288) Press coverage peaked between 1922 and 1924 before beginning a sharp decline. By 1930 and beyond, the Klan was rarely the topic of news stories.

Other major and unique sources of data included library collections. In this regard I am indebted to the manuscript and rare book collections of Emory University in Atlanta, and the University of Georgia in Athens. The microfilm collection of old Georgia newspapers in the main University of Georgia library holds a number of rare and important papers that are not readily available elsewhere. Lucinda Cockrell of the Middle Tennessee State University in Murfreesboro graciously researched the University's Center for Popular Music's collection for musical works on the Klan from the nineteenth and early twentieth centuries.

I am especially indebted to Col. John Shotwell whose unpublished Masters thesis on the "marketing" of the Ku Klux Klan is a beautifully insightful analysis explaining the order's rapid propagation in the early 1920s. Col. Shotwell was also kind enough to provide some of the unique photos that are included in this book. Steve Oney, author of *And the Dead Shall Rise*, was helpful in answering questions regarding the Knights of Mary Phagan. There were several individuals whose relatives were members of the Klan of the 1920s and who were willing to share their thoughts and experiences on the condition that their names not be mentioned. I will honor those requests while expressing my appreciation.

A number of individuals were kind enough to read and criticize the book when it was a work-in-progress. First and foremost in this regard, I must thank Dan Roper, publisher of *Georgia Backroads* magazine, for his input and support, not only of this project but also my writing in general. My thanks as well to Dennis Coxwell, Benjie Tarbutton, Frank Seagraves, Sarah Campbell Arnett, Mary Eleanor Wickersham, Tom Kennedy, and others who prefer to remain anonymous.

The time and effort devoted to writing would have been impossible if I did not have the support of my assistant, Brandi Taylor, and of my office nurse, Jessica Heldreth. Both were extremely helpful in allowing me the time and freedom required to complete this book. On a personal basis, writing—not to mention the days and weeks spent in various libraries or hunched over a computer—of necessity takes time away from obligations to family and friends. I am grateful to my wife and children for their patience and forbearance in this regard. Finally, I must thank my muse, the lovely Laura Ashley, for her ongoing encouragement and inspiration.

In the process of writing and drawing from then-current and primary sources, I have quoted material from a wide variety of newspapers, books, magazines, and other writings. It is my general policy to preserve the often stilted and sometimes complex verbiage in quoted material, even though the spelling, punctuation, capitalization, syntax, etc. would be considered incorrect by current standards. On rare occasions I have corrected obvious typos within quotes. If any changes beyond this were made to the quoted material, I have noted such in the text or in a footnote. The "Sources and Resources" section that follows contains several entries not directly quoted in the text, but consulted during the writing of this work. I have included these for reference as I consider them valuable and/or interesting background material for the reader wishing to further explore this topic or era.

I welcome feedback and comments. Feel free to contact me via email at dirkrawlings@gmail.com.

William Rawlings

Sources and Resources

Books, Pamphlets and Related:

Anonymous (Albion W. Tourgée). *A Fool's Errand*. New York: Fords, Howard & Hulbert, 1879.

Anomymous. *The Masked Lady of the Whilte House: Or The Ku-Klux-Klan*. Philadelphia: C. W. Alexander, 1868.

Anonymous. *The Nation's Peril: Twelve Years' Experience in the South. Then and Now. The Ku Klux Klan*. New York: "Friends of the Compiler,"1872.

Anonymous. *The Oaths, Signs, Ceremonies and Objects of the Ku Klux Klan*. Cleveland: Privately Published, 1868.

Avary, Myrta L. *Dixie After the War*. New York: Doubleday, Page & Company, 1906.

Bartley, Numan V. *The Creation of Modern Georgia*. Athens GA: University of Georgia Press, 1990.

Bickley, R. Bruce. *Joel Chandler Harris*. Athens GA: University of Georgia Press, 1987.

Blee, Kathleen M. *Women of the Klan: Racism and Gender in the 1920s*. Berkeley CA: University of California Press, 2009.

Brown, George A. *Harold the Klansman*. Kansas City MO: The Western Baptist Publishing Company, 1923.

Brown, William Garrott. *The Lower South in American History*. New York: MacMillan Company, 1903

Burton, Annie C. *The Ku Klux Klan*. Los Angles: Warren T. Potter, 1916.

Chalmers, David M. *Hooded Americanism*. Durham NC: Duke University Press, 1981.

Coakley, Robert W. *The Role of Military Forces in Domestic Disturbances 1789-1878*. Washington: Center for Military History, 1988.

Committee on Rules, U. S. *The Ku Klux Klan: Hearings Before the Committee on Rules*. Washington: Government Printing Office, 1921.

Cook, Raymond A. *Thomas Dixon*. New York: Twayne Publishers, 1974.

Coughlan, Robert. "Konklave (*sic*) in Kokomo," in *The Aspirin Age 1919-1941*, edited by Isabel Leighton, New York: Simon & Schuster, 1949.

Cutlip, Scott M. *The Unseen Power: Public Relations. A History*. Hillsdale NJ: Lawrence Erlbaum Associates, 1994.

Damer, Erye. *When The Klan Rode*. New York: Neale Publishing Company, 1912.

Davis, Susan L. *Authentic History: Ku Klux Klan 1865-1877*. New York: American Library Service, 1924.

De Tocqueville, Alexis. *Democracy in America*. 1835. Reprint, New York: Colonial Press, 1899.

Dixon, Edward H. *The Terrible Mysteries of the Ku Klux Klan*. New York: Privately Published, 1868.

Sources and Resources

Dixon, Thomas. *The Flaming Sword*. 1939. Reprint, Lexington: University of Kentucky Press, 2005.

Early, Jubal A. *A Memoir of the Last Year of the War for Independance in the Confederate States of America*. New Orleans: Blelock & Company, 1867.

Fahs, Alice, and Waugh, Joan. *The Memory of the Civil War in American Culture*. Chapel Hill: The University of North Carolina Press, 2004.

Fisher, William H. *The Invisible Empire: A Bibliography of the Ku Klux Klan*. Metuchen NJ: Scarecrow Press, 1980.

Foner, Eric. *Reconstruction: America's Unfinished Revolution 1863–1877*. New York: Harper& Row, 1988.

Foster, Gaines M. *Ghosts of the Confederacy*. New York: Oxford University Press, 1987.

Fox, Craig. *Everyday Klansfolk: White Protestant Life and the KKK in 1920s Michigan*. East Lansing: Michigan State University Press, 2011

Freeman, David B. *Carved in Stone: The History of Stone Mountain*. Macon: Mercer University Press, 1997.

Fry, Henry P. *The Modern Ku Klux Klan*. Boston: Small, Maynard & Company, 1922.

Gallagher, Gary W. "Jubal A. Early, The Lost Cause, and Civil War History." *Frank L. Klement Lecture (No. 4)*. Milwaukee: Marquette University Press, 1995.

Gallagher, Gary W., and Nolan, Alan T. *The Myth of the Lost Cause*. Bloomington IN: Indiana University Press, 2000.

Golden, Harry. *A Little Girl is Dead*. Cleveland OH: World Publishing Company, 1965.

Grady, Henry W. *The New South*. New York: Robert Bonner's Sons, 1890.

Grant, Ulysses S. *Personal Memoirs of U. S. Grant*. New York: C. L. Webster, 1885.

Harris, Joel Chandler. *Life of Henry W. Grady*. New York: Cassell Publishing Company, 1890.

Horn, Stanley F. *Invisible Empire: The Story of the Ku Klux Klan 1866–1871*. 2nd ed. Montclair NJ: Patterson Smith Publishing Corporation, 1969.

Hough, Emerson. *The Web*. Chicago: The Reilly & Lee Company, 1919.

Ingalls, Robert P. *Hoods: The Story of the Ku Klux Klan*. New York: G. P. Putnam's Sons, 1979.

Jackson, Helen. *Convent Cruelties or My Life in the Convent*. Toledo: Privately Published, 1919.

Jackson, Kenneth T. *The Ku Klux Klan in the City 1915–1930*. New York: Oxford University Press, 1967.

Jerome, Thomas J. *Ku-Klux Klan No. 40*. Raleigh NC: Edwards & Broughton, 1895.

Joint Select Committee. *The Condition of Affairs in the Late Insurrectionary States*. Washington: Government Printing Office, 1872.

Jones, Winfield. *The Story of the Ku Klux Klan*. Washington: American Newspaper Syndicate, 1921.

Knight, Lucian Lamar. *A Standard History of Georgia and Georgians, Vol. 5*. Chicago: The Lewis Publishing Company, 1917.

Knights of the Ku Klux Klan, Inc. *Klansman's Manual*. [Atlanta?]1924.

Knights of the Ku Klux Klan, Inc. *Proceedings of the Second Imperial Klonvokation.* [Atlanta?] 1924.

Lay, Shawn. *Hooded Knights on the Niagara.* New York: New York University Press, 1995.

Lester, John C., and Wilson, Daniel L. *Ku Klux Klan: Its Origin, Growth and Disbandment.* 2nd ed. New York: Neale Publishing Company, 1905.

Lisby, Gregory C. and Mugleston, William F. *Someone Had to Be Hated.* Durham: Carolina Academic Press, 2002.

MacLean, Nancy. *Behind the Mask of Chivalry: The Making of the Second Ku Klux Klan.* New York : Oxford University Press, 1994.

McPherson, James M. *Ordeal By Fire: The Civil War and Reconstruction.* New York: Alfred M. Knopf, 1982.

McVeigh, Rory. *The Rise of the Ku Klux Klan.* Minneapolis: University of Minnesota Press. 2009.

Mecklin, John M. *The Ku Klux Klan: A Study of the American Mind.* New York: Harcourt, Brace and Company, 1924.

Monteval, Marion. *The Klan Inside and Out.* Claremore OK: Monarch Publishing Company, 1924.

Moore, Leonard J. *Citizen Klansmen: The Ku Klux Klan in Indiana, 1921-1928.* Chapel Hill: The University of North Carolina Press, 1991.

Moore, William D., and Tabbert, Mark A.. *Secret Societies in America: Foundational Studies of Fraternalism.* New Orleans: Cornerstone Book Publishers, 2011.

Oney, Steve. *And the Dead Shall Rise: The Murder of Mary Phagan and the Lynching of Leo Frank.* New York: Pantheon Books, 2003.

Pegram, Thomas R. *One Hundred Percent American: The Rebirth and Decline of the Ku Klux Klan in the 1920s.* Chicago: Ivan R. Dee, 2011.

Pollard, Edward A. *The Lost Cause: A New Southern History of the War of the Confederates.* New York: E. B. Treat & Co, 1866.

Reed, John C. *The Brothers' War.* Boston: Little, Brown and Company, 1906.

Romine, W. B. *A Story of the Original Ku Klux Klan.* Pulaski TN: The Pulaski Citizen, 1924.

Rose, Laura M. *The Ku Klux Klan or Invisible Empire.* New Orleans: L. Graham Company, 1914.

Schmidt, Alvin J. *Fraternal Organizations.* Westport CT: Greenwood Press, 1980.

Shaff, Howard, and Shaff, Audrey K. *Six Wars at a Time.* Freeman SD: Pine Hill Press, 1985.

Shotwell, John M. "Crystallizing Public Hatred: Ku Klux Klan Public Relations in the Early 1920s." Master's Thesis, University of Wisconsin (Unpublished), 1974.

Simmons, William J. *The Klan Unmasked.* Atlanta: W. E. Thompson Publishing Company, 1923.

Singletary, Otis A. *Negro Militia and Reconstruction.* Austin TX: University of Texas Press, 1957.

Smith, John D., introduction to *The Flaming Sword* by Thomas Dixon, xv-xxvi, Lexington: University of Kentucky Press, 2005.

Stephens, Alexander H. *A Constitutional View of the Late War Between the States.* Philadelphia: National Publishing Company, 1868.

Thompson, C. Mildred. "Reconstruction in Georgia." In *Studies in History, Economics, and Public Law (Volume 64)*, 1-418. New York: Columbia University Press, 1915.

Tourgée, Albion W. *The Invisible Empire.* New York: Fords, Howard & Hulbert, 1880.

Trelease, Allen W. *White Terror: The Ku Klux Klan Conspiracy and Southern Reconstruction.* New York : Harper Torchbooks, 1972.

Tyler, Charles W. *The K. K. K.* New York: North River Publishing House, 1903.

Wade, Wyn C. *The Fiery Cross.* New York: Oxford University Press, 1987.

Wilson, Charles R. *Baptized in Blood: the Religion of the Lost Cause 1865-1920.* Athens GA: University of Georgia Press, 2009.

Woodward, C. Vann. *Tom Watson: Agrarian Rebel.* New York: Oxford University Press, 1963.

Wyeth, John A. *That Devil Forrest: Life of General Nathan Bedford Forrest.* Baton Rouge: Lousiana State University Press, 1989.

Journals, Magazines, and Related Periodicals:

Bell, Karen B. "The Ogeechee Troubles: Federal Land Restoration and the 'Lived Realities' of Temporary Properties, 1865-1868." *The Georgia Historical Quarterly* 85 (2001): 375-397.

Coulter, E. Merton. "Cudjo Fye's Insurrection." *The Georgia Historical Quarterly* 28 (1954): 213-225.

Duffus, Robert L. "Salesmen of Hate: The Ku Klux Klan." *The World's Work* 46 (May 1923): 31-38.

———. "How the Ku Klux Klan Sells Hate." *The World's Work* 46 (June 1923): 174-183.

———. "Counter-Mining the Ku Klux Klan." *The World's Work* 46 (July 1923): 275-284.

———. "The Ku Klux Klan in the Middle West." *The World's Work* 46 (August 1923): 363-372.

———. "Ancestry and End of the Ku Klux Klan." *The World's Work* 46 (September 1923): 527-536.

Formwalt, Lee W. "The Camilla Massace of 1868: Racial Violence as Political Propaganda." *The Georgia Historical Quarterly* 71, (1987): 399-426.

Frost, Stanley. "When the Klan Rules: The Plan to Capture Washington." *The Outlook*, 27 February 1924, 350-353.

———. "The Klan Shows Its Hand in Indiana." *The Outlook*, 4 June 1924, 187-190.

———. "The Klan's ½ of 1 per cent.Victory." *The Outlook*, 9 July 1924, 384-387.

———. "Nomination by Exhaustion: Political Side-Lights on Democratic Strategy." *The Outlook*, 23 July 1924, 464-466.

Greene, Ward. "Notes for a History of the Klan." *American Mercury* 5, (1925): 204-241.

Hux, Roger K. "The Ku Klux Klan in Macon, 1919-1925." *Georgia Historical Quarterly* 62, (1978): 155-168.

Jackson, Charles O. "William J. Simmons: A Career in Ku Kluxism." *Georgia Historical Quarterly* 50, (1966): 351-365.

Johnson, Julia E. "Ku Klux Klan." In *The Reference Shelf (Vol. 1 No. 10)*. New York, NY: The H. W. Wilson Company, 1923.

Lay, Shawn. "Hooded Populism: New Assessments of the Ku Klux Klan of the 1920s" *Reviews in American History 22*, December 1994, 668-673.

Literary Digest. "Quaint Customs and Methods of the Ku Klux Klan" *The Literary Digest,* 5 August 1922, 44-53.

MacKaye, Milton. "The Birth of a Nation." *Scribner's Magazine* 102, (1937): 40-46.

Merritt, Dixon. "The Klan on Parade." *The Outlook*, 19 August 1925, 553-554.

Moseley, Clement C. "The Political Influence of the Ku Klux Klan in Georgia, 1915-1925." *Georgia Historical Quarterly* 57, (1973): 235-255.

Percy, Leroy. "The Modern Ku Klux Klan." *The Atlantic Monthly*, 130, (1922): 122-128.

Shepherd, William G. "Fighting the K.K.K. on Its Home Grounds." *Leslie's*, 15 October 1921, 508-511, 526.

Shepherd, William G. "How I Put Over the Klan." *Collier's*, 14 July 1928, 5-7, 32, 34-35.

———. "Ku Klux Koin." *Collier's*, 21 July 1928, 8-9, 38-39.

———. "The Fiery Double-Cross." *Collier's*, 28 July 1928, 8-9, 47-49.

The Outlook. "The Klan as an Issue." 3 September 1924, 5-6.

———. "The Rise and Fall of the Ku Klux Klan." 15 October 1924, 237-238.

Uncle Remus's Magazine. "Principles and Scope of the Magazine." Vol 1., No. 1, June 1907.

Watson, Thomas E. "A Full Review of the Leo Frank Case." *Watson's Magazine* 20, (1915): 235-278.

Newspapers:
See individual footnote references.

Index